THE MYSTERY OF
THE LIGHT WITHIN US

THE MYSTERY
OF THE
LIGHT WITHIN US

*Illustrated with seventeen Watercolour
Drawings by Amy Wright Todd Ferrier*

By J. TODD FERRIER

THE ORDER OF THE CROSS
10 DE VERE GARDENS, KENSINGTON
LONDON, W.8

First Published 1932
Reprinted   –   1952
Reprinted   –   1967

Printed in Great Britain by
Percy Lund, Humphries & Co. Ltd, London and Bradford

AMY WRIGHT TODD FERRIER

Facing Dedication

DEDICATION

To

AMY

My Beloved Friend and Companion
whose Service on behalf of

THE MESSAGE AND THE WORK

could not be expressed in the
measure of Human Terms
though it was revealed in her
beautiful Fidelity to

THE MESSAGE AND THE WORK

amidst the Travail begotten of

THE RECOVERED VISION

and its restatement and unveiling to

THE HOUSE OF ISRAEL

and all who may be able to hear it.

From her
Friend

I

CONTENTS

PART FOUR

SOUL ESTATES: CELESTIAL AND DIVINE

PART FIVE

THE SUMMER SCHOOL OF 1931

LIST OF PLATES

PREFACE

The illustrations in this volume are a few of the Auric
Drawings painted by my Beloved Amy. Some of them
were painted many years ago, a few in more recent
years. They are an endeavour to express in form and
colour THE MYSTERY OF THE GLORY OF GOD WITHIN
THE SANCTUARY OF THE SOUL.

They are not to be regarded simply as artistic Drawings
and an Artist's concept of these spiritual states, for they
were the result of real Soul vision. Nor were they the
outcome of some passing clairvoyant vision; for they
belong to a realm far beyond that into which the
ordinary clairvoyant may look. Clairvoyance was not
unknown to her, but she never associated these Drawings
with such a lesser gift. Her vision was Soulic and of the
Inner Worlds.

When my request was made to her for a Painting
which would represent a Soul in certain spiritual experience and estate, I described to her the form and
auric glory of such an one. Bye and bye she would have
given to her the inspiration and vision necessary through
the opening up of the Heavens within her, and then the
Painting took form.

The exquisitely beautiful soft yet radiant colouring, so
characteristic of Spiritual and Divine Spheres, was her
own secret, doubtless brought through from past ages
when she was one of the great Religious Artists whose
works are still the monastic and ecclesiastical adornments

of certain centres in Italy, and the objects of wonder and admiration.

Had she sought a world recognition she might easily have won her way to it; for her gifts were varied. These she revealed in her Black and White Drawings, both Crayon and Pen and Ink; in Portrait paintings, Seascapes, Landscapes and Flowers. But she only found her true vocation when she began the Paintings embodying the Soul in its various degrees.

Yet though so gifted she was most diffident, and would never have chosen to have any of her work exhibited. She never considered it good enough. Yet she was so absolutely devoted to myself, to the Message I was here to give, and the Work that was to be accomplished, that she lived to further the Message and to help Souls to behold, and understand through beholding, something of the Divine Glory within them.

There were two Drawings she would have loved to finish: one was hurriedly painted in Sepia on ordinary paper as she had no other beside her at the time. This was done some years ago. The other was the last Painting from her brush. The former was the Head and shoulders of the Master as He was in the Days of the Manifestation. It portrayed Him in the midst of the Gethsemane—a face never to be forgotten. It was flashed into her consciousness and vision during a momentary recovery of that event.

This Drawing she longed to reproduce in Watercolour; but try as she might she could not. Then she essayed to do it in Oils; but what she had seen would not come. She was able to reproduce the outline, but the Mystery of Sorrow and Anguish revealed in the original, eluded her. Though she sorrowed over apparent failure, undoubtedly it was of Divine intent that that Mystery of Sorrow should not be unveiled to others.

Of the uncompleted last Drawing the same may be said. She was not permitted to finish it, for it portrayed the Anguished Countenance of The Master in the days of the Return.

These two *Mystery of Sorrow* paintings were quite distinct from Plate VIII given in Part III. In this latter the profound Anguish is hidden in the very manner in which the event is portrayed; though the auric outflow testifies to the deep grief by which He was moved, the effect of which is reflected upon the atmosphere around the ministering Angels.

How wonderful are the ways of the Divine Love and Wisdom! Such a Mystery as the Oblation, in the Burden of Sorrow and Anguish it entailed both before and after its accomplishment, is best left in such a veil as hides the Divine Travail.

The Divine Love and Wisdom are perfect in their way; and what the Lord of All purposes, is always sublimely beautiful.

To His Will we ever would bow.

J. Todd Ferrier.

THE TETRAGRAMMATON

B

A

THE LUMINOUS CROSS

The splendour of the Magnetic Light of the Inner Worlds is surpassingly glorious. Its Mystery is of the Eternal, and is the resultant of the motion of tremendous electric forces. It is also associated with the Macrocosmic Cross. The Cross is at the Heart of the Divine Mystery, and it is at the Centre of the Universe. In and by means of it are all things balanced. The Macrocosmic Cross contains GOD'S Secret. It expresses the Four Dimensions. In the Divine World, these are the Four Living Creatures or Eternities which are apocalyptically stated to be ever in motion, resting not, and who are full of eyes that look and see into the Four Dimensions.

The Balance of the Universe

The Cross expresses in and through its four right Angles, the balance of the Universe. And the motion of the Universe is signified by the intersecting Circle. Through the motion of the Cross all magnetic Light is derived. From the Centre of the Cross all power proceeds. The power is contained in the Divine Righteousness and Equity—the perpendicular and the horizontal, the upright and the equipoised.

The Cross is repeated in all embodiments of the Divine Mystery. It is at the centre of all Stars, and they all derive their magnetic Light from it. Its motion has the effect of making all their Ætheric Elements luminous. The alternating action of centrifugal and centripetal motion affects their Photosphere and causes their Chromosphere to reflect their inherent resplendence.

In this Mystery the Solar Body shares. The Divine Cross is at the Centre. From its magnetic pivot of balance its Four Dimensions proceed. The perpendicular geometrical line eventuates in its North and South magnetic Poles; and the horizontal geometrical line culminates in the Apexes whose office it is to hold all its Ætheric Elements in balance, and guard and control their distribution. These four dimensional Apexes were affected in their creative and distributive ministries when the present Photosphere had to be

3

*The Cross
and the
Solar Body*

fashioned to meet the special needs of the System as a result of the changes effected in the Celestial balance of the System through the Fall of the Earth. The present Photosphere is an accommodation. It was fashioned to be a means of guarding the Inner Angelic Heavens from the hurtful conditions prevailing within the Heavens of the Earth and upon all its materialized planes; and, also, that it should become a suitable venue for the Solar magnetic ministry essential to the needs of the various Kingdoms of the Earth, and for the preservation and sustenance of all her children.

The Photosphere as at present constituted was formed out of the Elements which at one time composed the Solar outer Angelic Kingdom. The Elements had to be reduced from their primal estate and partially changed in their Divine Qualities; but they were preserved from losing their inherent power of volition, like so many of the Elements of the Earth, so that they retained their volatility. The original Photosphere and Chromosphere extended hundreds of thousands of miles beyond those which now obtain; and all the Angels who served within the original outer Heavens had to be withdrawn to the intermediary Heavens. From these latter they have ministered for ages.

Whilst the Solar changes were for the general benefit of the whole Earth, there was one race of Souls whom the change very specially affected. These were the Sons of GOD who had been sent to aid the elder children of the Planet by giving to them Teaching on the Mysteries associated with the Divine Love and Wisdom. These Sons of GOD belonged to the Solar World. They were the Children of the Light. They were accustomed to commune with the Angels on the outer Solar Heavens during the days of their Earth-ministry. To them the loss was unspeakable when the Angels had to be withdrawn from the outer Heavens owing to the change effected of necessity in the Photosphere and Chromosphere. For thus one most important source of nourishment and power was lost to them when they most needed it amid the greatly impoverished conditions of the planes and Kingdoms of the Earth. These Sons of GOD were the Ancient Christhood upon this World, who in later ages came to be known as the Children of Zion and Israel.

These Souls knew the meaning of the Macrocosmic Cross as that appertained to the Angelic World. And in part, some of them

4

THE TETRAGRAMMATON

Facing page 4.

THE TETRAGRAMMATON

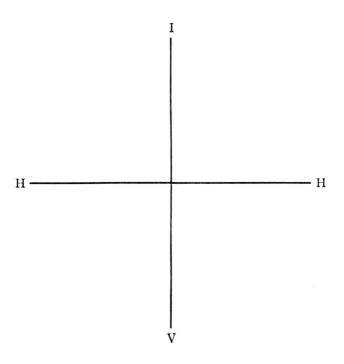

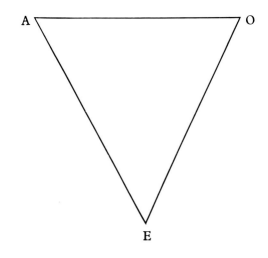

understood its relation to the Mystery expressed in Celestial balance and motion. And, as a race, they were the Divine Cross-bearers who had to carry much of the Planet's burden on the Human Kingdom and serve as redeemers. To them the Cross was the most sacred Sign of the Divine Mystery; and it became the most precious Symbol of His Presence with them.

These Souls also knew the Most Sacred Name. They had realized something of its Mystery. To them the Macrocosmic Cross expressed the Mystery. In its form it contained the unutterable hidden Name composed of the letters I H V H.

It expressed in the initial letter the Mystery—I AM.

In the double aspirates it signified the Breath in its dual motion.

In its Vau or V, it testified that the manifest world was the revelation from and the exposition of, I AM.

Herein was the FATHER-MOTHER testified of, and yet His Mystery veiled.

The Vowels E O A were necessary for the pronouncement of the Sacred Name; and these were related to other hallowed Names of I AM. They were the vehicles of the Sublime Mystery for the Great Manifestation.

It is thus that we have in our tongue the most adorable Name JEHOVAH.

When ADONAI makes manifest upon the Inner Kingdom or Divine Realm of the Solar World, HE appears as the Sign of the Cross. The Seer saw HIM filling the Sun. HE was known to the Sons of GOD as the Sign of the Cross. They themselves were Children of the Sun and bore in varying degrees that most sacred Sign. For, in the degree in which a Soul grows like ADONAI in its attributes, so does it take on the fashion of the Sign of the Cross. And a Messenger of high estate when mediating unto Souls such as the Sons of GOD, directly from the Divine World, has given to him the insignia of The Sign of the Cross. It was in this sense that the Master bore the Sign of the Cross and was known to the Sons of GOD in the unfallen days under that title as the Servant of the LORD mediating unto them upon other spheres, and also many ages later, amid the changed conditions.

5

Ioseph
Maria

This Title is associated with the Divine Names of I-O-Seph. For He Who bore the primal insignia of the Sign of the Cross was I-O-Seph Maria. And this most sacred name was bestowed upon the Master great ages ago when He was appointed to be the High Priest of Israel, to mediate unto that Ancient House of the Christhood through the Elders, of the Divine Mysteries which emanated from and gathered around the Divine Names I-O-Seph Maria.

As High Priest of Israel and the Divine Manifestor, He was crowned by those sacred names from the FATHER-MOTHER, and became known to the Sons of GOD as I-O-Seph Maria, the Messenger.

6

THE CROSS OF THE ELOHIM

PLATE II

Facing page 6.

LOVE

SERVICE

COMPASSION

DEVOTION

PITY

PURITY

B

THE CROSS OF THE ELOHIM

The Luminous Cross which speaks of the Eternal Mystery, reveals the sevenfold Glory of GOD when its Light is refracted. The Tetragrammaton whose Mystery is inexpressible as set forth in the four mysterious letters which the four magnetic apices of the macrocosmic Cross signify, becomes pronouncible and revealed when related to the ELOHIM. JEHOVAH, the sacred term for the FATHER-MOTHER who is in HIMSELF dual potency, becomes EL ADONAI, who again becomes the concrete fashion of the FATHER-MOTHER as ETERNAL CHRIST and, therefore, the sublime and glorious Trinity. But the distribution of the Eternal Potency of the primal Hypostasis and Pneuma or Spirit, is through the ELOHIM. These are the seven great agencies, the venues of the Eternal Mystery. The Primal Spirit discourses through them in creative acts, each of the seven representing a Kingdom. The Primal Ray is dispersed by means of them and broken into its seven component parts.

Thus is the Divine Spectrum revealed.

The Most Sacred Name

But the Spectrum of the Cross of the ELOHIM has a significance surpassing any outward scientific interpretation of it. It speaks of the seven orders of Ministry; of the seven great orders of Life; of the seven Human Races; of the seven Heavens; of the seven Angelic Kingdoms; of the seven Celestial Degrees expressed in the seven orders of Stars; of the seven great Archangels; and of the seven Realms and seven Spheres within the Divine World. It speaks of the work of the different Elohe as well as of the special Tincture of each; and it indicates how the various orders of Souls inherit the distinctive Tincture of their own Elohe. It shows also the sublimity of the Life to which the Soul may attain when, in addition to the realization of the full potency of its special Tincture, it has been able to partake of the potency of all the Tinctures and reach that Divine Degree wherein it can become the vehicle of its own Elohe, and also that of the ELOHIM for Divine embodiment and manifestation. For the realization of the Cross of the ELOHIM implies, in some

7

degree, Divine Christhood. In such an Estate the Soul is over-shadowed by the White Radiance. The Divine Cross is within it, and the Apex of the Eternal World rests upon its magnetic Pole. The auric glory is that of the Sacred Seven.

The Cross of the ELOHIM is multiple. It contains the Macrocosmic Cross with the Tetragrammaton and the Four Eternities or Dimensions. From the Divine World it becomes the Cross of Manifestation and Redemption, so that it is the Sign of the Messenger and the Redeemer. It likewise reveals the Threefold Path by which all Souls may attain to the realization of the Tincture of their own Elohe, ar.d, ultimately, to the Estate wherein they can partake of all the Sacred Tinctures, and come to know in high degree the over-shadowing of the White Light.

The Threefold Path is the way of Purity, Devotion, and Love. These contain the true meaning of Self-Denial, Self-Sacrifice, and Self-Abandonment, sometimes spoken of as the Great Renunciation. There is no other way of attainment. They form the three Degrees through which the Soul must pass to find the Crown of perfect Jesushood. But their inner signification carried the Soul through its three Ascensions and into the experience of the Great Metempsychosis concerning which more will be unveiled later.

The Cross of the ELOHIM was the insignia of those who were known as the Immortals. Many of these were sent to this world for the ministry of manifestation and interpretation, and some of these are upon the Planet, being specially ministered unto from the Heavens that they may again manifest the Christhood and contribute through their ministries to the Redemption of all the Planet's Kingdoms and children.

The Sons of GOD are the communities of Souls who have ascended from the various Planetary Systems into Celestial Estates. They are those who have so far attained that they need not return to the various Earths to be reincarnated, unless it be for some special Divine ministry. For all Souls in their growth and evolution return many times to the world which is their Planetary Mother, until they acquire the powers to function in Celestial Spheres, when they shall have risen above the need to return for experience.

For the Sons of GOD, the Cross of the ELOHIM was both Sign and Symbol—the Sign of the Office they filled, and the Symbol of the Presence with them.

Part Two

THE SOLAR MYSTERY

A THE SPECTRA OF SOULS AND STARS
B THE SOLAR KINGDOMS (Static)
C THE SOLAR FASHION (Active)

SOLAR SPECTRA

PLATE III

A

THE SPECTRA OF SOULS AND STARS

Spectra are associated with Stars. The Sciences of Astronomy and Physics have done much to enlighten the mind of man concerning the nature and constitution of the Stars. By means of the spectroscope much has been discovered in relation to Light. By means of the telescope a greater Universe has been revealed to man, and the motions of Planets and Stars explained. Through the spectroscope the Mystery of Light has been studied by earnest students, and many hitherto hidden potencies associated with the Spectrum have been discovered and explained.

The Stars Spiritual Manifestations

Yet with all its discoveries, physical science has only touched the outer fringe of the great Mystery of the nature and constitution of the Stars. Spectrum analysis has done much on the outer fringe, but it has not brought scientists any nearer to solving the Mystery contained in and expressed through the Spectrum. It still looks upon Stars as masses of elements and gases in a state of incandescency. The combustion is great and the potency tremendous. Light and heat are supposed to be the resultants of these. The Stars are living worlds in the sense of activity, but dead worlds when thought of in relation to habitation and ministering spirits. They are considered tremendous in volume and power, but without certain definite creative purpose. There is no home for Divinity in them; there are no Beings of an Angelic and Archangelic order filling the spheres, directing the elements in their motion, and generating magnetic and electric potency. Though it is recognized that there is some hidden power and law behind all the manifestations of potency and motion, yet there seems no place for a living and knowable GOD.

It is truly remarkable that physical scientists have never turned their thoughts to the essentially spiritual nature of the Universe Their definitions and interpretations are immersed in matter. As unconscious force is without purpose in its action, and as there is manifestly some sublime purpose in the Universe, potency cannot be without consciousness, and its activity and direction must have a

11

primal Source. The seen is the testimony of the presence of the
unseen. As truly as Man's works are the exposition of his thoughts
and purposes, so may it be truly said of the Universe. Its perfect
manifestations are the revelations of Divine Thought and Purpose.

The Universe is one, though manifold in the exposition of the
Secret Presence. All embodiments are related to one another. One
great Principle is expressed in them and the same purpose revealed
through them. All true high conscious Life is from the one Source,
and in manifestation is the ever varying reflection of the Eternal
Mystery. Life in manifestation is a resultant. It must be the
exposition of the Secret at the heart of the Universe. Man
must be related to the higher orders of embodiment as these
latter are related to the Divine Secret Source. As these are, so is
Man in fashion and potency. As there is something kindred in all
manifest Worlds, so is there in man to those we name Angels,
Archangels and Gods. The Secret of the Eternal is at the heart of
them all.

The Human Soul, having kinship with the Unseen Universe of
Being, shares the elements out of which all things became manifest.
For the nature and constitution of the Human Soul are one with
the elemental states and constitution of the Stars. All have proceeded
from the same Source; and though the processional of each Star and
each Soul differs according to the degree of manifestation and order
of ministry, yet the purpose behind each and all is the same. It is to
embody and interpret the most Sacred Mystery.

As the Light given forth by the Stars is inherent in their elements,
so is the Auric display inherent in the elements of which the Soul is
built up. They have in common their origin in and from the Divine
Ætheria. It is the Divine Ætheria which gives the resplendence to
that portion of the Heavens we speak of as The Milky Way; for the
Divine Ætheria has within itself the properties of Life and Light,
and is a container of the universal consciousness, and is, therefore,
the reflector of the Eternal Mystery we name Omniscience, and
which we postulate of the FATHER-MOTHER.

The process of the Creation and generation of a Human Soul
is the same as that of a Star. The Soul is in this respect a miniature
of the greater creation. They have this in common, that both are
built up out of the Divine Ætheric Elements, and both are fashioned
like a Spiral.

The way of the fashioning of the Human Soul is through the motion of the Divine Breaths amidst the Elements composing the Divine Ætheria. It is built up out of those Sacred Elements which contain within themselves the potency of Life and Light, and that are of the Divine Mystery of universal consciousness and related to Omnisciency.

The Origin of Light in Souls and Stars

From its inception the Human Soul has within itself the Principle of Life-Eternal and the potency of the Eternal Light. In its Spiral are the two mysterious magnetic Streams whose alternating action build the Life-forces and enrich the attributes by means of a process of ingathering from the Divine Elemental Kingdom; for these have Systolic and Diastolic action. They proceed from and return to the Divine Centre.

As the Soul grows its consciousness expands and deepens; then, periodically, that brings about an ascension of Life, enabling the Soul to function upon higher planes and more inward realms. And thus does it continue to grow and ascend until it can be magnetically and dynamically lifted up as high as the Angelic World of its own system; then into Celestial realms; and ages after, on to the threshold of the Divine Kingdom.

As it thus grows, the Light within it becomes more and more intense. And as the Light falls upon its magnetic plane, its auric resplendence becomes manifest. The Light within it is the resultant of the polarization of all its Ætheria; and the degree of intensity of the Light is commensurate with the magnetic status it has attained to. The Auric Light is its true nimbus; but it is not simply a single circle of light around the head, such as the great spiritual artists put around the head of the Madonna and the saints. It is a wonderful compound globular Light which gradually changes from white Light to first one and then another of the colours of the rainbow, and finally to reveal all of them: for they are all contained in it, even as the spectrum is contained in the primal ray.

Then, according to the age of the Soul, the Spectrum becomes less or more intense in its manifestation. For the age and estate of a Soul may be known through its Aura. But the age of a Soul is not determined by the ages through which it has persisted and manifested; otherwise all Souls of the same number of cycles would have Auras of equal degree and intensity. Age in the Divine Sense represents the quality and quantity of the Soul's ingathering of potency, and its attainments. For, through drawing into itself during the magnetic action resulting from Desire, Prayer or Flight to the Heavens, Purpose and Love, the streams of Divine Ætheria, it grows in stature and grace; and through these it becomes so deeply affected that it not only essays to attain spiritual heights of consciousness and power, but it actually achieves the summits of the Hills of GOD in its Initiations. As these latter are Angelic Degrees, in this way it passes upward in estate from Kingdom to Kingdom and becomes as a brilliant Star in the firmament of its own Sphere. Henceforth it is ensphered in the Cloud of its Radiance. Its Aura is now as the true Chromosphere of the Sun and the Stars. It shares with them the revelation of the Glory of the ELOHIM. The latent qualities of the Seven Sacred Tinctures of the ELOHIM are now to be made manifest through it. In the measure in which it has appropriated the qualities of these Tinctures, so shall its Aura express the Divine Mystery.

So much akin to the Solar World is the Human Soul, that its Aura not only contains all the elements of the Spectrum as seen in the refracted ray of Light, but it contains likewise those mysterious invisible rays of which scientists speak concerning the Solar Ray. It has invisible rays preceding the red. These are related to the heat rays of the Solar Body. And following the Violet ray there are invisible rays of a disintegrating nature, rays that find their way to the heart of things. These invisible rays preceding the Ruby Tincture and following the Violet Tincture, have for their service the transmission of the life-forces for generative ministries, and the transmutation of the elements. In their action they generate dynamic force by which the whole Being is raised and endowed; and they give the Soul power to negative the effects of certain deleterious elements, and even to disintegrate evil images and scatter impure elements.

In the possession and exercise of this power the Soul's kinship with the Solar World is made manifest; for the Sun has many unseen rays which contain secret power for generative and transmutory ministries. Some of these have been discovered by the apostles of physical science and put to medical and healing uses. But the true secret hidden in those unseen rays is not known, and the unenlightened uses of them may lead to disastrous results—which indeed has happened more frequently than is generally known. To try to wrest the secret of these potencies by the means employed by material science is to violate the Divine Law. For the Secret of GOD can be known only from within, and is a knowledge which is gifted to the Soul through high realization of the Mystery of Life and Light. Even the humblest flower of the field retains its secret. No scientist has come at the secret of its Life-principle. Only the phases of its manifestation are observable and can be known. For the secret associated with the realm of the Spirit whose intelligent motion produces the flower, belongs to the Eternal Mystery we name the FATHER-MOTHER. If science fails to wrest the hidden secret of the flower, how can it expect to wrest from the Solar Body the Divine Secret of its unseen rays?

The Divine Nimbus

The Human Soul has derived its auric splendour from the ELOHIM. The ELOHIM are the Seven Spirits of GOD. They are the distinctive and operative powers within the Eternal Light. They are as Seven Altars of Fire the flames of which make up the Seven Sacred Tinctures. They are also the Light within the Seven Sacred Lamps in the Divine World. When the Soul fully attains, all its planes are reflectors of the ELOHIM as expressed in the Seven Sacred Fires. For in such an attainment the magnetic pole of the Being is overshadowed by the Presence who becomes accommodated to the individual; and the effect of the overshadowing is such that the Soul becomes clothed in auric Light. And when the Presence is greatly realized, the display of the Aura is such, that it is as the Rainbow around the Throne. Here the Soul takes on the Fashion of its LORD. Here is made manifest its relation to the Eternal Light. Henceforth it dwells in that Radiance; yet not as in an atmosphere of Glory that is external to itself. It is enshrined in the Cloud of HIS Glory as one who is altogether transfigured. But as such transfiguration is the outcome of the transmutation of the entire fabric of the Soul, and the raising of all its elements, attributes and planes by a dynamic process which gives it power to function within the Divine Kingdom; so does the Aura become more intense in its radiance as the result of the intensified magnetic conditions and action, until, at last, the Aura is as the Divine Cloud of Radiance enveloping the whole Being in the Eternal Light, and clothing it with the ineffable garment of Divine resplendence.

Such is the Mystery of the Light Within.

Such is the Share which the Human Soul has in the Mystery of the Stars, the Gods, and the Law of Being.

And in such wise may the Eternal Light be revealed in and through the Human Soul.

15

THE RETURN FORCE (CENTRIPETAL)

THE SOLAR KINGDOMS (STATIC)

PLATE IV

B

THE SOLAR KINGDOMS

The glorious Sun is little understood. The telescope and the spectroscope have done much to assist students of Astronomy and Physics along the path of observation of the phenomena manifested upon the outer Kingdom of the Sun. But these phenomena are as mere fragments of the full story of the Sun. And they are mostly related to the present state of the outer Kingdom. Indeed, all ascertained knowledge through observation and analysis relates to the glorious body in his present state of divinely imposed limitation, and not to the real Sun who was complete in the days of his perfect manifestation; for the Sun known to Science is not the glorious perfect Divine Embodiment of ADONAI, but that resplendent realm accommodated to the needs of the whole system as this latter became affected through the Fall of the Planet Judah, now known as the Earth[1].

The Solar Divine World

In the unfallen days the Sun occupied a larger place in the Celestial Heavens. It had no such Photosphere and Chromosphere as it has now. Spatially it covered nearly double the arc of its present measurement. It had a fourfold constitution. The simple drawing will illustrate this, though it is altogether too inadequate even as an illustration. But it sets forth the interior majesty of the Solar Body, and its glorious Heavens. These latter may be thus expressed. The first seven innermost circles represent the Planes and Kingdoms of the Divine World. Through these the innermost Divine centre directly ministers to the cosmic whole. And it is through these Kingdoms and Planes that the Solar Body as the compound representative and therefore Vicegerent of ADONAI, ministers to the Sons

[1]In Old Testament history, Solar and Earth Mysteries are hidden in the terms Israel and Judah. For, though the histories of the Kingdoms of Israel and Judah have been related to the Jewish Race, yet are they wholly of a mystical significance, and contain much Planetary and Solar Story. The rending of the Kingdoms of Israel and Judah and the antagonism between the two, relate to Planetary Catastrophes and Solar adjustments; and the great Diaspora which resulted, was concerned with the dispersion of the Sons of GOD and the dissolution of their Brotherhoods. For these were the centres of the Christhood manifestation and the Angelic and Celestial ministries to the Children of Judah—the Earth.

*The Solar
Celestial
Rainbow*

of GOD within his system.   Indeed, it is through the Divine approach by means of these Kingdoms and Planes that the more advanced of the Sons of GOD who minister upon the Earth, are nourished, upheld and directed.   And it is also through those Kingdoms and Planes that the Central Authority of the Universe of the System to which the Sun belongs, communicated the Divine Purpose and Decree.   The Tinctures of the Kingdoms and Planes reveal the fields of ministry of the ELOHIM, each Elohe has one Kingdom with its planes: and there are seven planes within each Kingdom.

*   *   *   *

Then follows what seems to be space, but which represents the magnetic Plane of the Divine Kingdom. By means of this Plane the Seer looks into the Divine World, and through it he receives communications. By means of it those who have attained Celestial Christhood but have not passed their Degrees into the Divine Christhood, receive illuminations and instructions concerning the Divine Purpose and ministry, and are thus prepared for the still higher Initiations into the Divine Estates even whilst they render ministry of a Celestial and Angelic order.

Beyond this magnetic circulus there are seven more Kingdoms and their Planes. These circuli represent the Celestial Realm within the Sun. They also are interfused with the sacred Tinctures of the ELOHIM; for the ELOHIM operate through them, rendering Celestial Solar ministries, and also receiving such from the Sun's central authority—its own Divine World, as well as from the various members of its Celestial System, and likewise from Mazzaroth. As it is held in state from the Divine World through its corresponding Divine Centre and Magnetic Poles, so is its relationship to the Celestial Divinities upheld, and its power to render Celestial Service continued. Those who are in the estate of Celestial Christhood derive their illumination within the various Kingdoms through the operation of the ELOHIM, their illumination varying according to the Kingdom upon which they function and the ELOHE who serves them.

*   *   *   *

This Solar Celestial Realm is a projection from the Divine Centre for purposes of manifestation and ministry. It is inherently present always in the Solar constitution, but is not always obviously manifest. It acts likewise as a Defence to the Divine Kingdom, for no one can

18

reach the latter except through the former. Thus, no one who has not entered the Divine Kingdom by means of the Divine Initiations, and through the observance of its most sacred Ritual, can approach that Kingdom by other way than the path of the Celestial Realm. For the Soul can approach and enter the Divine Kingdom only when it has accomplished all its degrees upon the Celestial Realm.

The Solar Celestial Magnetic Plane

Here it may also be observed that the various Tinctures of the ELOHIM are transmitted into the Solar Celestial Realms, but in reduced intensity compared to the degree of those Tinctures upon the Divine World; for all Celestial creative acts within the Celestial Spheres are the outcome of the motion of the ELOHIM. And these Tinctures in their varying degrees also signify the state of the various Kingdoms and those who dwell and minister there.

* * * *

Beyond the Celestial World of the Sun there is another of its Ætheric Heavens which again looks like empty space like the wide circulus that divides the Celestial from the Divine World. This second circulus is the sphere through which the Celestial ministrants communicate with the Angelic World. It is the Celestial Magnetic Plane.

Souls who are able to transcend all Earth influences and rise into the higher Angelic World, have messages sent to them upon that Plane. Thus is it with those who are on their way to become Seers and Prophets of the Divine Kingdom. They receive instruction through that Plane to enrich, illumine, and strengthen them for ministry. As they rise in state, so does the communication to meet their growing need. In this way Souls acquire the potencies represented by all the Celestial Kingdoms and Planes, and attain to the estate of Celestials.

* * * *

Outside the Celestial Magnetic Plane we have what seems to be another repetition of the Spectrum shown in the Divine and Celestial Kingdoms. Again there are seven circles, each taking the colour of one of the Seven Sacred Tinctures. Here again the intensity of the Tinctures is less in degree. This part of the Solar constitution formed, at one time, the Angelic Kingdom. It extended far beyond its radius of the present day. It was originally the Solar Angelic World from which the Hosts of the LORD of Life ministered. It formed the true Chromosphere and Photosphere of the System of the

Sublime
Solar
Sacrifices

glorious Divine Being who is in charge of the Sun. During the long ages concerning which it has been mythically written of that the Gods visited the Earth and the Immortals dwelt with man, the ministry of the Solar Body was perfect; for it had a perfect Photosphere through which to minister, and a perfect Chromosphere through which the ELOHIM could reveal. In those days the Angelic World was very near and was most real to the Sons of GOD and even to the elder children of the Planet. The Angelic Heavens of the Earth were pure and equipoised, and responsive to the attraction of the Divine World; and this enabled the Angels to give continual ministry, and for an unfailing communion to be kept up between the Earth and Sun. Then was the Earth a glorious body also in the System. It was clothed in its own magnetic Light as its Poles were affected from the Solar World. For the mysterious elements out of which Light becomes manifested in the Solar Body and all Stars, are also in the Earth, and perfectly fulfilled their office in the unfallen days.

Through the sad fall of the Earth, or the land of Judah the Planet-Soul, in its elements, Kingdoms and Planes, and in a very special way all the circuli of its Heavens, it became necessary for the Divine World to make great changes in the outer Kingdoms of the Sun's constitution. The Divine World purposed to make a tremendous sacrifice to save this Planet and all her children. It revealed a majestic stooping of the Divine Love and Wisdom to give effectual ministry to the Earth. The sacrifice was contained in changing the elements which composed the Chromosphere and Photosphere, and reducing them from their primal state to one that was greatly denser. This meant a process of contraction till the Chromosphere and Photosphere ceased to have their original place. The Angelic Heavens had to be suspended in their ministries through the various circuli of the Chromosphere and Photosphere. The Angels had to be withdrawn to the lower Celestial plane, and many elements to be indrawn from the Angelic to the Celestial Realms. Then the present Photosphere was formed out of the changed elements, and accommodated to the ministries required. Thus it became a vehicle for the operations of the Divine World on behalf of the Earth. And it is so unto this day, though solar changes are now taking place as the outcome of the change effected in the Heavens of the Planet by means of the Oblation.

20

During this Naros much will be accomplished within the present Photosphere and Chromosphere towards the restoration of the Ancient Angelic Heavens. The operations through the Solar Celestial Kingdoms are most potent, and by means of the unceasing changes effected, the Celestial Realms are drawing nearer to the Sons of GOD. Through this ministry the Angels of the outer Spheres are now able to encompass the Earth. They are the Hosts of the LORD proclaiming the Avatar. It is also now possible for the Presence of the ETERNAL ONE to overshadow the Sons of GOD and for the Divine World to directly affect them. With the accomplishment of the Redemption of the Planetary Heavens, as one of the resultants of the Burden of the Oblation, the Angels are now able to approach those Heavens and minister unto many. And the Earth herself can be ministered unto more directly and with fuller and intenser magnetic streams poured forth from the Divine World through the latter's Celestial Spheres. For this sublime purpose are the great rents in the Photosphere kept continuously open and special ministry sent through them. The mystery of the Sun-spots has quite a different meaning, both as to their origin and purpose, from that assigned to them by physical scientists. That they are enlarged from time to time, though the enlargement may seem to be related to the effect upon the Photosphere of the Planets Jupiter and Saturn in their perihelion, is the confirmation of this great Celestial ministry; for with the enlargement of the cavities there is an intensification of the Divine Streams poured forth from the Central Kingdom. The whole of the Planet is more acutely affected at such times. What are named electric storms, which are multiplied and intensified during such periods, are the resultants of the intensive ministry of the Divine World, and the fruitage of the transmutory work accomplished by the Divine magnetic streams within the Earth's atmospheres and elemental Kingdoms.

With the dawn of this Naros there is heralded new hope for this member of the system; for its complete healing is assured. And the great and glorious ONE whose sublime sacrifice has accomplished so much for all its members and very specially for this world, shall once more be able to gradually reduce to the first estate the glorious elements of His ancient Angelic Heavens, and unveil His transcendent glory.

The Day of God's Sabaoth

21

THE OUTGOING FORCE (CENTRIFUGAL)

THE SOLAR FASHION (ACTIVE)

PLATE V

Facing page 22.

C

THE SOLAR FASHION

The interior of the Solar Body is entirely different from that guessed at by Physical Science. A voyage to the interior of the Sun would be most remunerative to Science. If the Mind, as a sacred Argosy, could sail the etheric sea from Earth to the glorious Orb, it would truly be a voyage of great discovery. The inner Spheres would reveal the most wonderful superstructure. It would be found that though the Sun appears to the human eye as globular, yet in the inner spheres it was like a tremendous Spiral containing seven great Planes and seven Kingdoms; that the Planes had dual motion upward and downward upon the Spiral, and outward and inward from the Spiral, as they rendered creative ministries; and that the Kingdoms designated the field of action where the creative ministries were rendered, and the degree of realized Life and Power by those who dwelt and served in them.

The Solar Planes, Static and Active

The Divine Mystery contained in the Sun's Fashion has had to be guarded from all who have not attained to that degree of Divine Life which would enable them to rise into the Solar Cosmic consciousness, and become citizens of the glorious Celestial World, able to dwell and serve within its Kingdoms, if so commanded from the Divine World. Therefore, no illustration of the Mystery may be given: it is not permitted to unveil it. The story can be told only in a general way, yet sufficiently clear to explain many things concerning the strange appearance and action of the Sun. The illustrations given in the two plates entitled "The Return Force" and "The Projecting Force" set forth, whilst still veiling the Mystery, the inward and upward motion of the planes, and their downward and outward motion. They are centripetal and centrifugal. The latter speaks of the projection of Divine Potency, and the former indicates the return. They might be termed the masculine and feminine forces. The feminine is in repose as if quiescent, though not really so; the masculine is the active aspect of the creative force, projecting through all the Kingdoms and Planes the potent magnetic mysterious force out of which Life and Light are generated.

The Presence at the Centre represents not only the One who is the Head of the Sun System as Vicegerent of ADONAI, but also speaks of the Sum of all the high Beings whose home is in the Sun, and who serve in it for the ELOHIM. For, though the glorious Orb has One presiding as the Divine Representative, to whose Divine Counsel all render sweet obedience since it is obedience unto the Will of the Divine World, yet it is a great and resplendent system of Souls in Celestial Estate. In an individual sense it can and does represent and embody the Divine Man, or ADONAI made manifest in and through the Head; but also in a communal sense is that glorious One envisaged. For all who dwell in the Sun's innermost realm, have known the Mystery of EL ADONAI in the Eternal World. And, whilst individually realizing HIS most transcendent Mystery, even as their Head; in a Corporate Body they concretely embody HIM. The meaning here may not be easily apprehended, but it is of immense importance. For where it is known that there are millions of glorious Beings in the inner Realms of the Solar World, and that together they form its Divine Kingdom and, therefore, represent EL ADONAI in embodiment, it will be the more readily understood how the united action of such a glorious company upon and through the highly magnetic elements, causes the outer Kingdoms and Planes to be clothed resplendently in magnetic Light. For the real glory of the Sun is the resultant of their action, producing through the action of the Divine Elements, the magnetic radiance; and it is in no sense the outcome of combustion of fiery elements as physical science believes.

This should aid the illumined to more fully apprehend the significance of the apparent spherical appearance of the Sun; for even in the age of perfect manifestation, before the drastic and tragic changes had to be effected in the Photosphere and Chromosphere, the embodiment gave the appearance in the Celestial Heavens of the globe. But the globular form was the outcome of the Aura. This latter encompassed the glorious body like a cloud of radiance. It enshrined it. As a Divine Spiral it was never seen except to the Divine Seer. And to him its Eternal Mystery was held as a Secret.

The present appearance of the Sun in the Celestial Heavens is globular. But this form is not the result of the Aura, but of the shape of the Photosphere. Looked at scientifically, this appears to be an encompassing sheath of fiery elements in a state of high incandescency.

The surface seems like a molten sea, never at rest and ever changing. But this phenomenon is the result of the play of intense magnetic streams upon the elements of which the Photosphere is composed. In this way does the Divine Centre project through the Photosphere the necessary accommodated elements and electric forces for the nourishing of all life upon the Earth, the disintegration of false states, conditions and elements, and the transmutation of many of her elements as forerunner of her complete Redemption and Restoration. Such is the cause of and the reason for the many phenomena observed by students of Astronomy and Physics. In this way can the reason for the molten sea in the Photosphere, the great prominence apparently upon the surface of the disc, and the immense streams of fiery elements projected for thousands of miles beyond the Photosphere, be understood and explained. And with such an understanding of the phenomena, there remains no longer any room for haphazard theories which fail lamentably to explain the Sun's Mystery—and find no place for the LORD of Being and of Hosts—the LORD GOD of Sabaoth—for the operation of HIS perfect Law throughout the Universe, for HIS manifestation in and through all staral embodiments as living vestures of HIMSELF and glorious conscious exposition of HIS Own Mystery.

The Divinity of Man

One of the outstanding gifts bestowed upon Man by the Creator is the inheritance of the same Mystery common to the Sun and all the Stars. The Divine Macrocosm is repeated in Man. He is a Divine Microcosm. All the Kingdoms are in him. He shares the Spiral, the Balance and the Planes. When he accomplishes certain degrees of his growth and evolution, the Gods can speak to him. He can enter their Spheres. He can receive from them. Even the Son of the Highest can approach him. He can attain to enter His Sphere. He can walk with the Son of GOD. He can come to know the Eternal Mystery. The Glory of the Divine World can be reflected into him. He can be enshrined of GOD. The magnetic streams of the Divine Innermost can cause the Radiance of the Resplendent ONE to ensphere him. And in this experience the radiations will cause his own Aura to melt into and become one with the Spectrum of the ELOHIM.

Such, then, are the high endowments of man. He is the possessor of the Divine Magnetic Principle, which relates him to the Divine World. He has the nucleolus which gives him a correspondence with

*The Divine
Possessions
of Man*

the Celestial Realms. He has the nucleus by which he is associated
with the Angelic Kingdom. And he has the outer fields for experience
and ministry. In a most real sense he is indeed the replica of the
Heavens. And when he is grown up and crowned with the fulness of
his manhood, his Aura would not only be a glorious magnetic display
upon his outer magnetic plane, but it would reveal to the Seer of the
Divine Kingdom the estate entered into and the office filled.

In this way are Souls known.

IN HIS EARLY DAYS

PLATE VI

A

IN HIS EARLY DAYS

PLATE VI

It is somewhat difficult to write of the Master in a way that would appear altogether impersonal, for the human mind does not find it easy to think impersonally; to differentiate between the inner Spiritual and the outer manifest. Yet the glory that may envisage the outer manifestation, must have its cause in the inner Spiritual Realms. In the Celestial Realms even, the manifest is but the garment of the unseen inner World of Divine potency.

The Seen and the Unseen

Therefore, what has to be said of the Master will relate entirely to the inner Life, however great the glory of it may appear to the human vision. The magnetic Light is divinely begotten. It is the radiant manifestation of the result of the Soul's magnetic Pole being overshadowed by the Divine Presence in great degree; for in such an experience the Soul is raised into high estate.

In its constitution the Soul of Man is built up out of the most beautiful spiritual elements. The quality of these is like that of the Gems of the First Water. They are pure Divine Elements. According to the degree of the polarization of these, so is the manifoldness and intensity of the Aura. For all Light is the resultant of polarization of the elements within an embodiment, whether Star or Human Soul; and the polarization is effected through the overshadowing of the magnetic Poles of the embodiment by the Divine World.

It will, therefore, be readily understood that the Aura of one in Christhood is not only beautiful, but is likewise manifold and intense; and that a Soul in the Estate of Divine Christhood is clothed with an Aura of such intensity that it reveals the Divine Resplendence. Such an Aura would have the power of repulsion. It would by its own magnetic quality, when in positive state, repel those who were out of harmony, or who were in opposition to the Soul; whilst it would, in its negative or static state, draw to its atmosphere those who were needy and seeking for true spiritual alms. For such Souls, the Cloud of Radiance would be full of healing and comfort.

Now, the Master was in the Estate of Christhood. He had passed

The Aura
Revelatory

through its manifold phases. In the Heavens He took His degrees in the various Masonic Schools of the higher Spiritual Realms, becoming an Angelic Christ and then a Celestial Christ of high order. And then He rose to be a Divine Christ. By Angelic, Celestial and Divine Christhood it is to be understood that, in addition to having the capacity to receive high illumination from those realms, He was likewise able to function upon their Kingdoms and become a citizen of them.

During the days of the Manifestation, the Divine Christhood of the Master was obvious to all who knew what Christhood stood for. Even in His childhood the glory of the Heavens shone through Him, though few beheld His Aura. There was an entire absence from Him of anything savouring of the phenomenal and spectacular. The Divine World does not thus reveal itself in and through those who are its Christs. Its potencies and the glory of them are inward and hidden. The power, illumination, and radiance of one in Christhood, have to be discovered.

The accompanying Plate will illustrate such an Aura as was seen by the Seer around the child Ioannes, generally spoken of as Jesus. The radiance is great, though the Spectrum tints are not so emphatic in their manifestation. The Light revealed is that of the Christhood, but as yet only in the degree of perfect Jesushood. Later, the radiance becomes more intense, and the Tinctures of the ELOHIM more fully revealed. Indeed as the Plate which follows that of the childhood will show, the Mystery of the Light within the Soul deepens with the Soul's ascension into the Celestial and Divine Spheres. For with every degree taken on the ladder to Christhood, the Radiance of the Divine increases, the Soul shares the Divine Resplendence, and the Bow of GOD—the Rainbow of the ELOHIM— becomes manifest in the Aura.

How beautiful it will be and how good for this world when the children can all be born of parents who are pure in their desires and ways! When all the Souls returning for new manifestation, and especially the older Souls, can be born into the conditions of life associated with the Jesus state! When those who are to come as leaders and teachers of the children of men can have such conditions to grow up in, that they will not require to travail, as Souls do now, to attain the Jesus and Spiritual Christhood states, but will grow up into them full of hope, vision and joy! Unto such an end is this message given back to Israel.

30

DURING THE MANIFESTATION

PLATE VII

B

DURING THE MANIFESTATION

PLATE VII

As already intimated, Christhood has many degrees. The Soul *In the* passes through many heavenly Masonic Lodges, each more advanced *Bosom* than the other, ere it reaches the estate of a Divine Christhood. *of the* And when it reaches that estate, the Divine power it has gathered *Father-* on the way, causes such an intensification of its Aura as to make *Mother* the latter beyond description. Plate VII gives a faint idea of the inner Sanctuary of one in Divine Christhood. When such an one is functioning entirely on the inner realms, the realization is of an order that lifts the whole Being into *oneness with the Indwelling Presence*. The Soul becomes One with the FATHER-MOTHER.

This accounts for many Sayings by the Master, and explains how He not only came out from the Bosom of the FATHER-MOTHER for the purpose of the Manifestation and Oblation, but how, in the high Christhood He always dwelt in the Bosom of the FATHER-MOTHER. The Auric Glory of the Soul in whom such a Divine Union takes place is ineffable. It is more than transfiguration; it is the real Ascension into the Cloud.

Herein also is revealed the real meaning in the stories of the Baptism, Transfiguration, and Ascension into the Cloud from both the high Hill in Galilee and the Mount of Olives. For in the Baptism the Cloud is *above* the Master; the Voice speaks from out of its midst; and the Dove is gifted unto Him from out the Glory: in the Transfiguration the Cloud overshadows Him for a time; transcendent fellowship and counsel take place; the Voice again speaks not only to Him but concerning Him; He becomes transformed and transfigured in the Divine Presence, and enshrined in the Glory: in the Ascension, the Cloud awaits His coming; he passes into it; He is received out of sight, because no longer is He separate from the ETERNAL ONE in His consciousness, but is ever one with the FATHER-MOTHER; henceforth the whole Being becomes as the Body of the LORD, one with the cosmic whole; the Servant is no longer apart

31

from His LORD, He has become the Messenger for the Eternal World whensoever and wheresoever He may be sent. He is girt about with the band of Gold which is the insignia of His Degree; and He has given to Him the crown of Gold which bespeaks His Office. He is now named a High Priest after the Order of Melchizedek. He stands in the Eternal Light; and all about Him there are the Cherubic and Seraphic ministries. The glory behind Him is that of the Eternal Mystery. Within that Eternal Light He stands. Henceforth He is a Divine Prism for the refraction and dispersion of the Glory of the ELOHIM.

Such was the Estate of the Master great ages before He came for the Manifestation and the Oblation. His real Baptism, Transfiguration and Ascension, were accomplished elsewhere than upon these planes or within this System. Because He had taken such High Degrees in Divine growth and evolution, He was equipped for His Mission.

Many have desired to know who He was before the days of the Manifestation. Many have conjectured and have been led astray. Those who had known Him prior to the Earth-Manifestation, had lost the memory of Him. The obtaining conditions had so dimmed their vision till many of them came to think of themselves as children of this Planet. In a most real sense (though the interior significance of the saying had relation to the ADONAI) *He came unto His own, yet His own received Him not; but to all who heard His Message unto the understanding and following of it, He showed the true way to regain the power to make manifest as Sons of God.*

Those who had known Him of old time and who came to recognize Him again, did not do so in any personal way. When they themselves functioned on the personal and mental planes, they became troubled by some things He found it necessary to do, and many things which He had to say to them: then they questioned amongst themselves concerning Him. But when they functioned on the spiritual planes they knew Him and His Message. Then they could truly say to Him, "Thou hast the Word of Eternal Life."

AMID THE GETHSEMANE

PLATE VIII

Facing page 32.

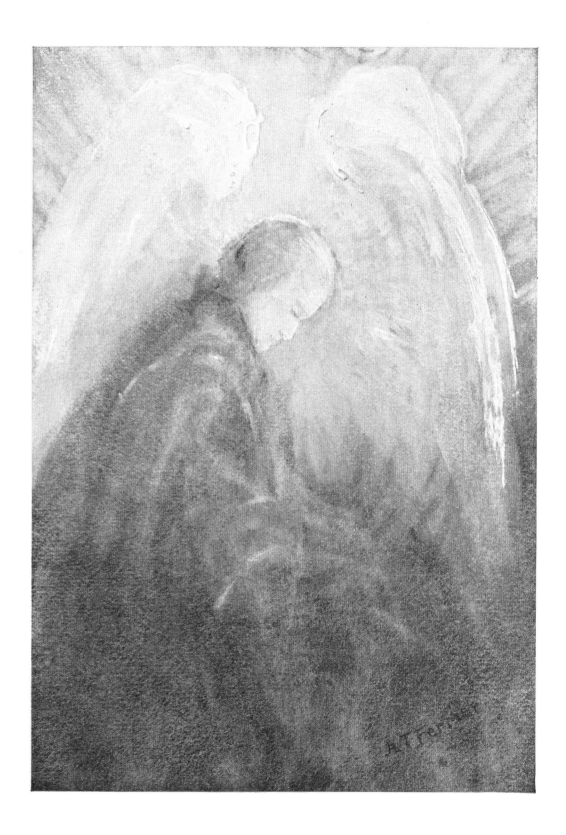

C

AMID THE GETHSEMANE

PLATE VIII

"Now when His anguish was passed away, He was ministered unto by Angels; and these accompanied Him unto the hour of His Passover when He entered upon the work of Ransoming which the Father-Mother had given him to do."

The Shadows of Sorrow

Between the Auric manifestation of Plate VII and that of Plate VIII there is a great contrast. In the latter it is as if the Glory had departed. Even the Angels who minister have their Auric Glory dimmed. The whole atmosphere is one of sorrow. When great sorrow overtakes a Soul the radiance of its Aura becomes veiled. And though sorrow does not visit the Angels as the outcome of their individual travail, it does affect them in sympathetic way when they have to minister to those who are in sorrow. In a very special way was this so in the Master's travail in the Gethsemane as He looked out upon the path along which the Oblation would take Him. For, as those appointed to minister to Him beheld the veiling of the Glory that had been His and the profundity of the sorrow that overtook Him, they themselves became affected; for in His Travail the whole Heavens were bowed down with grief because of the Burden He had to carry on behalf of this world.

The Light within Him had to be veiled. To His vision it was as if the glorious Presence were being gradually withdrawn. The realizations which had been so transcendent and blessed, grew less and less. He could no more dwell in the Cloud of Radiance until the Oblation was fully accomplished. The Cloud could not follow Him in the path of the Travail; it must await His Return. From out the Glory He had to be let down. The Heavens found it necessary to take away the consciousness of His LORD, so that He knew not where to find HIM amid the Travail, though He was the Vehicle of the Passion of the LORD. The transit from Divine Christhood to the Soul-empty state of a Bondservant, was from the

*Gethsemane
A Divine
Mystery*

summit of Divine Glory to the deep sunless valley. All the Divine Forces whose motion caused the Auric Glory of Divine Christhood to pour itself forth unseen, except by the Seer, in revealing ministry and sublime manifestation, had to be changed in their motion so as to operate within a realm foreign to them and Him in order to affect the prevailing conditions within the Planetary Heavens and effect their purification and redemption. Who may guess or imagine what it meant to Him who had been a dweller within the Glory of the Cloud of Divine Radiance, to have to take passage on the great Astral Sea of spiritual death and make His way into the land where the Eternal Light shone not, and where the ages of the ministry of the Oblation would be passed amid the deep darkness of a moonless and starless night? For the Mind would be un-illumined, and the Christs would be absent. It was even so that only those who had been appointed to minister to Him amid the Travail knew the contrast in Him between the glorious state of Divine Christhood and that of the Redeemer. It was absolutely necessary that Angels should minister to Him, for He could not rise into the Cloud of Radiance. A way of communication had to be kept open during the Lives of the Oblation so that the Divine World could mediate unto Him through the Celestial and Angelic Realms; for the ministry had to be of a very special nature. He was mysteriously upheld through the operation of the Law of the Kingdom to which He belonged; for He was held by His magnetic Poles by means of the magnetic stream flowing from the Divine World. In like manner, through His Poles He was affected from the Divine World to carry out the Will of the Heavens upon the place whither He went and into whose evil conditions He had to enter. And the action of the magnetic stream upon His magnetic Poles had to be of such a nature, that these latter would not be so affected as to cause His Divine Aura to make manifest. For He had to be veiled. Indeed, He had to be hidden from all those who were enemies to the Christhood manifestation, and the work of the Oblation. Truly there was a "veiling of faces."

Even the ministry of the Angels to Him could be rendered only after certain phases of the Work had been undertaken and the Burden borne. For during the process of such work, the Angels could not approach Him; and it was only afterwards, in the hours of His loneliness and sorrow, that they could give Him direct ministry

34

of comfort. The Divine World, however, held Him always by His magnetic Poles. That World could always communicate with Him; influence the direction of the work He had to do; give Him, as long as need be for what had to be done within a given time, the Divine Urge to proceed; control Him in the spending of His auric forces and energies so that His hand was stayed; turn His thoughts and desires from the active and tragic processional by which the graven images were blotted out and the elements within the Planetary Heavens transmuted, to that static state wherein in passive but introspective mood He could contemplate what He had done, and, in doing so, have the floodgates of His Being opened for the sorrow begotten of the nature of the Burden and the Work, to pour itself forth from the flooded fountain of His Soul.

It was at such times that the Angels could approach Him and minister of the Divine Balm of the Eternal Love. But the perfect healing of His sorrow could be realized only after the Oblation had been fully accomplished. For, until then, He could "no more drink of the fruit of the Vine" as in the Estate of Christhood, and know the joy of entering into the consciousness of the Divine Overshadowing and Indwelling, and ascend once more into the Cloud of the Divine Resplendence and share its Glory.

It was not an easy thing that the Angels had given them to do who were appointed to minister unto Him; for He had been accustomed to receive direct from the FATHER-MOTHER by means of the Archangel of the Presence. Indeed, He lived mostly in the Eternal consciousness; and, because of the transcendency of this estate, the loss to Him was unspeakable amid the new, strange, and most evil conditions. And such difficulties were greatly increased when He had to enter into those awful states which miraged the inner vision and made Him captive to fear and doubt, bound Him to the pillar of Pilate's Judgment Hall where the callous spirit of denial and negation flagellated Him and made Him even doubt the goodness of the FATHER-MOTHER in the Angelic ministry.

35

THE SACRED HEART

PLATE IX

Facing page 38

A

THE SACRED HEART

PLATE IX

The story of the Sacred Heart is full of profound truth. Though to many it will be related to the traditional superstitions of Rome, and be circumscribed by the personal application of it, first and specially to the Master as the Sacred Heart of Jesus, and then to Mary as the Mother of the LORD; yet it has a more far-reaching meaning, and touches every spiritual man and woman. For that which it signifies is in the Soul's constitution. The true Society of the Sacred Heart is something transcendently greater than any ecclesiastical community. Indeed, the seeker would often look in vain for the real Sacred Heart in the fellowship of the Societies that have assumed the name.

Playing at the Mysteries

The title is associated with the Master to signify His love and compassion. Pictures and statuary represent Him with the Sacred Heart upon His breast. These may seem the expressions of children when they play at the Mysteries. And truly they are. But most men and women are only little children in their religious outlook, beliefs, and experiences. *They play at the Mysteries.* Certainly the great Church whose Altars are many, and whose symbols build up its spectacular, only plays at the Reality. Though it makes use of Altar and Symbol continuously in its mystery-dramas, yet its real understanding of them is almost nil. Its spectacular is amongst the gods of material images. Its realm of ministry is outward though it claims to speak for the Heavens. Its Kingdom and conquests are largely of the Earth. Yet its Altars claim to speak of the Soul and the LORD of Being. And all its symbols are proclaimed to be the living language of the Heavens, though inarticulate. Its devoted adherents are asked to believe in the Sacred Heart of Jesus, to worship at the Altar named after it, to pay tribute to it; yet no one of them, not even their Priests, appear to be in the least degree conversant with the language for which the Symbol stands, nor with its hidden meaning.

Yet the Symbol is of Divine appointment. It speaks of the Divine potencies within the Sacred Heart or Chalice. It is

39

The Sacred Chalice

reminiscent of the Divine Love. The Wisdom of the Most High is revealed in it. The Secret of GOD is contained in its Mystery. For the Sacred Heart, when applied to any Soul, signifies a high state of consciousness; and when predicated of a Messenger, as in the case of the Master, it shows forth His Divine Office. It is of high mediatorial character. It is as the insignia of Divine Appointment. For it reveals the quality of the ministry to be rendered, and the sublimity of the gift to be given.

The Symbol is age-old. In the Human Love estate it is an echo clear and vibrant of events in the Celestial and Divine realms. The Sacred Heart of Jesus is the concrete exposition of the Divine Love's outflow from the Chalice of Eternal Being. Jesus is GOD's revelation of Love embodied. Even the Sacred Heart of Mary the Mother of Sorrows, is an unveiling of the "Motherhood of GOD."

The Human Soul is of Divine Formation. It shares with the Solar World the Mystery of the Spiral. That Spiral has its sacred centre. Within the Southern Dimension the Divine Heart of the Soul has its place. Its dual motion is the result of the magnetic stream which flows from the Divine Centre of the Microcosmic Cross within it. That action affects the Apex of the right-angle formed by the perpendicular and horizontal streams of magnetism set in motion by the Principle when active. The Apex likewise forms a magnetic Orifice through which the Divine Heart can pour its magnetic Life-stream. That stream may be observed in the illustration, Plate IX. It proceeds from the bosom as an intense stream of white light, when the Soul is in Divine Christhood. In the lower degrees of Christhood it is present. And in one who has attained the Estate of Jesus, Christ, and the LORD, it is most powerful as a vehicle for the communication of the Divine World Life-stream, named, The Blood of the Lamb. For when a Soul is in high Christhood, it has become so much a part of the Body of the LORD that it can be used, even as the Divine Elements of a magnetic order are used, for the transmission of the mysterious Life-stream of the Divine Love and Wisdom.

Though this high Estate is couched in the Drawing (Plate IX), yet originally it was meant to illustrate the spiritual estate of the Divine Motherhood; and in less degree, such a state of Soul attainment as was associated with the Mother of the Master, and Souls in kindred estates.

THE ANNUNCIATION

PLATE X

Facing page 40.

B

THE ANNUNCIATION

PLATE X

Those who are familiar with the works of the greatest spiritual artists, will recall their portrayal of the most sacred theme of The Annunciation. Two of Fra Angelico's pictures will be specially remembered. The place of announcement; the tender grace and diffident attitude of the Madonna; the wonderful features, form, and attitude, of the Archangel Gabriel; make a most harmonious and impressive setting to such a Divine, Imperial Theme of the Soul. Yet with the perfection of arrangement, place, embodiments, and colour, there is an earthly element in the presentations difficult to eliminate, which tends to divert the mind from the Spiritual, and make of the event, which belongs entirely to the Kingdom of the Soul, something that took place upon the historical planes, and objectively. For it is thus that the Annunciation is regarded in religious stories and believed in and taught by Priests and Scribes.

A Divine Soul-Drama

But the Annunciation was of another nature than that portrayed in religious history. It was and must ever be a purely mystical story. It is most real to the Soul who is honoured with the experience. It is essentially inward though it has its outward manifestation. The scene of its enactment is within the cloisters of the Soul, and the out-working of the drama is within the Sanctuary of the Being. The dialogue is always between a Virgin-Soul and the Angel of the LORD. The Message is that which religious story associates with the Mother of the Master; yet it is no human conception and birth that are foretold, however beautiful and poetic the idea may be; rather is it the conception and maturation of a new and higher Life in the Soul which in manifestation after birth shall attain to be crowned, Jesus, Christ, and the LORD.

The Annunciation is one of the great Mysteries. Where it is heralded to the Soul it testifies of the Soul's attainment. For only to one who had reached a certain degree of spiritual estate could the

41

*The
Message
of Gabriel*

Angel of the Lord speak and be understood. Because it is both an illumination to the visited one and a call to rise up into Divine Estate. The Angel approaches those only who have known the Christhood in ancient times. No other Souls could endure the approach of Gabriel. None others could understand the message of an Annunciation. There is so much implied in it. There is the Vision of things transcendent calling the Soul upward. There is the recognition of the Angelic World and the Messenger from it. The voice of Gabriel has to be recognized and endured. And the burden of the announcement has to be borne unto the fulfilment of the Divine Will.

In Plate X these are shown. The Vision has broken upon the Soul, and the whole Being is arrested. The recipient is no mere child, but one full of the Light of Wisdom. The potency of the Divine Love is great in action, hence the magnetic rays streaming from the face and bosom, which here represent the countenance and Divine Heart. The Being is intent upon the Divine Vision, and is hearing the Divine Message. Gabriel is communicating, for he is the Archangel of illumination. That which he has to transmit from the realm of the Elohim is of supreme importance to the one so honoured.

All hail, Maria! My Lord hath sent me unto thee to inform thee that thou art honoured and chosen by Him to be the vehicle of His Manifestation. Henceforth art thou to be consecrate unto Him; for He shall overshadow thee through His Holy One. Thou shalt conceive, through His overshadowing, that which shall be named Son of God. And thou shalt bear and bring Him forth into manifest Life as Jesus, Christ, and the Lord. And it shall not be of any man that thou conceivest and bringest forth; for that which is to be born into manifestation from thee, is from the Lord of Glory.

The Glory of Love is expressed in the countenance. The joy begotten of the Vision fills the Cup of Life. The amazement of the honour gives Divine Soul intensity to the look, and whelms the Heart with deepest emotion. Gabriel is not visible to the outer eye, but the Soul beholds him. The drama is inward; its acts and scenes are within the realms of the Gods. The Aura breathes Angelic Atmosphere. It is of Solar order. And it is of the resplendence of the spectrum as it filled the Solar chromosphere in the Earth's unfallen days.

42

The importance of a right understanding of the Annunciation should be recognized by Israel. All the members of the ancient community of the Sons of GOD who are now within the spheres of the Earth for ministry must recover the Annunciation, and pass through its experiences in the recovery. For the conception, maturation, birth into manifestation of Jesus, Christ, and the LORD, can be alone made in and through them. They of old time knew the Christhood estate. They were of the great company of GOD's Christs. They were children of the Sun, of the Radiance, and of the Heavenly Wisdom. They loved much, even to the giving up of all for service. They were no strangers to the visits of Gabriel. He had frequently to communicate with them. They had even looked into his glorious spheres. It is to them he again speaks. His announcement is of and from the Law of Wisdom and Love. He foretells what is to be for them and through them. It is now for Israel to respond, to regain their ancient Inheritance, to arise and make manifest the Christhood, to restore the regnancy of Jesus, Christ, and the LORD.

Gabriel's Message unto Israel

Arise! Shine forth the Light that is within thee, O Soul of Israel! For the Glory of thy LORD hath arisen within thee.

The coming of Gabriel is now. He has come and is coming to all who possess the Sacred Heart in their Estate and Manifestation. He is seeking for the House of Maria, the Virgin-Soul, the one who is in the state of selfless love; for unto such an one may he foretell the coming of the LORD into Manifestation in the holy estates of Jesus Christ.

It is the Day of the LORD; the day of Gabriel's appearance unto the House of Israel.

It is the Day of the Great Annunciation of the coming of Christ Jesus to heal the world of its hurts. It is the Day of the regathering of Israel for such a Manifestation of Jesus Christ as will bring the true Redemption to mankind, the healing of humanity's wounds, and the concrete exposition of the Presence of GOD with HIS children.

Hear, O House of Israel, this Word of the LORD!

43

THE ASCENSION

PLATE XI

Facing page 44.

C

THE ASCENSION

PLATE XI

The Ascension as told in the New Testament, is an arresting story. *A Soul's*
It is entirely associated with the Master, and is supposed to describe *Divine*
the manner of His farewell to the Earth and flight to the Heavens. Its *Experience*
interpretation has not been easy even for the best scholars, exegetes
and expositors. The passage of the Master through the Celestial
Heavens is not the only difficulty to be overcome; for in addition
there are the three accounts of the Ascension, and these are amazingly
contradictory. In each of the statements there would be the same
Celestial problem; for in an Ascension through the various atmospheres
which mantle the Earth, it would not make any difference whether the
Ascension took place from a high hill in Galilee or from Bethany, or
from the Mount of Olives. But the Ascension of the Master could
not have taken place from the three geographical situations at the
same time. Nor was He likely to have made any display of such a
spectacular order, giving to the mind of the disciples an entirely
outward interpretation of facts which to Him were absolutely spiritual
and Soulic, and had no relation whatever to a transit from the Earth
to the Solar Body, or to another Celestial system.

The Ascension was a spiritual fact. It was a Divine experience. It
took place amidst Æthereal Atmospheres. It had three great degrees.
Its way lay through the Galilean Porch upon an exceedingly high hill;
by way of Bethany, the House of Mary and Martha where the LORD
loved to visit; and from the summit of Olivet.

It was a spiritual fact for it was an ascension of the whole Being in
state. It relates to the experience of every Soul who passes into the
higher and more inward Kingdoms. For all who share the Body of
the LORD through the realization of the Presence, do so by the Divine
process, dynamic and empirical, of the elevation of all the bodies,
from the Soul or higher Ætheric, to the outer body. In such an

45

Galilee,
Bethany
and
Olivet

experience the Soul transcends the Earth. It takes its flight through the Earth's Atmospheres, rising far above them in state of Life and Consciousness, till it enters the Atmospheres of the Celestial Kingdoms. That is the first great Degree of the Soul's Ascension. It is the Degree of the Eternal Love.

In taking its second great Degree, it passes through the Portals of the Home at Bethany. It is the Home of Divine Wisdom where the Soul, Maria, learns the Mystery of her LORD as she sits at HIS feet; and as Martha, learns *how* truly to serve HIM. For when it is said that "He led them as far as Bethany and was parted from them," it is not the LORD who leaves the Soul in the House of Wisdom and Service, but it is the LORD in the Soul who parts the Being from its undue attachments to the merely individual relationship in the House of Wisdom to HIMSELF, and the personal character of the Soul's service. He parts the Soul even in such a state as the Degree implies, from all the bondage of merely individual relationship and personal devotion, and bears it up and into the Atmospheres which pervade the Divine Heavens. And thus it rises beyond the House of the Divine Wisdom as a Divine Centre of learning and acquisition, and enters into the House of the LORD.

It is the second great Degree. Here Wisdom is realized.

But the Degrees of the Divine Love and Wisdom through the Soul's Ascension from Galilee and Bethany, lead to that other Ascension which is associated with Olivet. To take the Celestial degree and ascend into the realms of the Gods through the realization of the Divine Love in sublime fulness, prepares the Soul to receive with true understanding the Mystery of the Divine Wisdom, and together, these Degrees empower the Soul to take the next Degree wherein the Love and Wisdom become so united in the Being that that Ascension is taken and accomplished in which the supreme Sacrifice of Being itself is made unto the LORD. In that Ascension Nirvana is reached. The Soul becomes one with the LORD. And it is thus so unified in Love and the realization of the Wisdom and Spirit of the LORD, that it is henceforth the vehicle absolutely for manifestation and sacrificial service. Whatever sacrifice the LORD of Being purposes, the Soul seeks full share in it. In the measure of its capacity it gives as the LORD gives.

46

The Ascension from Olivet is into the Divine Kingdom of Sacrifice. Here Love and Wisdom are revealed in their perfection as the Soul moves, serves, and gives supremely. It is the Degree of the Son of GOD.

The exquisite Drawing, Plate XI, reveals more than is apparent. The Aura is magnificent. The quiescent and active solar states are present. The static Balance, named "the Rest of GOD," is expressed in the outstretched arms with lovely drapery. The active state or centrifugal motion is testified of in the upright figure, which speaks of the Divine Righteousness, or the Standard of a Son of GOD. The base of the Standard is lost in the chromatic Atmospheres wherein is hidden the Mystery of GOD; and the Apex of the Standard is glorious in its magnetic radiations. The Head is as a Divine Chalice that is full of the Eternal Light; the Countenance reveals the Soul's joy in the attainment through ascension to the Eternal World; and the eyes are luminous through the realization of the Mystery of EL ADONAI.

The Estate of the Elders of Israel

The drawing is illustrative of the exalted state into which those who were designated The Elders of Israel, had attained. They had "Ascended up on High." They had taken the three great Degrees of the Ascension. They understood the meaning of the High Mountain in Galilee. The Wine of GOD had been their drink and the Wisdom of GOD their daily Bread, when they dwelt upon the heights of Zion, or Christhood. For the dual Mystery of the Divine Love and Wisdom had been accommodated to their estate, and they were able to celebrate the most Holy Eucharist. They had visited Bethany as catechumens and become the friends of the LORD, and had learnt much there concerning the Mystery of the Fig-tree. And they had even been on the slopes of Olivet though not on its summit, and had heard of many sacred things from Him who was the LORD's Servant and Messenger; and, as the result of such fellowship, they had ascended still higher in their estate and consciousness.

Such were the three Degrees of the Ascension, to Israel of old; and such must they become again to the whole House of Israel in these days. The Return and the Regeneration are the prophecy of such high realization.

THE METEMPSYCHOSIS

PLATE XII

Facing page 48.

D

THE METEMPSYCHOSIS

PLATE XII

The term metempsychosis has often been used to signify the descent
of the Human Soul from its own kingdom to that of the Creature.
This was called the transmigration of the Soul, either voluntarily
undertaken for some redemptive purpose in the Soul itself, or something imposed upon the Soul as a judgment for its evil deeds.

*The Law
of God is
Perfect*

Such transmigration has taken place many times in the past ages.
Many of the spirits or Angels who fell from their first estate and
became rebellious against the Laws of the Divine Love and Wisdom,
had to be shut up within forms beneath the Human Kingdom—not
as punishment for their sad and disastrous conduct, though as a
protection to the Planet and her children, as well as the guarding of
other spiritual and Divine interests. And for the healing and redemption of some of these it was necessary that they should learn lowliness
of mind, obedience, and gentleness through suffering. And for those
who most cruelly betrayed and destroyed the weak and the humble,
it became the only path, the treading of which might have a salutary
and restorative effect upon them. The Law of GOD is just; and HIS
mercy is revealed in the just and healing operation of HIS Love.
Those who persist in dealing out unkindness and cruelty to other
Souls, have to be taught the true way; and if they will not learn that
way upon the Human Kingdom, then it becomes necessary for them
to learn by the path of transmigration to a lower Kingdom. Rulers
might learn much if they would, what the oppressing of a people
may bring to them. Sportsmen and sportswomen, and scientists who
oppress and torture the creatures in the name of knowledge for
remedial purposes, may be assured that all cruelty practised must be
undone in its effects and its ignoble spirit redeemed, even should it
mean the going down into the state and conditions of the hunted, or
entering and passing through the like tortures within the vivisector's
laboratory. There is no escape from the Law that governs
Righteousness and Equity. The Eternal World works to the Balance,
and all Souls must express that Balance.

But transmigration may have another meaning. It may relate to the

E
49

Soul's Ascension. Wheresoever the Soul is it must have vehicles. Its liberation from the physical body and its translation to higher realms does not mean that it ceases to have a vehicle through which to manifest. Therefore, to transmigrate may also mean that the Soul knows translation; and to be translated is also to be exalted in state. Enoch is said to have been translated; for GOD took him.

Now, metempsychosis is translation. It is the process by which the Soul passes from the limitations of the outer vehicle, and rises into another realm where a new vehicle, corresponding to that realm, is assumed for functioning through. It is the process of The Regeneration wherein the Ætheric Body becomes changed in its texture and fashion. The transmutory process prepares the Soul to function upon the more inward kingdoms. From state to state it can ascend; but in each Ascension a fresh metempsychosis is passed through. The overshadowing becomes greater and more intense. The glorification is increasingly transcendent. The vehicle appears to be more fragile, though actually it is more potent. The garments grow quite diaphanous, and the whole fashion of the Being takes on a fuller radiance. It is a scene of sublime transformation; for the fashion and countenance change. It leads on to perfect transfiguration in which process the Being takes upon itself the likeness of the LORD. Henceforth all the vehicles share in the Sacred Tinctures. Each becomes clothed in its own garment, from the Ruby to the Amethyst. When the Soul attains full Divinity, its final metempsychosis has been accomplished.

But for ministry it might have to descend from an Estate so high, as in the case of the Oblation. In such an experience there has to be a laying down of acquired powers and regnancies. A Body of humiliation might even have to be taken. But such a metempsychosis would be on behalf of others, and so for redemptive purposes. It would be a voluntary vicarious burden.

The wealth of meaning in Plate XII cannot be written of; but the process of Divestment and transmutation is indicated. The Divine Glory is enveloping the entire fashion, and in the cloud it is changing. It is a translation of the Soul by the Divine World; and the veil, diaphanous though it now be, is gradually withdrawn from the countenance. The Soul is now free to soar in its vision, and to look upon the glories of the Divine World. The Drawing is wonderful in what it reveals and in what it veils. It testifies of the Soul changing its Kingdom; but it hides from the curious the Secret.

THE HOLY GRAIL

PLATE XIII

Facing page 50.

E

THE HOLY GRAIL

PLATE XIII

The ever enchanting story of the Holy Grail is shadowed forth in Plate XIII. Its association in the Artist's mind with a Divine Eucharist, is obviously portrayed. Its scene is the Temple of the Knights. The Altar and the Presence become one. The over-shadowing Glory and the Elements of Eucharistic Blessing, are blended, whilst the latter remain sufficiently distinct and apart to reveal the individual character of each part of the Mystery.

From the Altar Table there is an ascending arc of Divine Revelation. The first arresting sign is the Monogram. It contains the three letters I.H.S., so greatly reminiscent of the crucifixion, and the insignia and ritual of the Church. The letters are usually translated in the world memorable terms—Jesus the Saviour of men (Iesus Hominum Salvator). But in the Greek form they stand for the first three letters in the name of Jesus; and in their innermost mystical significance they represent The Sign of the Cross, the dual mystery of the FATHER-MOTHER, the Altar of Divine Oblation, and the Secret of the Spirit. They speak of more than the Servant of the Manifestation, or of His Cross, or of the Redemption accomplished by the Oblation, and the Salvation that is to come to man. They belong to the Kingdom of the innermost Mysteries, and are related to Ioseph Maria. They form the Divine Monogram engraven upon the Altar of Being. An under-standing of the significance of these letters will help to make clear the Holy Grail.

Of this latter, the first part of the Mystery meets us in the Sacred Loaf. It is the Sacramental Cake said to have been broken by the Master at the Last Supper of the LORD. But it has also been associated with the Knight-Templar. For in the Home of Templary the Grail was conceived of as The White Stone upon which the name of every Knight was written. It was also the Luminous Stone: it gave forth

The Divine Knight-Templar

51

radiance. There was iridescent motion in it. And in like manner it became the mysterious Bread of the hungry.

Thus the mysterious Stone of Living Fire seen upon the Altar, and handled by the Seraphim in acts of Blessing, was regarded as the Living Presence of the LORD of Being. The Loaf became the Bread of Life, the Radiant Testimony, the Keeper of Seals, the Insignia of Divine Knighthood. To have a portion in it was to be consecrated absolutely for the Service of LORD ADONAI.

Following the Bread of the Sacred Seven upon the Altar, we meet the Chalice on the way. It is the Cup of the New Covenant. To overflow it is full of the Wine of GOD. From the fruit of the Eternal Vine the sacred energy proceeds: it is even as the sacred Fire of GOD. The potency of the contents of the Chalice is manifest in the radiance which emanates from it. There is Life indeed in that potency, and there is Light in its elements. To drink of it is to receive the Blood of the Lamb of GOD.

In the outer history of the Grail as seekers have conceived of it, the chief value is given to a pewter, bronze, silver or golden chalice. Indeed by most writers upon the theme, the Grail itself is confounded with the chalice. But merely to find and possess the Cup supposed to have been used by the Master in the Last Supper, could be of no value whatever other than archæological and sentimental; and to imagine that it is the Chalice of the Grail is to materialize the most Holy Mystery. Even mystics who have not come into the true and full vision, though seeking for it, attach undue importance to the objective symbol, and not infrequently mistake the symbol for the Reality.

The Holy Grail was and is nothing objective, though its glory becomes manifest in and through those who find it. The Chalice of GOD is in us, and HE fills it with HIS sacred Wine. But the Wine is the Fruit of the Vine, and is HIS own glorious Life-stream. The Grail is HIS Holy One as HIS Presence within the Chalice of our Being. That Presence is often glimpsed by the seekers as they journey on their way to the Christhood estate; but it eludes all who have not reached the Christhood. They may not touch to hold it until their hour is come when they enter into the Guest-chamber and share the Holy Mystery. In that Fellowship they will eat of the Bread which is the Flesh or Substance of the Son of GOD, and drink of the Cup which contains the Wine or Blood of that Holy One. In that act they will be the possessors of the Holy Grail. And they will become one with its Mystery. Its inherent power they will share. Its glory will shine through them. Their flesh will become as the Flesh or Substance of the Son of GOD. Their Life-stream will merge into His Life-stream; henceforth He will energize them and be their Life. They will walk with Him in white. At His Altar they will mediate for Him. To them will the Heavens be ever open, and upon them will the most Holy Gift descend to clothe them with Divine Power for High-priesthood. Such is the story told in Plate XIII.

The Soul becomes one with The Host

53

THE SOLAR GARMENT

PLATE XIV

F

THE SOLAR GARMENT

Plate XIV

It is difficult to record in writing the Mystery of the Woman clothed with the Sun. There is a sense in which this is true of all the Mysteries; but in this instance it is very specially so. The Solar potency is tremendous, and its resplendence is ineffable. How any Soul could endure its full potency, or live in its resplendence, is not easy to apprehend. The Sun clothes the Earth with light by means of magnetic action; and physical Science has helped many to understand in some small degree how that is accomplished. But Science has nothing to say about the Human Soul receiving light from the Sun; for the story of the Soul is outside its domain. Few Scientists seem to know whether man is a living Soul. From the standpoint of physical Science it would be an impossibility for any one to be clothed in the garments of Solar splendour, beyond the measure of the Earth's illumination by day.

How the Sun Garments the Soul

The above articles on "The Solar Mystery," should help those who read with open perceptions, to apprehend something of the Mystery of the Solar Light, and the way in which a Soul can possess it and be clothed by it.

The Woman clothed with the Sun is an event of Celestial significance, and one to be experienced only by the Soul who has entered upon Divine Christhood. It represents the triumph of the Soul along the path of ascensions as it has risen from Kingdom to Kingdom and glory to glory. It signifies that the Soul has risen to be a citizen of the Sun in high degree, and that through its own Solar Centre all its powers can be and are affected. It indicates that the Soul has acquired the power to receive direct from the Divine Kingdom, the magnetic stream; that the influx of that stream has raised it to the rank of a Son of GOD; that its Solar Orifice is the venue through which the influx proceeds to flow into the Spiral and through the various planes, affecting the magnetic Pole so greatly that its action results in the Soul becoming clothed in the auric magnetic Solar Light.

55

The Crown
of Stars

Thus it will be perceived that the Soul is clothed from within and not from without; that the Solar resplendence ensphering it is generated through the influx of the magnetic stream, and the action of this latter upon the magnetic Pole. For when a Soul attains to this estate, its Aura takes on the appearance of the Solar Glory. The effulgence of the radiance of its Aura is great: indeed it is ineffable. Even in the static state, such a Soul's Aura would be glorious though passive; and in its active state, the centrifugal force would be tremendous. The appearance of such a Soul would be as one who was garmented, through its auric cloud, with the golden radiance of the Sun.

In the Drawing the Woman stands upon an arc of Light such as the Moon would make in the Celestial Heavens. In the Apocalyptic Vision the Woman clothed with the Sun has her feet resting upon the Moon. Mystically the Moon represents the Mind, especially the Celestial Mind, called also the Higher Mind. The beautiful feet are associated with the illumined Understanding. When the Understanding is illumined from the Sun or Divine Centre, the whole Mind is lit up. It becomes an arc of sacred Light.

In such an Estate of conscious realization, the Soul has power to transcend all the lower and intermediary spheres, and ride upon the chariots of the Heavens—the Solar Breaths. It has power to move from sphere to sphere—Angelic, Celestial, and Divine. It has power to move and serve in all the realms through which it has passed on its way to the Divine; therefore, it can descend for ministry through the Mind in its various aspects, clad in Divine resplendence. On its mission it would appear in the Celestial and Angelic spheres, through the intensity of its auric glory, as a Star in the Firmament. And like the stars in the skies that are named variable, growing more luminous at times and then less intense in the manifestation of their glory, so would such a Soul manifest in the Heavens according to the nature and degree of its ministry, and whether it was in its Static state with all its magnetic streams quiescent, or in Active and centrifugal motion wherein its streams were projected for ministry. For it is in such wise that Stars change in the Celestial Heavens, and the glory of their radiance appears great or dimmed; and it is in like manner that Souls who attain their Divinity, shine in the Spiritual Firmament, varying the manifestation of their glory

56

according to the nature of the ministries to be rendered, and the capacity to receive of those to whom the service is rendered.

All this is implied in the Drawing (Plate XIV). And there is an endeavour to express something of the Static and Active states.

Yet there is more. The attained Inheritance of such a Soul is Regal. It has given to it the Royal Diadem. Its Crown contains Twelve Stars. The Inheritance breathes Celestial Atmospheres. The Soul in such estate becomes the Centre of a system. In miniature it has Mazzaroth. In reality, the Twelve Stars are only its Attributes. But the Attributes are essential members of its constitution. They are the original Twelve Knights of the Round Table. And the Round Table is the Divine Planisphere of the Soul. Around it the Knights take their places to hear from and respond to the central authority. It is indeed the Zodiacal Belt of the Soul. For in the fully evolved Life, the Attributes correspond to the Celestial Mazzaroth. In Divine Christhood the Soul has taken into itself all the qualities of Mazzaroth. The powers of the Soul are in harmony with the Zodiac. The Twelve Systems can communicate with the Soul. And thus such a Soul, whilst clothed in Solar Light and reflecting the resplendence of ADONAI, at the same time becomes crowned with the Twelve Stars whose light and ministry speak of the Celestial Mazzaroth. The Divine dignity of the Human Soul was never more majestically set forth nor its glory more wonderfully revealed. It is so enrobed and crowned as to be henceforth named a Son of GOD. And its ministry gives to it the status of Celestial Lordship, as a member of the Fellowship of the Gods.

THE MESSENGER

PLATE XV

G

THE MESSENGER

PLATE XV

All that has preceded has its culminating resultant in the status and *The Estate* ministry of The Divine Messenger. For even one who is chosen to *of a* be the Messenger of the LORD, has attained to the estate which such *Messenger* an office indicates. All powers realized become cumulative. As the Soul passes through all the Kingdoms, taking the initiations and degrees necessary, it becomes an initiate of each Kingdom, and then a Divine Alchemyst having power to fully appropriate all that has been received, and thus gain the cumulative resultant.

The Messenger thus acquires the power to function within the various Kingdoms to which he may be sent on Divine Service. It is an office of grave responsibility. It is also full of danger in a fallen system. The Messenger is the Servant of his LORD. Though he must needs be richly endowed for his office, yet he may not claim anything for himself. What he has to do he accomplishes in the strength of his LORD. The Message he may have to proclaim is the Word of his LORD. In this service he is guarded. If he is from the Divine Kingdom, he will be Overshadowed from ADONAI. If he is a Celestial Messenger, an Archangel will accompany him. In addition, the Hosts of the LORD will encompass him.

Since this fallen world began the Messenger has had many difficulties to overcome. He has had to meet and overcome the conditions generated by the continued actions of those who brought the Planet and her children down from pure spiritual elements and atmospheres to materialized substances and fixed conditions and Planes. These conditions have made it difficult for the Messenger to function upon this world's Planes, and to give the Message from the Heavens in a way to make it clear to those for whom it was sent, whilst at the same time guarding it from those who have set their faces against the Divine Love and the restoration of the Christhood. And the Messenger has not only to protect the Message from those who would destroy it and himself, but he has to set a

59

*The
Messenger
of the
Manifes-
tation*

guard upon himself so that the materialized conditions do not hurt him and prevent him from fulfilling the Divine Purpose of his mission.

It is no sinecure, at any time, to fill the office of a Messenger; and to be the Servant of the Lord unto those to be ministered unto upon this world, concerning the past and future of the Christhood, is one of dangerous responsibility and burden bearing.

The Drawing (Plate XV) represents the Messenger on the more feminine side of the office. It is an exquisite picture of one sent from the Divine World, and who has held high office there. The insignia proclaim the nature of the service and the subject-matter of the Message. Both in the form and the insignia the Sign of the Cross is revealed. To bear the Sign of the Cross signifies the estate of the Messenger. To be the Messenger for the Sign of the Cross is to be the Vicegerent of Ioseph Maria, He who is known on the Divine Kingdom as The Sign of the Cross. The Sign implies Sacrifice. In relation to this world it had redemptive significance. The one who fills at any time the office indicated in the Drawing, is crowned with the Solar Glory and the Fiery Cross. The Message he has to give is concerned with the ministry of the Cross. It will speak of the Divine Love in His Holy Passion. It is the Message of the Manifestation recalling the Children of the Cross to their ancient inheritance with its Life and Service. It is also the Message of the Manifestation concerning the Divine Purpose in the Oblation to redeem the Planetary Heavens and recreate them. It is the Message of the Christhood, and its presentation is Angelic, Celestial and Divine: these latter are implied in the Drawing. And it represents the Master as He filled the office of the Manifestor, both in the Heavens and in the days of the Manifestation. For He had been crowned a Son of God, and was therefore clothed in the Glory of the Lord. He had been crowned with the Solar Estate so that His auric revelation was Solar Radiance. And He had been exalted to the Divine Kingdom to bear the Insignia of the Royal House of Ioseph Maria, and to have conferred upon Him for His office, the most sacred title, as Vicegerent, The Sign of the Cross.

To be the Messenger of the Most High is to be of great Estate; great in power for Service; great in radiance; great in Divine Realization; and great in lowliness of mind, heart and spirit.

WITHIN THE SANCTUARY

PLATE XVI

H

WITHIN THE SANCTUARY

PLATE XVI

This Drawing and the one which follows, seem of a different order to those already given. And to many they may appear to be of much less importance. Yet their value is equally great. Indeed the realization of all the high spiritual states and Divine qualities expressed in the previous illustrations, is dependent upon the full realization of that of which Drawing XVI speaks. For the path of high realization is that of Devotion within the Sanctuary of Being. And all the Devotion in service through any avenue, is the concrete exposition of Devotion of Mind, Heart, and Spirit.

The Path of Divine Attainment

There can be no attainment without Devotion. Prayer and pure aspiration become the motive power of all ascension. The graces of the Spirit are the steps upon the Ladder GOD has let down from the Heavens to Earth by which the Soul must climb to the apex of Life. On the Spiritual realms those graces make up for the Soul the Steps of Jacob's Ladder. These also have their correspondences upon the Celestial and Divine Kingdoms. To attain Spiritual Christhood the Twelve Graces must be acquired. To reach Celestial Christhood the Twelve Houses must confer their Degrees upon the Soul. To enter through the portals of the Divine World, the Seven Kingdoms of the ELOHIM must write their mystery within the Soul, and give to it the insignia of Divine Christhood.

The path to the summits is that of service. But service is the expression of Devotion to Truth ; to the Divine Wisdom as revealed in the Divine Creation ; and to the Divine Love in its sublime sacrifices. True Devotion is full of reverence. It speaks of the Sacred Mystery with bated breath. It approaches the High Altar deeply conscious of the Presence of which the Altar speaks. It enters the Sanctuary to worship. It comes in the attitude of kneeling, bowing in all the Being. It looks Eastward for the Light to break over the High Altar, for it would be illumined from the LORD. And in the

61

midst of prayer there enters through the window of the Northern Transept, the Glory of the LORD. For the Cross of the Presence appears to the vision of the Mind, and illumines that part of the Being's Sanctuary. Bye and bye the Glory will be observed above the High Altar. The Macrocosmic Cross pours its radiance upon the Mind ere it reveals its Mystery upon and above the Shekinah. The Soul must learn of the Divine from the Divine; and it can so learn only within the Sanctuary in and through beautiful Devotion, Worship and Service. If it would wear the Girdle, it must also wear the Image of HIM Who bestows it.

The Path of Devotion is also the way to the interior knowledge of the Secrets of GOD. Through right Approach, reverent Aspiration, true Prayer and Blessing, Worship and Adoration, and the full sacrificial consecration of the whole Being, the Soul is accounted worthy to receive those Mysteries from the Archangel of the Soul's Elohe. In such an hour it begins its greatest Initiation. This event leads it on to that other great event in which it becomes the inheritor of the Great Realization.

In the Drawing, Devotion, Consecration, Illumination, Reverence, Worship, Adoration and Vision, are all expressed. And the Priesthood of the Adorer is revealed in the Celestial Sapphire Garment.

THE ALTAR OF OBLATION

PLATE XVII

Facing page 62.

I

THE ALTAR OF OBLATION

PLATE XVII

The ultimate of the Soul's processional is the Altar of Oblation. *Beneath*
It is the gateway to the Heights of GOD; to the Depths of HIS Mystery; *the*
and to the realization of the Length and Breadth of HIS Love. It *Shekinah*
opens the Four Dimensions of the Eternal World; it unveils the
Shekinah; .it reveals the Glory of the Overshadowing Presence; it
opens the Tabernacle containing the Host; it brings the Soul into the
immediate Presence of the Most Adorable ONE. Through it the
Divine Initiate reaches the high court of the Royal Arch where there
is entrusted to him the Key of all the Divine Mysteries.

The Altar of Divine Oblation is the Mercy-Seat.

The Sacred Lamp burns as if suspended from the Sacred Arch.

The red Flame of the Eternal Life casts its glow upon the Inner
Sanctuary.

The Cross and the two Witnesses are there. They adorn the Altar
of the Most High, and testify that HE is the Alpha and the Omega;
and also the upbuilder of that Templary which makes the Soul the
place of HIS Habitation.

The Luminous Cross reveals its Mystery and perpetually stands as
the sign of HIS Presence and the outflowing streams of the ELOHIM;
and the Divine Love and the Divine Wisdom bear witness to the
Mystery of all Divine Oblation.

The Host is there wrapt up in the Glory of the Overshadowing
ONE, testifying of the Most Sacred Mystery of the Divine Substance
and Life-stream, the invisible yet most tangible Holy Grail, which,
when the Soul finds and partakes of, makes it one in Substance and
Life-stream with the Body of the LORD of Being.

In that hour the Soul enters into HIS Glory. Henceforth the
Cherubim overshadow its Altar, and the Seraphim minister unto it of
the Most Holy ONE. For its sublime Oblation has been made. In
completest and most holy sacrifice it has offered its very Being unto

63

the FATHER-MOTHER for HIS Service. Whatsoever is demanded of the Soul, that also is freely given. Whatsoever is commanded, that also is most lovingly fulfilled. If it is called upon to ascend into the highest Heavens to serve before the LORD, there is joyful response. If it should be asked to leave the Glory and descend into other spheres, states and conditions to serve in redemptive ministry, with equal joy is such request responded to. The honour is the same. The Heights and the Depths are one in service to the FATHER-MOTHER.

In such an Oblation upon HIS High Altar, the Soul seeks no honour for *itself*. To do HIS Will is to be honoured of HIM. To make sacrifice; to give up all in Life; and, if it were necessary, to give up Life itself in HIS Service, were honour indeed. In apparently losing everything it had acquired, the Soul would in reality be gaining everything. To be absolutely One with the LORD Who gives us all, is to gain the summit of the Mountains of GOD.

Before this Altar, the Stars and the Soul are one in substance and spirit. The Solar Mystery is the Soul's Mystery. To understand the one is to be illumined concerning the other. Whether the Soul be in static or active state, it is an oblation unto the LORD for service, even as are all Stars and Systems. At this Altar it is linked to the Universe. The degree of realization and the outflow of auric glory are in the measure in which the attainment has been made and the oblation accomplished. Here the Soul becomes a sharer with all the Gods, in the Divine Glory.

PART FIVE

THE SUMMER SCHOOL OF 1931

A A HOLY CONVOCATION

B THE MYSTERY OF JACOB'S LADDER

C THE ADAMIC RACE

D VICARIOUS SACRIFICE

E THE SECRETS OF GOD

F THE WORSHIP OF THE MOST HIGH

G THE GIRDLE

H THE BLESSING OF ISRAEL

AND

I A DIVINE RHAPSODY

(An address given to friends in the Sanctuary at Headquarters on April 10, 1932, which, in response to many requests, is included; and also because its sublime theme is a suitable closing cadence.)

F

A HOLY CONVOCATION

THE NATURE OF IT

THE SIGNIFICANCE OF IT

THE QUALITY OF THINGS SIGNIFIED

THE CALL TO EMBODY THESE

THE DIVINE CHARACTER OF THE
 FESTIVAL OF THE HOLY EUCHARIST

A HOLY CONVOCATION

The purpose of this School is not one of propaganda in the ordinary meaning of that term. It is not a conference even, nor a congress of ecclesiastical or ordinary religious order. It is a convocation of some of the one-time members of the household of Israel, with a view to real fellowship, and through that fellowship the deepening of the spiritual life and the enrichment of the heart's love. And, through the exposition in the life of each one of the motion of the Divine Love and the blessedness of the communal fellowship, the coming into larger and fuller vision of our LORD and of HIS Will concerning us individually and collectively. We are come here for a holiday, that is, for a Holy Day, a day of consecration, which I hope will also be full of the Earth's sunshine, and Divine sunshine expressed in human joy and gladness. The word holy, as I have ofttimes said to you, means sacred. So we have come together for the sacred purpose of learning more concerning ourselves, of our past and what our LORD would have of us in the coming days. So it is a Holy Convocation. What I have to say to you I would thus unveil to you:—

The nature of the Convocation.

The significance of it.

The quality of that which is signified.

The call to that which is signified.

The real nature of the festival culminating in the holiest of Eucharists.

The nature of this Summer School or Holy Convocation is, that it is an assembly in part of some of the ancient Children known at one time as the Ancients of GOD, at another time as HIS Peculiar People, at another time as the Sons of GOD, and then as Israel and the Children of Zion. It is the coming together of a few of those who were called through the ages by all the prophetic messages and revelations sent from the Heavens through the true seers, and the interpretations of the Divine Mystery as given by the real priests of GOD who were able to mediate of HIM because they knew HIM, and could speak of HIM as those who knew HIM. It is a regathering of those unto whom the Prophets spake, and for whom the Master came in the days of the

The Purpose of the School

69

Manifestation full of the motion of the Divine Purpose to seek unto the finding of Israel, or as many of the real Israel as could then be found and called. For the purpose of the Master's coming to this world was not to be a world teacher in the sense in which that expression has come to be occultly used through the ages, and very much emphasized in these latter days, to teach all the world how to change its politics, religious life and outlook, and ecclesiastical organizations. He came for the direct purpose of finding the few who could respond to His Message, a Message which came from out the heart of the Fire which was upon the very Altar of GOD. He came to seek unto the finding of Israel. He emphasized the fact that to be an Israelite indeed was no mean thing; that the life represented was no easy accomplishment; that the vision it called to was no earthly vision but that of the FATHER-MOTHER, and thus transcendent as the Heavens.

The nature of this School is to emphasize the Message of the Manifestation. It is a Holy Convocation unto such of the House of Israel as can respond to it, to hear anew the Message sent from the Heavens concerning the ancient Christhood to be rehabilitated in these days wherein we ourselves are manifesting. It is what the Master came to seek unto the finding of in the days of the Manifestation, and would have found more effectually but for the betrayal of the Message He had given to Him to give unto them. What He came then to accomplish He comes again in this Message to accomplish, to seek unto the finding of the Children of Israel. For it is essential to this world that they be found. It is essential to this world's redemption that they arise. It is essential, as you will hear during this School, to the whole Planetary constitution that they be found. For the awakening of all the divine attributes in them and the coming forth of these into sublime manifestation, and this, not only in the manifestation of life, but also in the divine quality of service, is absolutely necessary for the Redemption of life in this world and the restoration of the Planet. The nature of this school is, therefore, that of seeking unto the finding of the attributes of Israel in all who have heard the call in some degree and responded to it unto the manifestation of that Life and Service for which Israel stands, that in such a manifestation they may become the interpreters and revealers for GOD.

You will therefore see now in the second aspect, the significance of this School as a Holy Convocation; for it implies the profound meaning of being an Israelite. It is a great claim. If it were a human claim it would be of mere pride and vanity. No real Israelite can think himself great in the world sense of great claim. There is no such thought in the Celestial and Divine Realms of greatness. For the greater a Soul is the less is it conscious of being great in estate or service. It knows itself to be as one possessing nothing apart from HIM Who is all and in all. Its greatness is not begotten of its own thought, nor its consciousness of its own attributes, nor the depth of its own desires and its realizations, nor even of the measure of its own ingathering of the Divine Glory. Its greatness is in the measure of its capacity to embody HIM; and to manifest and reveal HIM naturally and unconsciously. Because if you be conscious that you are like HIM and reveal HIM, it would be as if you were calling upon people to look at yourself, and to see that you were different from themselves and others who pass by.

An Israelite a Son of God

Beloved ones, I cannot impress this Divine Truth upon you too deeply—a Truth that will have to be emphasised in some of the unveilings that are to be given you—of the need in each one for absolute humility; the need in each one of the consciousness that we have nothing apart from HIM, and that we are only great in HIM, and will never know that we are great in HIM, if so be that we attain. Even a God, one who has realized Life to the estate of one of the Gods, able to function within the realms spoken of as the Realms of the Gods, feels but a child in the universe of conscious Being.

The significance of being an Israelite indeed is this, that a true Israelite has the Divine Inheritance. *A true Israelite has that Divine Inheritance which is the crown or resultant of great ages of Realization of Divine Estates.* What that inheritance is we shall see. For what reason do you think the Master went to so much trouble to pass out from glorious conditions within the Heavens to function upon these outer planes for a period, making manifest as the FATHER-MOTHER gave unto Him of Love and Wisdom, and in the degree in which such could be unveiled amidst the conditions through which He had to minister? Why did He seek specially unto the finding of Israel? Because to find Israel was not only to find a man or a woman, nor to find merely a Human Soul—all which would have been beautiful. The Master touched many during His ministry who were not of Israel, and would not be in such an estate for many ages, but who were, nevertheless, equally dear to Him so far as His ministries

71

unto them could be rendered. For there were other sheep which were not of the Fold of Israel. He sought Israel because the true Israelite represented a Soul who had greatly acquired interior knowledge of the Divine Mysteries; one who had attained to great realizations of the Divine, whose attributes had been so cultured that at one time they were able to interpret the Divine, not only in embodiment but also in ministry. The House of Israel were Souls who in their magnetic light were at one time glorious, and whose light shone in even the Celestial realms. The Master came to seek unto the finding of them. His ministry was unto the touching of their attributes, the awakening of the emotion of their heart, the recalling of their Being into a state of Remembrance—The Paraclete—through the Message of the FATHER-MOTHER's Love and Wisdom.

The significance, therefore, of being an Israelite is the momentous truth of having held within one's self the Divine Inheritance. Most religious men and women think of the Divine Inheritance as something to be acquired in the spiritual realms when they pass over. It is like the views they hold concerning Eternal Life. They think they will have it after they pass from these planes. But that is an erroneous concept of things. They may not have Eternal Life there any more than here; they will not, unless they have realized it here. For Eternal Life is the quality and quantity of Life within our Being wherein we realize HIM Who is the Eternal Life, always and in all realms as Universal Being. Even when functioning on the planes of outer manifestation, the Soul can be conscious of the Eternal Life. It can rejoice in the consciousness of the Presence. There can be the consciousness of having this Light within; and of the auric glory of it pouring, in great degree of consciousness, of itself forth through the Being. Israel had the Divine Inheritance. The spiritual momentum of such a consciousness is tremendous; for the quality of that Life relates to the degree in which the Soul has realized the Sacred Mystery. For the possession of the Divine Inheritance is the attainment to the consciousness of HIS Indwelling. It is not a great reward poured out upon a Soul as a gift from without. You might possess a world without having the capacity to rule it, as many men have owned kingdoms without the gift of true administration. That is not real possession. The Divine Inheritance is real estate. It is the possession of the consciousness of HIS Overshadowing and Indwelling.

The quality is the quality of the Eternal HIMSELF. To know HIM thus wise is to have attained oneness with HIM. To be an Israelite indeed is, therefore, no mean thing. It is of high quality; yet it is a lowly thing. To be an Israelite indeed is a great and glorious estate. Yet the possessor must ever be humble. It could not be otherwise. You cannot possess GOD without being humble. If you imagine you possess HIM and you are yet full of pride and vanity, you may be assured from this Message—for it is from the very Altar of HIS Love and Wisdom—that you have made a mistake. If the pride of ages affects you and you recognize it, you have to cast it out; it is of the enemy, as you will have again to learn. And in its relationship to the Ancient, Peculiar People of GOD, known as Israel, I will have many things to say during this school. Beloved children of the FATHER-MOTHER, this I say unto you: to inherit HIM and HIS Kingdom is to be like HIM.

The Quality and Quantity of Life

That is exactly the spirit and the substance of the Divine Inheritance which is in store for Israel here and hereafter, in this world and all the worlds wherever the Soul may travel: it is to be like HIM. The quality of the Life is one throughout the Universe. The Eternal Life is the same in all the worlds and all systems. The quantity of the Life, however, differs; it varies according to the degree of realization by the Soul. For its quantity can be the measure only of that which has been possible of realization within the world where it has grown up and evoluted towards the realm of the Divine consciousness. For the Soul may expand beyond that to the circumference of such a realization as is expressed in the system to which the Planetary member belongs on which the Soul has grown and evoluted. Thus a Soul can have a Planetary consciousness of HIM; and then it can attain to the possession of a Solar consciousness of HIM. But even a Solar consciousness of HIM, understood correctly, is comparative. So that a Soul can grow and ascend until it has the universal consciousness of HIM; which means, that that Soul's consciousness of HIM would enable it to be commanded to function anywhere for purposes of HIS ministry unto HIS children. Thus, though the quality of the Life is always the same, the quantity differs according to the degree of the Soul's ingathering, ascension, realization, comprehension, power of penetration and endurance, as it receives the involution of the Divine Immanence.

73

It is, indeed, a great thing to be an Israelite. To be an Israelite indeed is to be one in whom is no guile, no world deception or self deception, in whom is no pride, no haughtiness, no self upliftment and glorification, but just the exquisitely beautiful Soul who is full of the consciousness of lowly childhood before HIM, in HIM, and for HIM. *The great ones on the Earth and in all the Heavens are lowly ones.*

*   *   *   *

Seeing the nature of this Life unto which ye are again called, you will surely recognize that this is verily a Holy Convocation, a sacred time, a day of great consecration. The Message has not come out of the heart of any system on the Earth, nor council, nor scholastic centre, nor through any ecclesiastical venue. It has come right from the very heart of the Inner Worlds. Who could have restored the Vision of the Christhood, but the Christ of GOD within the Eternal Heavens? Who could have triumphed over all the opposing forces, material and occult, that have been in opposition to the establishing of such a manifestation of the Life Eternal as Christhood called unto, but the Eternal LORD of Being? Who could have accomplished such great things in the Planetary Heavens that it has become possible to bring through this Message—a Message that concerns itself with the Message of the Manifestation days, the Message of the prophetic times, and the history of Israel in ages long antecedent to the prophetic days? Who could have accomplished so much but the Great Love and Wisdom through the operations of HIS Eternal Christ?

Therefore the call is GOD's call. It is no man's call, though the Servant has to proclaim it. If you knew what it meant in the early days of the re-unveiling of this Message to the world; if you knew what it meant of fear lest it should appear to be the call of a man, you would understand the Divine Passion that fills my Being to-night when I look upon the countenances of so many who have responded to the Message. For only Israel could respond to that Message so as to make an embodiment of it. Many may follow Israel out of Egypt to the border of the wilderness and go back again. Many may follow thinking they are coming to receive something great and new, but go back again because the life unto which this Message calls is a life of embodiment, a manifestation of the attributes of HIM Who is our LORD. Many will hear but only the few follow. Many will follow part of the way who will fail to become Israelites indeed. Many of those who fully follow will feel the burden of the travail which the Message brings. But those who endure unto the end, those who allow the Message to work its full effect within and through them, shall be as those who will be counted worthy to be, by involution from the Eternal World, the manifestors of GOD'S Christ, the revealers of GOD'S Love, and the shedders of the glory of HIS Wisdom.

The Call of the Servant

My call is from HIM. HE called me to bring it back to you. It is not my call though it is given through me. HIS Voice has not been heard in the public thoroughfares nor in the great centres, calling. It has had no ready-made avenues for it through which its glory could pour itself forth. It has had no ecclesiastical system awaiting the birth of such a vision; nor the rebirth of it; nor even the echo of the Divine Voice through the chancel, as well as the nave and transepts and galleries of the earthly sanctuaries. It had to begin as the despised Message. It was repudiated by thousands unto whom the first of "the Heralds of the Cross" were sent. It was greatly condemned, repudiated, and even ignominiously scorned, till it seemed as if there could not be in this age any tangible response to such a Message.

But the Heavens waited; and they worked whilst they waited. They encouraged the Servant and the few noble ones who held up his hands. They filled his heart with hope when it seemed a hopeless task; and with joy also when the sorrow was overwhelmingly great. When one wrote responding to the Message, there were tears of joy to think that out of the hundreds of thousands who had contacted the Heralds even one would respond to this Message unto Israel. Even in this hour I look upon the lovely countenance of one in our midst who, more than twenty years ago, wrote saying how the Message had arrested and held her; and what joy there was in the hour of that communication unto me and those who bore the burden with me! It was even as the joy that comes to the Angels of GOD. It was HIS call: I could not refuse it. The Message is written within me; it is in the fabric of my Being. Its motion is in my own motion. Its Passion is in my lifestream. HE spake; I but responded.

And this is HIS call to you; it is not mine. I can give you nothing that HE does not will and permit me to give you. It is thus that the Message has been gradually unveiled to you, even unto this day. It is a call unto the Ancients of Israel. This Holy Convocation is to give opportunity again for that call which comes directly from HIMSELF. You come here, not to hear me only who am HIS Servant,

75

but to hear what further HE would unveil through HIS Servant to help you in the coming days and years in your ministry unto this world.

It is a call to the Vision Sublimest. The Vision is of HIS own Altar. Oh, the glory of that high Altar! I often wish we could make our earthly Sanctuary Altars even in some degree reflect the glory of that Altar. To be before that Altar is to be mediated unto from HIM directly within the Being. To learn to mediate from that Altar is to stand before it and look from it unto those to be mediated unto. It is never behind though it might seem as if it were so. In giving Blessing, it should overshadow us. The Divine Altar is always within, and to stand before that Altar and mediate from it, is to endure the vibrations which play from the Shekinah above the Altar, vibrations which are set in motion by the activities of the Elohim who are the mediators and interpreters of the Sacred Mystery. The path to that High Altar is the way of the Message. To come to that High Altar in high degree is to be absolutely the LORD'S. It is easier to use language than to make it realistic to the vision and in the vision; and it is difficult to find terms to express what it means to anyone to be altogether the LORD'S, and to realize HIM in sublime fulness.

*   *   *   *

And now I would lead you farther on the way to being HIS. This is the Holy Convocation. It is a new celebration of the Passover. The fellowship is the Passover Supper. It is a fellowship full of memories. The memories are pregnant with travail of great ages. For it is a fellowship of the past as well as of the present. It is a fellowship reminiscent of the heavenly places where once we all dwelt. It is a fellowship vibrant with the motion of ages within us, the ages through which we have passed in our manifestations and burden bearing. It is a commemoration of our own passover; of this world's passover; and it is also a commemoration of the passover of our LORD.

Here, in this very hour, there is the resurgence of Egypt. There dioramically passes before the vision the shadows, the pains, and the sorrows of the wilderness journey. There is not one of you free from bearing some degree of the pain and the shadow of the ages. But in this celebration of the Passover there is a note of Divine triumph. You do not celebrate it in Egypt—that is, within the state of bondage which Egypt represents to-day. You do not celebrate it in the wilderness amidst the great trial and sorrow and anguish of travail that are the outcome of the fallen conditions, and which make your life to be full of incertitude because of the ever-changing states within and around you, together with the bitterness of the waters you have had to drink, and the languishing of your Being for Hidden Manna. To-day it is a Holy Convocation, the celebration of triumph over all the past; yet heralding that greater triumph which is to witness the full and perfect restoration of all Israel, when, individually, the members of the Ancient Congregation shall once more be in Christhood, and, communally, the whole Household of Israel will be as the city set on a hill. For it will be such a concrete exposition of that high Life which can alone save the world. And remember this, that whilst this Convocation commemorates your own passover through the ages, it also commemorates the triumph of the LORD's Passover. For, but for that Passover which was the Travail of the Divine Love, it would not have been possible under any circumstances to have restored the Message to you, and enabled you to give to it such an embodiment as will make effectual the Redemption of this world and all her children, and the Redemption of those who were at the head of the Planetary administration. As the result of the Divine Passover there is to be the Redemption from the bondage into which they were drawn down, of all those who were at the head of the administration of this once most glorious Planetary system. For every member of the Hierarchy is to be restored.

The Sublime Sacrifice of the true Eucharist

*　　*　　*　　*

Now, unto this end we would have this Holy Convocation nothing less than the most Holy Eucharist. A Eucharistic sacrifice is a sacrifice of thanksgiving. It is a sacrifice of praise. Real praise is in the motion of the Being. It is not simply singing songs, either individually or communally. We can express the praise of GOD individually and communally, and should ever do so when opportunity offers itself. But the real spirit of praise is in the motion of our Being. We praise HIM in our motion, our gait, our deportment, our action, our attitude to one another, our attitude always to HIM. That is praise. I praise THEE, O GOD! By sharing the motion of THY Love to such an extent as I may share it, even unto the fulness of my Being, I praise THEE! Love is ever perfect in its motion; through THY Love in me I praise THEE!

*The
Perfect
Way of
Divine Love*

The Holy Eucharist is sublime sacrifice of praise and thanksgiving. The outer symbol we shall again make use of during this School. That outer symbol speaks of that which should ever be offered in our lives. Our very substance and our very lifestream should be made a Holy Eucharist unto HIM. The motion of our Being should express the praise of HIM. How can I best praise HIM? By growing more like HIM and thus revealing HIM more; by doing to the extent of my ability through my attributes what HE would do; by saying to Souls, according to my capacity, that which HE would say, and in the like beautiful way; even in discerning and separating action, to discern and judge and act in the way that would reflect HIM. And here you will observe that, in being like HIM, there would be an absence of the spirit of blame; there would be no sitting in judgment upon anyone; there would be no grumbling, nor criticism (you will bear with me for saying this); nor would there be any distrust; there would be no subtle influence casting shadows. Because Love is perfect. It thinketh no evil; it feeleth no evil; it sayeth no evil; it doeth no evil. When it finds evil it touches it to change it. If it will not be changed the evil must pass from Love's presence. Love never condemns. Now the whole purpose of this opening address to you, which is like the opening out of my own Being to you as HE has moved me (for HE does move me), is to bring you, through your own history reflected in the latent memories and in the visions which you have, to HIS High Altar, to hear HIS Voice, to follow HIS way, to make consecration of yourself absolutely unto HIM, and so make this school, from this night of its inception unto the closing service of it, a Holy Eucharist of praise and service unto HIM.

Bear with me. You know how I love you. That I sorrow that I have not more power to make HIS Love for you manifest; sorrowing that I am not able to have all the opportunities I fain would for the revelation, for the manifestation, for the interpretation of that Love. But I love you with all my Being because I am HIS. Anything I have is HIS. I am all HIS, even if it had to be in the bearing of an Oblation. And because I so love you, and I know how you love me, for it is so manifest, I ask you to make this verily a Holy Convocation, an Assembly of Israel, by offering your life Eucharistically to HIM. Let your note be praise, praise, praise; in everything, in every condition at all times, the praise of HIM. To praise HIM is to bless!

78

But we cannot in our hearts bless HIS Name without blessing HIS beloved ones. In HIS Name I bless every one of you. I ever bless you. Even in the hour begotten of deepest travail, I bless you. It could not be otherwise. It is not of man, it is not personal. Oh, if it seems so put that thought away forever. I speak not in any personal way, but of HIM as HE moves within me to bless you.

And now as I would have this service close Eucharistically we will unite in the communal prayer.

THE LORD'S PRAYER

OUR FATHER-MOTHER IN THE HEAVENS, MOST HALLOWED BE THY NAME UNTO US.

MAY THY KINGDOM COME WITHIN US.

THY WILL BE ACCOMPLISHED BY US: EVEN AS IT IS DONE WITHIN THY HEAVENS, SO BE IT ACCOMPLISHED UPON THE EARTH.

GIVE US THYSELF THE DAILY PORTION OF THE BREAD OF LIFE.

FORGIVE US OUR SINS, AND HELP US AS WE PASS THROUGH, TO FORGIVE OTHERS.

AMID THE GREAT TRIAL LEAD US, THAT EVIL OVERTAKE US NOT.

FOR THE KINGDOM WITHIN US IS THINE, WITH ITS POWER AND ITS GLORY, EVEN FOR EVERMORE.

THOU ART THE ARCHE AND THE AMEN.

B

JACOB'S LADDER

G

THE MYSTERY OF JACOB'S LADDER

This morning I am moved to unveil to you yet more fully something of the mystery of the travail of the Planetary Angel, Ya-akob-El, and all the heavenly Hierarchies, as well as your own travail which ran parallel to theirs.

The story of Jacob's Ladder is one of the most familiar in the Old Scriptures. There is something arresting in it for the individual Soul. Jacob is represented, in the way that story is set forth, as being of such a nature that his characteristics appeared to be essentially human. The story has had an individual application in Soul history since the great mystery was permitted to be told. But in the form in which it appears in the Old Scriptures, it is not as it was told. Some parts of it are not correctly stated. For though that old world story seems so apt in its application to our own life in our life's travail, and there is so much that is beautiful and hopeful in it wherein it speaks of the ministry of the Heavens unto the Soul, yet the story is cosmic. It is cosmic because it has relation to the Planet. It has also relation to the Celestial Hierarchy. Its ramifications are so great that it has relation to the Eternal Mystery of Living Fire.

The first act of the drama is set forth as a dream; the second as an awakening vision; and the third as a time of great travail.

Do angels dream? Do archangels dream? What are real dreams which so imperfectly come through into the consciousness as the consciousness becomes operative in the personal equation? What are real dreams but heavenly communings, heavenly revealings, and heavenly communications to the Soul, and the unveiling of the Soul's history to itself in a covert way? For it may not learn too much at a time lest the vision should overwhelm it. Many of the beautiful dreams are nothing less than intimate Angelic communings by the Soul with the Angelic World. Whilst its vehicle rests it is borne along in its consciousness to historic places where it has passed through great and blessed experiences. What are Soul dreams that are full of travail but dreams of a like order? But in this latter the places bring to the Soul such memories that it even agonizes in the night watches. And such travail is so often reflected into the vehicles when the hours

83

of earthly awakening come, that the mind, operating through the outer vehicle, becomes fearful and oft-times dreads for the time being, to go to sleep again.

This story of Jacob is a story of the Angel of the Planet. He was in a high position. He was a patriarch in vicegerent estate or he could never have been appointed to be the Angel of the Planet. He was Ya-akob who is known in the realm of his ministry as Ya-akob-El or the Lord's plenipotentiary and vicegerent for this world.

Now in the unveiling of this mystery I would have your thoughts gather around these aspects of it:—

1. The travail of Ya-akob-El.
2. The cosmic character of his dream.
3. The revelation of the Countenance of Living Fire.
4. The Angelic ministry unto Ya-akob-El.
5. The coming of the Avatara (though then only prophetically anticipated).
6. The vision of the great reconciliation.

In the old story you have Jacob in conflict with his brother Esau. His travail begins with Esau, and it continues owing to the state of Esau. And you will notice in the simple form of the story, though its meaning is covered in the terms, that Jacob went out from Beersheba and went to Haran. Now Beersheba was the place of the Seven Wells, or the Divine repositories containing the Elohistic central magnetic forces through which each Elohe operates. And to go out from Beersheba and make one's way to Haran was to descend in state from the glorious realizations, fellowships, and applied potencies associated with the Seven Wells of the Elohim, and go into a land that was barren. When this Planetary descent was fully accomplished, Ya-akob-El, as the great administrator and director of the Celestial Hierarchy whose members had been appointed to mediate within the Planetary constitution unto and through the Planetary Hierarchy whose members operated within the Occult Realms of administration and direction, found himself, because of the necessities of his ministry and the state into which his kingdom had gone down, deprived of the perfect fellowship and ministries which had been his by the Wells of Beersheba. It was thus he went down into the hard and stony conditions, suffering because of his own inherent properties and realized potencies, and one time glorious fellowship with the Presence. Can

84

you conceive even for a moment what it must mean to a Planetary Angel to be in the state wherein he feels as if, Celestially and Divinely, he were alone, because his kingdom has become so changed through evil influences being introduced into it, that the Heavens themselves are under the necessity, owing to the conditions, to change their ministry?

Doubtless you think yourselves alone at times, and very lonely in the world. And the deeper your travail in your return, the more alone you will feel, until you attain to that consciousness wherein you walk forever with that Presence Who is your LORD. It does not mean that there are none by your side during your consciousness of aloneness, none to respond to your call, none waiting upon your message to them, none willing to pour out of their treasure house of Love upon the altar of service for you. This loneliness is of an entirely different order. You may be in the midst of these presences and yet be conscious of being absolutely alone. Here I would remind you of sayings in the Old Testament which of late days I have read to you concerning the Divine appeal to Ya-akob-El, asking of him whether he had forgotten that the LORD never fails in HIS remembrance of HIS children; along with the appeal to Israel who also came to imagine and affirm that the LORD forgot HIS children. But amidst difficult conditions it is not easy always to remember, not even for an Angel. An Angel is one who ministers. Most men and women think of the Angels on the other side as the ministrants of the other side only; and of the Archangels as the greater ministrants there. But Angels minister to Souls here and now; and the Archangels are those who have realized more fully the Divine Omnipotency, and Omnisciency, and realized such through the realization of the Mystery of Love. These great Ones are dwellers in the radiance of HIS Wisdom, and are appointed for ministry to Systems, Planets, and even individual Souls. Even upon the earth planes we have met Angels by the way, and known the attendance of Archangels.

Now, the cause of the travail of Ya-akob-El was through Esau. Who then was Esau? Who was this brother? Recently I said to some of you when speaking of Esau that he represented the earth man, the man who is thoroughly immersed in earthly conditions. He loved the mess of potage. He was a warrior. He loved venison. All these things are symbolical. Esau represented a state. The state was more fully expressed in the term Edom. The Edomites were the descendants

85

of Esau. They were and are those who follow the life which Esau represented. Esau represented a state of mind in the Planetary constitution wherein the birthright, the sacred heritage of divine childhood, was sacrificed and sold. Esau had to do with the materializing principle that was introduced into this system and which caused the glorious volatile elements, substances, and planes in their magnetic motion, to become changed, so that the world became Esau's world rather than Ya-akob-El's. You will understand that the fear which filled the heart of Ya-akob-El was the fear begotten by the action of this materializing spirit, lest it went still further and further until the whole Planetary constitution might become so fixed that it would be ultimately lost as a volatile member of the Celestial realms of the FATHER-MOTHER. Oh, an Angel can travail. He can travail in the measure in which GOD has been realized by him; for all such travail is of GOD. The measure of even a Soul's travail is just commensurate with its power of realization of HIM WHO is the great Travailler in the Universe. Anyone appointed to fill the office of the Angel of a Planet such as this is, must have the capacity to divinely travail, if the need should arise. Aye, even the glorious ONE appointed as the Angel of the Sun, must have the capacity to travail. For even the Solar Body has travailled in and through the travail of Ya-akob-El. This was occasioned through the changing of its glorious Angelic Heavens into their present state. This state was at one time more accentuated than it is at present. But the present state of the photosphere, or what is known in material science as the photosphere, was the outcome of the changing of the once glorious, perfectly volatile, luminous and divinely magnetic elements of the Angelic Heavens of the Solar Body, in order to provide an atmosphere through which there could be accommodated the magnetic ministry necessary for the restoration of this Planet and other members of the system who became affected as the result of the going down of this land of Ya-akob-El. But even the Planetary Angel, with all the Hierarchies in the Solar Body, have had to share in the travail. Men and women, as a rule, think personally. If they rise above it they think individually. If they get outside of themselves they get into a tribal vision, or a racial vision, or a national vision. But how few of them are able to rise out of the circumscribed state of the personal and the individual, the tribal, the national and the racial, to be as children of GOD who think universally and divinely, first in a Planetary way, and then in a Solar way, and then in a

86

Universal way? I would have you understand how it comes to pass that the Divine Mystery we name the FATHER-MOTHER can travail through the LORD of Being. For the LORD of Being can and does travail through one of HIS glorious Celestial embodiments. And ADONAI can and does travail even through one of HIS Sons in the estate of The Son of Man. This is the inner meaning of the conflict of Ya-akob-El with Esau conditions. So great was the travail that he was overwhelmed through ages, and became fearful lest his kingdom should go utterly out.

The Dream of the Planet's Archangel

Do you say this could not happen in any Divine World? Oh yes, it could. A world can go out from that state and ministry for which it was created, though there would be nothing lost except its ages of history associated with its growth and evolution, and all the history of its children. The spirit is never lost. But the embodiment may have to change; and all the elements reduced and changed, be regathered, refashioned, and re-impregnated with that holy Mystery we name GOD'S Spirit. There can be the loss of great ages. There can be imposed upon the Divine World great grief. HIS Divine and Celestial children can know great sorrow begotten of profound travail.

It was in a startling epoch of this order that Ya-akob-El, himself full of dismay and wondering what could be the ultimate, in his tarrying had his dream vision restored to him. And in this you will see that the vision of the Ladder is also cosmic. It is not simply a dream of a ladder being let down from heaven to his kingdom. It is a vision of the still living active ministry of the Celestial Hierarchy. Ya-akob-El was full of sorrow, even unto the despair of his Being, because of the state into which this world had gone down. Then, behold, there was a ladder rising from the world, from the realm of his administration; and it reached unto the Heavens. In the true story there were twelve rungs or steps to that ladder, and at each step there were Cherubic Presences. On each side of each rung there was a radiant countenance. There was an ascending arc of this glory, until at the top of it Ya-akob-El saw a vision, the Overshadowing ONE, Who appeared to him as a Living Fire, the Divine Sacred Flame in motion. From that Flame the countenances of the twenty-four Cherubic Presences were illumined.

It is a cosmic drama. Therefore we must lift up our vision from the littleness of our own personal limitations and outlook to witness the grandeur of the Divine way, the Divine ministry, the Divine Over-shadowing, and the Divine appeal even to a Planetary Angel. For even as the Divine appears to you as one of HIS Angels or Ministrants in less estate of manifestation and ministry, so does HE to HIS Celestial Children. It was a time of uplifting of the heaviness that overhung the whole of the Planetary atmospheres and elements, issuing in such changed conditions that Ya-akob-El, even amidst the stony or hard elemental states which still prevailed, could have given to him, as a restorative, a vision of the glorious Celestial ministries that had once been constant in his consciousness and vision. Thus he might see again how the FATHER-MOTHER, as the Living Fire or LORD of Being, could send forth HIS energy unto the ultimate healing and redemption of all the kingdoms over which Ya-akob-El reigned but which had become forfeit through having lost their heritage, and had become so changed that they went down into a great night wherein no light shone to illumine the Planetary planes. Verily the recovered experience was the Gate of Heaven unto Ya-akob-El! Verily he was, even amidst his hard conditions, once more on the threshold of Bethel! The Great Love had come back to him in consciousness. For even ourselves see these things in consciousness. We hear them in consciousness. We feel them in the motion of the lifestream of our Being. For all Divine things are realized in consciousness. And although that which we are realizing may at times seemingly become, as it were, objective, it is a subjective objectivity. It is the realization taking form within the Being. It is the realization itself beheld. It is thus ADONAI is seen. For ADONAI is no man, no ordinary human form, not even an Angel, nor an Archangel. HE is all the Angels and Archangels gathered up into HIS own Universal Being. ADONAI realized in vision, is the subjective realization becoming objective to the Soul's sight.

Thus you will understand what it meant to Ya-akob-El to witness again the cosmic ladder, the way of the Divine ministry, and the twelve-fold nature of it. It was the ministry of those glorious Elders who are said to have been seen around the Throne. It represented the Divine and Celestial ministries unto the Planet, the services of the Divine Hierarchy expressed through the Celestial Hierarchy to the Celestial Angels of this Celestial member.

Great and marvellous are THY works, O LORD of the Heavenly Hosts. Who is to be likened unto THEE?

The Great Love could not fail where there was the least response. Ya-akob-El is assured through his dream-vision. Henceforth the conditions on which he has rested amidst the long night of his travail shall be changed. In and through his recovered memory shall the hard conditions even become as a living altar for his LORD. The memory of the Divine Goodness will bring back life to the hard and lifeless conditions.

In the application of such a thing to life you will see the meaning at once, even in your own experience amidst conditions which you think so stony and lifeless, unresponsive unto your endeavour, or, if responsive, seem to rebound upon you unto the smiting of you. Learn from the dream-vision to lift up your head. Lift your head above them. Arise out of the night which they have signified. But do not leave them. Take them and raise them; pour the oil of your Being upon them and change them; make of them verily upon the Earth an altar unto the LORD of Love.

*   *   *   *

Then followed the vision of the Living Fire of the Sacred Mystery. How wonderful it was to have such a culmination to the vision. The Ladder represented the twenty-four members of the Divine Hierarchy as those glorious members of Divine estate ministered Celestially unto this Planet. They ministered to the Planet's own Celestial Hierarchy, and originally through that Hierarchy unto the Interpreters of the Divine Will who were the administrators of the intermediary realm, and who came to be known as the Occult Hierarchy. These administrators formed the Hierarchy that had to do with the direction of the elemental things. It was through the members of this Hierarchy that the great descent of the whole Planet was accomplished, after Lucifer, the Angel of the seventh sphere of the Planetary constitution, had been brought down. The majesty of the dream-vision lies in the discovery again on the part of Ya-akob-El, that the LORD, the GOD of the Living Presence, was still with him, notwithstanding the conditions into which his kingdom had been brought. This was verily an inspiration to him. *This is none other than the House of GOD.* It was a coming back again to the place of HIS Presence. It was the very gateway back into that Kingdom from which the whole Planetary Household had gone out.

Behold how HIS Cherubim and Seraphim minister from HIM! Behold how HIS Angels come with the tokens of HIS Love, bearing

*Administra-
tion
through
Hierarchies*

within their censers the sacred incense, and in their lamp the Living Flame to fill the members of the Hierarchies of the Earth with the sweetness of HIS Presence, and to impart to all HIS ministrants the energy of HIS undying Love!

Beloved ones, be sure of this in your own experience, that above you there is HIS Ladder at the top of which HIS Presence awaits you. Though you may not be able to see HIM as Ya-akob-El saw HIM; yet you may behold HIM in the angel-faces upon the Earth, and the angel-faces that come to you in your night dream, and HIS Angel who may appear before you in your day vision. Be sure HE is ever thoughtful for you, even if you do not accomplish all you want nor gain all you desire. Look around you; look within you; look above you; then ask yourself how it comes to pass that you are able to accomplish so much. Is it not because HE is at the top of the Ladder sending down the magnetic potencies of HIS Eternal Fire to energize you, to enrich you, to illumine you, to empower you, and to clothe you with the garments of HIS own sacred Priesthood, garments full of the very essences of HIS incense and the potencies of HIS most Holy Flame?

★   ★   ×   ★

Here is an interesting thought for us all. It is revealed in this cosmic drama that even an Archangel is ministered unto. Angels have to receive ministry as well as give it. Even a Planetary Angel is angelically ministered unto. This is clearly unveiled in the dream story. Ya-akob-El saw the Angels descending and ascending[1]. He saw them come to him. He felt them approach him. He was conscious, even as it is said Elijah was when in the wilderness he lay under a juniper tree, of being touched by the Angel of GOD. Lo! it is no dream. It belongs to the realm of the great *reality*. It is no mere vision external to one's self, but a great and holy experience within the Sanctuary of our Being. It was thus Ya-akob-El beheld it through recovered realization.

You may not have seen Angels descending upon you, but at times you have felt them. You may not have been conscious that the Angels were blessing you; yet often you have felt Angelic atmospheres and inhaled Angelic breaths. Perhaps you have had that most sacred

---

[1]His name was Ya-akob, the term corresponding to the Greek Iacchos, the Planetary Angel. But when an Angel became Viceregent for the LORD, the suffix El was added; for this denoted regnancy.

90

and blessed experience of inhaling the very fragrance of the incense from the censer upon the Golden Altar, which is said to represent the prayers of the saints. If so, how great must have been your blessing. But though that exalted blessing may not have come your way, still you must have felt the Angels, even if you have not seen them and been conscious of their touch. When you have been desperate in yourself, thinking and feeling you would do something hurtful to yourself or others; or that you would go further away in your spiritual estate and repudiate HIM Whom once you believed, because you are conscious of having as resting places only hard and stony conditions, in such hours have you no remembrance of having been touched by an Angel, of awakening to look into the face of an Angel, of coming back to consciousness, even in the personal life, to hear the voice of an Angel?

The Peculiar People of Jehovah

I know how many of you doubt amidst Life's difficult conditions. You doubt whether you are really true to yourself and to HIM. You doubt whether you really were ever of the Children of GOD, of that Peculiar People named HIS Elect Children who were sent to this world as HIS interpreters. You wonder whether you were ever an Israelite indeed, one in whom there is no guile. But why do you doubt HIM Who never failed you? Earth conditions are difficult. The places are oft-times hard and stony. Much of the world's spiritual soil seems beyond bearing fruitage for you. Yet amidst the most difficult experiences, have the assurance through knowing HIM that HE is ever the same. HE is true. Do not think for a moment that HE looks callously on your Life's struggle; that HE is a stoic far removed from the travail of HIS worlds and HIS children upon them. Do not think HE is far removed amid the Celestial Universe from those here who seek unto HIM. HE is ever near. HE is Universal Being; therefore you cannot get away from HIM. Wheresoever you go HE is. If you fail to realize this it is because you have forgotten HIM. "Whither shall I go from HIS Presence?" wrote one of old time. Why, you cannot go from HIS Presence. You cannot lose HIM except in consciousness. You can fail to recognize HIM. You can refuse to permit HIM to affect you. For myself, if I want HIM to affect me, if I want HIM to touch me and reveal HIMSELF to me, then, wherever I am, I am with HIM. He touches and affects me.

★   ★   ★   ★

91

*The
Travail of
the Angel
of the
Planet*

In this cosmic drama you share. That which was given ages ago to Ya-akob-El to recall him to the remembrance of the Divine Love, has been given to Ya-akob-El through all the ages since. And it is given to you also. For, remember this, that the ages of the travail to which my vision has gone back, preceded the Divine Purpose to accomplish the Redemption of this world by the Oblation. For, away back in those ages it was hoped that this distraught Earth could be recovered. And the Divine World's hope would have been realized but for the insidious work of those who hated the way of the Divine Love and Wisdom. In this spirit they approached the children, unseen but full of magnetic power; and, affecting them, got them to go still further down, even until they reached the Sodomic state and brought into the world the outer darkness of Gomorrah.

Little indeed do you yet know the history of the æonial travail of this world, yourselves involved in it, and all the children who belong to it; and likewise the travail of the Great Love for the healing of this distraught member, and the restoration of the Celestial balance of the whole of the system. Little do you even understand the forces that have been playing throughout the ages of the Oblation to defeat it, and thus to make impossible the restoration of Ya-akob-El's kingdom through the restoration of the long lost Sons of GOD. These Mysteries have been cryptically stated in the "Heralds[1]." Then they had to be most guardedly touched upon. Ofttimes they are so stated that none but the initiated unto whom it might be given, could discern the meaning. It was given me to so record these Mysteries, that, bye and bye, they should be discovered by those who would become illumined and thus be able to discern the heavenly secrets hidden for great ages. It is only now that it is possible to unveil these Mysteries in a more open way. For, in our ministry, nothing is unveiled but by the Will of HIM Who is our FATHER-MOTHER. Even this story has been spoken of by me many times, but not until now in relation to the cosmic drama. Of HIM alone am I able to thus speak to you in these days.

And now consider this. That the ministry of the Angels and Archangels unto Ya-akob-El through that glorious Divine Hierarchical revelation, prepared him and this world for the Avatara.

Now an Avatar is ofttimes confounded with the appearing of a

---

[1]"The Herald of the Cross," Vols. i to vii.

messenger in human estate. No doubt the messenger is the vehicle of his LORD or her LORD. But the servant-messenger is not the Avatar; he is only the vehicle of the message. For there is one real Messenger; HE is the LORD of Being. But, just as Ya-akob-El had given to him the title of Lord Ya-akob—that is the meaning of the El at the end of the name, given because of the regnancy and the position he was placed in —so the Messenger is designated in some way with that which will express the message. Within the Heavens the Servant will be known by that name. But the Avatar is the coming of the Presence in a cosmic sense. If the coming be to a system, then it is solar. If it be to a Planet like this, it is planetary; and it is cosmic in a planetary degree. In this lies the meaning of Mahanaim. Ya-akob-El's vision was clarified: his outlook was made luminous. He beheld meeting him in the way the Angelic Hosts. They signified Celestial and Divine things for him. They announced the Avatara, or the coming of the Messengers. They spoke of the encompassing Heavens. They heralded the Maranatha. Oh, many have been the Messengers sent to this world! Those of you who have read the Mysteries as set forth in the philosophies will remember that many Messengers are supposed to have come. They are generally considered to have been eleven, and the twelfth was now due, and he would gather up into himself that which the ninth revealed and which the twelfth should represent. Thus the representative of the Avatar would be the ninth and the twelfth Messengers in one. In other words, he would be Moses and Elijah. He would be the revealer of GOD and the Interpreter of GOD's Righteousness. But there have been many, many Avatara sent to this world. There have been, in a few instances, the greater Messengers who have had to convey the greater messages. But the last Messenger of very special import is to combine in his Message, Moses, Elijah, and the Master Ioannes known as Jesus.

The Hosts of the Lord God

That which is said to have been beheld by Ya-akob-El at Mahanaim, was the two camps, the Celestial and Divine encompassing of the Hosts of GOD. He beheld the Hosts of the LORD GOD of Sabaoth. He beheld the coming of those Hosts to ensphere the Earth, to accomplish her healing and enrichment. It was a prophetic vision; but it was one sure to be realized. The result of the Avatara would be this, there would be such a re-manifestation of the glory of the Divine Love and Wisdom that the Earth would be healed of all her

93

darkness and her sorrow, her woundings through her evil states, and brought back to be once more the one-time pleasant and glorious land of the Planet-Soul Judah. A fellowship that was indeed reflective of the fellowship of the Ierusalem which was always above, would again be restored, so that the whole Earth would become as that Holy City.

It is only now, notwithstanding that the Avatara as GOD's messengers came and went, through great ages, and gave their messages and manifestations from the Divine World, that the two camps of the Hosts of the LORD are able to encompass again this Earth; it is only now they are able to pour out of the fulness of the magnetic streams from that Divine Presence of Living Fire WHO is the sacred Mystery in the Life of all embodiments—each Human and Angelic Soul, each individual world, each solar embodiment, each glorious multiple Celestial system wherein are many suns. It is only now Mahanaim can come to pass. That which could not be accomplished four and five naronic cycles ago, can now be accomplished because of that which the LORD of Love did for this world by means of the Oblation, and is still doing unto the effecting of its full Redemption. For, because the Planetary Heavens have been purified by the motion of that Love in its Divine Passion through the blotting out of the evil images, and changing the conditions, by the throwing down of the principalities and powers of evil that dominated even those Children of the Kingdom who desired to walk uprightly and to go in the way of the LORD of Love; and also, through the accomplishment of the Oblation; the Planetary Heavens are now filled with the magnetic streams flowing from the two camps—the two great enspherings of Angelic Avataric ministrants. One of the great painters was moved, in an hour of sublime illumination, to paint the ensphering heavens in a three-fold way— the Divine Heavens, the Celestial Heavens, and the Angelic Heavens, though at the time he did not realize all he was putting into his picture[1]. Here, I would say to you, and you will not think this personal in the least degree, for you know I wish not to speak personally in any way whatsoever, for all I have is of the Great Love, and I have nothing worth having that is not HIS;—in vision I have seen those spheres crowded with the Hosts of GOD, even as that noble one so many years ago endeavoured to portray. I have seen the Angelic Hosts encompassing the Earth, and beyond them the Celestial and Divine.

[1]Fra Angelico

94

It was the coming of the Avatara. To me it was not a reflected vision, but the appearing and motion of the actual thing. It was a revelation of how those glorious ones encompass now the Heavens of the Earth, and pour into them for all who are there the glory of the FATHER-MOTHER in such degree of magnetic power as those within the Earth's heavens can endure to receive and to be the transmitters of down even on to the outer earth planes. And it is the effect of that Avataric movement which is disturbing the whole world, physically, racially, nationally, commercially, and religiously. There never was a time, it is said, such as this upon the face of the Earth. Verily there never was, though there was a far better time, before the Earth needed the special solar ministries in the way it does to-day, and when Souls were able in their consciousness to pass into the Angelic World at will and behold its glories and enjoy its communing.

The Great Reconciliation of Esau with Ya-akob.

That which is true in the Planetary life for Ya-akob-El is true for all Israel. For that which is to be realized for Ya-akob-El can only be realized upon the Earth through Israel. That is how it comes to pass that Israel, in the old Mystery and prophetic statements, is so involved with the House of Jacob. And you will note such expressions, thought to be simply reminiscent of Jewry, as are found in the Old Scriptures, and especially in the Psalms, where a psalm prayer will close thus— "O GOD of Jacob!" For here it is the LORD of Ya-akob-El. The saying refers not to a man, nor to an individual, but to the Divine regnant state represented by Ya-akob-El.

*   *   *   *

The Avatara are coming: the Avatar is come. The Avatara are coming in the glorious Messengers from the Inner Worlds: the Avatar is come in the encompassing of the whole Planetary life from the LORD of Being. As the result there is taking place that which was prophetically shown to Ya-akob-El and heralded by the prophets, though when it was first shown to Ya-akob-El it was hoped it would be realized without the Oblation: but as that could not be, the Oblation was projected. And you now know that it has been accomplished and the great reconciliation effected. How? Through the healing of Esau. The meeting with Esau is Soulic. There has taken place the healing of his opposition and his hate. You do not heal conditions by continuing in dread of them. You do not heal oppositions by fearing lest they overwhelm you. No; you can only heal them by giving the gift of your love. Jacob is said

95

*The effect
of the
Avatara*

to have given Esau gifts. It is not happily put in the story of the Old Scripture. But in the real story it is most happily set forth. What has Jacob to give to Esau? Why, that which he has of the Divine Love and Wisdom. What he has of Divine Potency he gives unto the healing of the elemental realms and elemental conditions. He gives of himself unto the healing of the Planetary Mind, and the restoration of Esau which is also the restoration of Lucifer. There are profound inter-relationships here referred to which may not be further unveiled at this present time; but the indications will show you how full those Old Scriptures are, not only of travail, but also of the Divine Mysteries— truths belonging to the most sacred Mysteries of the Planetary and Solar constitution and administration.

As the great Reconciliation could not be effected without the Manifestation to be followed by the Oblation, the Oblation was projected. The Manifestation was made; the Oblation has been accomplished; and now the reconciliation is to take place. How is Esau to be reconciled to Jacob? How is this world that sold its birth-right for a mess of potage, to be recovered so that it shall share the Divine Inheritance? Through Divine Sacrificial Service on the part of the Children of Israel. Unto them Ya-akob-El looks for the gift of their love. He needs the magnetic principle of their love to be in motion through all their attributes, so that every attribute will interpret the Divine Love and reveal the Divine Wisdom; every attribute to interpret the FATHER-MOTHER and express HIM in service. As there is no such thing as hypothetical redemption for a Human Soul, neither is there for a planet, nor for a celestial system that goes wrong. Redemption is practical. It affects the life that requires to be redeemed. It is accomplished through the changing of conditions, the healing of woundings, the restoration of impoverished states through enrichment, the rehabilitation of the standard of life to be one with the Divine Righteousness. Thus there is to take place a resti-tution of the spiritual uprightness of the Being and the rebalancing of all the planes. Thus for the individual life, and thus for the Planetary constitution. The planes have to be healed; the elements to be purified, the emotion and the magnetic streams flowing through the emotion to be healed. The kingdom of Ya-akob-El has to be restored through right thought and action everywhere and in everything. But that restoration can become effective only, indeed it can be accomplished only through such a restoration taking place first of all in every Son of Israel. The Avatar encompasses the Planetary Heavens. The Celestial Avatara are active in pouring forth the Divine magnetic streams into the Planetary Heavens, charging those Heavens as reservoirs are charged from the streams which flow from the heights around them. There must be some who can respond, otherwise all this charging of the Planetary Heavens will be in vain. The Earth itself, as you can witness, reels under the outpouring; and the outpouring could never have taken place but for that which has been accomplished by the Divine Love for Israel. Now the Heavens await the arising of Israel. All Israel must be restored through the reconciliation of themselves to HIM. They must come to know HIM again, that they may be reconciled even to their burden-bearing instead of complaining about it. They must cease contending with the burden, and rejoice to bear it. Instead of desiring to fly from life because the burden of sacrifice seems too heavy to carry, they must delight to do the Divine Will. The Divine FATHER-MOTHER, through the LORD of Being, Who is HIS embodiment, travails in the very magnetic centre of HIS Own Being. HE travails through the Divine Hierarchy. He travails in and through the Celestial ministries of accommodation. And then through the Planetary Hierarchy. All this travail is unto the healing of the world. What the Heavens ask is, that Israel shall share that travail as the Nobles of GOD, the ancient spiritual aristocracy who were HIS Peculiar People. Those are HIS people who realize the Divine Inheritance, who rejoice in their sonship before HIM, who are rejoiced by fellowship with HIM, and who are now seeking to commune together as one great family in HIM, in various degrees of age-long experience.

This cosmic story calls to everyone who hears the Message. If you can respond, then you may witness the great Mystery in the third vision, which seems to have been such a human and individual reality to Jacob. For it is none other than an unveiling of the Divine Passion in the Oblation, the Divine Love travailing with the kingdom of Ya-akob-El unto its healing, and the restoration to the estate wherein it can again be ministered unto and named after Israel. It is through such travail the great Planetary reconciliation is to take place, and the kingdom or land of Edom once more become an integral part of the realm of Ya-akob-El.

Israel's Penuel and Peniel

H

Human
Inadequacy
to reveal
the Lord

The honour of being called to have part in that most noble redemptive, healing, uplifting and illumining ministry, is indeed great. It is to be glorified by the FATHER-MOTHER. Ya-akob-El named the place of the third vision, Peniel.   He had seen the Divine Presence face to face. Then he came to Penuel. As he ascended its height the Sun that had so long ago gone down, arose again. The glory of his LORD in resplendent vision broke once more within HIS consciousness. That which was then unto him prophetic, is to-day unto him realistic. It is the Day of the realization. So great has been the restoration in the Planetary Hierarchy as the result of the Oblation, that the joy is already glorious indeed. That which was then prophetic is to become in this day an empirical experience to you through being realized within you. You also must see GOD face to face in your travail. You must look upon HIS countenance. You may ask HIM what is HIS name and HE will tell you it is an unutterable name, but that it is written large within you. The day breaketh. It has broken. The Sun is emerging from the night. It is now Peniel for you. GOD has spoken to you face to face. Now are ye to go forward to Penuel. The Son of GOD in the full resplendence of Divine Fashion is to arise within you, to set no more. Then shall it come to pass that from HIS glory ye shall no more go out, but dwell forever within the Eternal Light.

I am conscious how fragmentary the unveiling of the Mystery has been; yet I hope the fragments may be gathered up by you into your baskets and preserved as precious elements of the Divine Bread broken unto you, that ye may understand the LORD of Being and HIS way, and rejoice before HIM; and rejoice in HIM, which is a far greater thing; and make the world glad for your coming unto it and your travailling in it, your sharing of its burden, your mediation unto it of the glorious heavenly ministries.

*   *   *   *

O Transcendent One Who art the most glorious Lord of all Being; my Lord, and the Lord of Ya-akob-El and Israel; my Father-Mother, and the Father-Mother of all Thy Children; how inadequate we are for these things, even with the endowments Thou hast given us. How inadequate are the best powers of Thy Servant to express Thee, and interpret Thee, and reveal all that may be revealed concerning Thee! Yet Thou blessest Thy Servant with Thy most blessed Benediction, and dost cause its wondrous streams to reach Thy Children.

We would bless Thy Name forever, O most Sacred Heart of Love!

THE ADAMIC RACE

THE PROEM OF CREATION

WHO WAS ADAM?

THE ESTATE OF THE ADAMIC RACE

THE TREE OF KNOWLEDGE MYSTERY

THE FALL OF THE RACE

THE MYSTERY OF THE TWO ADAMS

THE RESTORATION OF ALL ISRAEL

THE RESTITUTION OF THE EARTH

THE TRIUMPH OF CHRIST

THE ADAMIC RACE

This morning I am led to speak to you on another old-world story closely identified with the history of Ancient Israel, and therefore with the history of yourselves. It is the mystery associated with that dramatic part of the story of creation in which it is said the ELOHIM created man, and that there was given to him by the Divine FATHER-MOTHER the name, Adam. The title of the address is, therefore, The Adamic Race.

Sublime Proem of Creation

The proem of creation, even as it is found in the book of Genesis, is sublime. The Divine processional, if I may so name it, from out the heart of the Divine Mystery into the Celestial realms of manifestation, is there indicated; and we have a series of dramatic pictures associated with the coming into manifestation of star systems and our own Sun and Moon. Then the earth that seemed to be formless takes motion and becomes a formulated and concrete exposition of Divine activity. As the story is told in the Old scriptures, there follows the creation of different orders of life; and the culmination is reached in the statement that the ELOHIM communed together, and as a resultant, purposed to fashion a higher order of Being named man, with capacity to reach unto the heights of the realms of the Elohistic ministries, and to drink of the streams of those realms and thus come to the understanding of the Mystery couched in the ELOHIM, and take on by means of various attributes the likeness of ELOHIM, and grow and evolute, and still grow and evolute, until through the eternal ascensions of the Being, man could image GOD.

To see that drama, even in the tiniest miniature vision, is to witness something of the transcendent nature of the Divine Love and Wisdom, the sublimity of the Divine Purpose, and the glory of the Divine activity.

Then there is introduced another part, supposed by scholars to have been written by an entirely different hand, causing to arise in the schools through the ages the controversy as to which account was correct, whether the Elohistic or the Jahvistic, because of the different names that seemed to be used for the LORD and GOD. The second part of the story, however, is the introduction of other elements of spiritual history which belong to great ages after what is set forth in the proem

101

had been realized in the fashioning of the earth and the generation of mankind. For great history had been written through the operation of the law of growth and evolution before the Adamic Race arose upon the earth, so that there is in the second story a great history implied. But as a result of the loss of an important part which originally belonged to the story, there is confusion, and this has led readers and scholars to confound the Adamic Race with the first human race upon the earth.

This will become clearer to you as the mystery of that Race is unveiled, in so far as I may be permitted to do so in this hour. I would essay to do this under these aspects, so that they may give you pivots around which your thoughts may move:—

Who was Adam?

The estate of the Adamic race.

The mystery of the Tree of knowledge (concerning which a warning was said to have been given).

The fall of the race.

The unveiling of that mystery as set forth (through having been glimpsed in the Teachings of the Master) by the Pauline writers concerning the two Adams.

The restoration of all Israel and the world.

For, as in Adam all died, so in Christ, the second Adam, shall all be made alive again.

* * * *

Who was Adam? In many of the occult philosophies where they have dealt with the Mysteries, it is believed that Adam represented a different race from the human race as understood in the story of creation. In some parts of the interpretation of the ancient mysteries as taught in the schools of occult philosophy, Adam is believed to have been the first Messenger sent to this world. That he represented a race, is self evident, even as Christ is said to have represented a race. I am using the term Christ as it is thought of historically, theologically, ecclesiastically, and even occultly, in so far as the application may be given to the Master. For it is quite true, as we shall see, that He who came, or was sent as the Master, did belong to a race of Souls concerning whom He spake. For it is reported of Him that He said: *"Those whom the Father-Mother gave unto me shall come unto me."* Those who were of HIS race, whom HE knew, would return to HIM as the representative of the Christhood, which did not mean to Him personally. They would come back to the Christhood through the

Message. They would return to the regnancy, of which He had to speak, and therefore which He represented.

In like manner there are those who believe that Adam represented a higher race, and that he came as the first Messenger to the human race to teach them concerning the Divine Mysteries. Indeed, in many of the occult schools it is believed that he laid the foundations of the Mysteries which have been studied in occult and spiritual schools all through the ages, in so far as such Mysteries were known in the schools. Was he a Messenger? He was undoubtedly one in high estate. Was he the father of a race? He was, in a patriarchal sense. Undoubtedly he stood as one crowned with a high degree of consciousness. The tiniest flower can drink the sunbeams; but the measure of its receptivity is far less than the flowers that are greater in their manifestation and service which also drink in the sunbeams with a greater fulness. Thus all Souls can drink of the sunbeams of HIM Who is ever the Sun of our Life; but they can only drink of such according to the degree of their capacity. And as capacity is a thing that grows and expands, deepens and enlarges and ascends so that the Cup of Life becomes vaster in its measure, thus the human race in the early days of its beginning, and long ages after those early days when the human race had grown and evolved, ascending from one degree to another of spiritual consciousness, even then had not reached the estate which is represented in that old-world dramatic story of the creation of the Adamic Soul. Here one of the great difficulties confronting us is to get you all to think impersonally. That is the difficulty in unveiling many things to you. I would help you to get rid of the merely personal and human equation when you think of a Messenger. The Messenger is the Presence Who is with the Servant, without Whom the Servant is no Messenger. He is the LORD's Messenger only through the Presence Who is with him, illumining him, exalting his Being to the realm where he can see and know. And he can see and know in realization in that realm only because he is able to enter into oneness with His LORD.

*   *   *   *

Adam came from the hands of the ELOHIM as a Son of GOD. It is worthy of note that in tracing Adam's heritage in the genealogical histories in the two Gospels Records attributed to St. Matthew and St. Luke; that in St. Matthew's record man is taken back in his descent

*Amid the
Garden of
Eden*

only as far as Abraham, the claimed founder of Jewish story; but in St. Luke he is traced back to Adam, "which was the Son of GOD." Adam is called by the writer, the Son of GOD. And so he was a Son of the GODS, of the ELOHIM, and therefore a Son of GOD, the FATHER-MOTHER Eternal Mystery. This is witnessed to in the further dramatic presentation in the story.

Adam knew the Mysteries, such at any rate as might then have been unveiled. The Adamic Race belonged to him. The Adamic Race was comprised of Souls who could understand that which the Messenger was able to unveil to them. These Mysteries had become part of himself. They were great realizations. We will pass from the particular to the general, and think of Adam as representing a race known as the Adamic Race. In the story of the Garden of Eden we actually find a race of Souls so highly developed and unfolded that they are able to walk with GOD, which implies that they were able to live in the consciousness of GOD, to hear HIS footsteps, to be conscious of and have the power to endure HIS vibratory motion through HIS Angelic and Archangelic ministries.

The picture of Eden is the picture of every Soul. But the vision of Eden realized is the vision of the Adamic race. The story of Eden embodies the divine qualities which are latent in every human Soul. These are revealed in the story of Eden perfectly realized, wherein it is said GOD walked "in the cool of the day"—an expression full of wonderful tenderness and mystery. Man was able to hear the Voice. He was able to understand what the Voice said. Nay, he had attained to that state of conscious realization wherein he had the right to the Tree of Life—not only the right by his creation, but the right by his attainment. He was in that state wherein he could approach the Tree of Life in the midst of the Garden—which was the Tree of Divine Mystery—and partake of it. The estate of the Adamic Race is therefore revealed in this, that they had attained to such a spiritual and even divine consciousness that they were able to partake of the Tree of Life consciously, and to eat of its fruits. For the Tree of Life represents the central Mystery of Being. It represents that Mystery in the Eternal Heavens. It represents the same Mystery at the heart of every Celestial embodiment. It represents the magnetic centre by which all staral systems are held. It represents the magnetic pole of even a world like this. *It represents the magnetic pole of God in you.*

For it is only through the magnetic centre of your Being that you are able to touch the Tree of Life and appropriate its fruits unto the enrichment of your Being. The Soul becomes like GOD only through willing to be like GOD. It does not attain through false ambitions. It could not become like GOD in that way. It attains through willing to be everything that is Godlike. So that a Soul does not actually approach unto and touch the Tree of Life until it can cognize, and then have realized that which it has cognized, the Divine Mystery within itself.

The Mystery of the Tree of Life

The Adamic Race walked with GOD. They had the right to the Tree of Life, so they entered into the Holy City—that is, they rose to have the consciousness of HIM of Whom the Tree of Life spake. For you will understand this, that the Tree of Life is not only the magnetic Principle within your own Being, and within all worlds and all systems, and which is at the very heart of the Universe itself, but it is the Principle at the heart of the Sign of the Cross. It is the Sign of the Cross in the Eternal Realm. It is expressed in manifold degrees from that Divine Centre throughout the whole Universe of Being. The Mystery is concretely embodied for purposes of ministry.

Thus does it come to pass that in the Human Soul it is planted, because without it the Soul could never know GOD; could never touch HIM; could never hear HIM; could never attain the power to appropriate HIM. It is the Sign of the Cross within your own Being. We become in fashion like the Sign of the Cross in the measure in which that Tree of Life becomes our very Being. We grow like it. We grow rich through it. We become one with HIM Who is at the heart of it. To bear the Sign of the Cross in the fashion of HIM Who is known as THE SIGN OF THE CROSS, is to bear within us the Tree of Life, the fashion of GOD; first the likeness of ELOHIM through our attributes; then the image of GOD in our spiral, in our consciousness, and in our vision; all our attributes being impressed with the majesty and the beauty and the glory of HIS own Mystery.

Thus do Souls at last become as Gods. But to do so does not in any sense produce self-upliftment and self-glorification. How frequently I have to impress this fact upon you, that self-exaltation and self-glorying are utterly at variance with the Divine World and with the purpose of Life itself. They are at variance with the Angelic ministries. When we read that Moses spake these words: "Said I not unto you ye shall be as Gods," we may know that it was not spoken to fill heart and mind with pride. Yes, ye shall be like GOD. For, as the Master said and the disciple John recorded:

"Beloved ones, now are ye the children of God. And although the mystery of the manner of how ye so became is not yet fully unveiled to you, yet know ye this, when He shall have fully become in you, ye shall be in fashion like unto Him, and ye shall know Him as He is."

*   *   *   *

The Adamic Race made Eden. They made paradise. The Tree of Life was their magnetic centre. The most Sacred Mysteries were unveiled to them. They were the expositions of GOD in this world.

In the story it is further said there was counsel given to them containing a warning, which seemed to throw a shadow. It is recorded that they were counselled through Adam not to eat of another tree that was in the garden, the Tree of Knowledge of good and evil. For in the day in which they did partake of that tree they would fall. Why should such a tree have been in the garden if there was danger in its presence? And why should such a command have been given from the Divine World to the Adamic Race not to partake of that tree?

Here there is evidently indicated a danger zone, and anxiety concerning it. The story is cryptographic. The mystery naturally is hidden. It had to be; and much implied in it will still have to be hidden; for the full mystery behind it must remain a little longer guarded. And the mystery of it can be fully unveiled to you from the Inner World only as you are able to receive it and realize all that it signifies. But there are some elements in the story which may be unveiled now.

It is of the very nature of the Divine Love that there should be the Tree of Life, the sign of the Sacred Mystery we name the Sign of the Cross, at the magnetic centre of our Being, as well as in the heart of all worlds and systems; and it is also of the nature of the Divine Love that within the Divine Principle which the Tree of Life represents at the centre of our Being, there should not only be the Law of GOD operating, when untramelled, unto the perfecting of that which has been created and fashioned, but that there should also be in the unveiling of our Life, and even in our interpretation of the Life in our ministry, perfect liberty of choice and action within certain circumscribed areas, the latter limitations being absolutely necessary for the balance of the universe. Thus, unto individual Souls, a race cosmically expressing

Life (for the Adamic Race did give a cosmic expression of life), perfect liberty was given in the unfolding of the life before the FATHER-MOTHER. There is no growth where Life is in bondage. There is only growth through perfect liberty. That is the liberty of the Sons of GOD. Freedom is not license. Even in life many things might be lawful which are not expedient, because of the state of the world. But in an unfallen world all things lawful find their exposition in the manifestation of the individual, the communal, and the racial life.

Divine Law and Soul Freedom

Now, "the Tree of Knowledge of good and evil" is a cryptic statement concerning the uses of our *will* which is at the magnetic centre of our Being. Through our will we have power to choose and differentiate, not only in a mental way, but of a far more serious and far-reaching character. The mind ofttimes makes decisions on the spur of the moment and amid difficult circumstances which it finds have been mistakes; but it only finds those mistakes through the accumulation of results in the outer life, or it discovers the mistakes when the Soul goes into the Silence to commune before the High Altar of the LORD of Being. For the Divine LORD is within the Principle of our Being, and through our *inner will* which has the power of Divine judgment and choice, instructs the mind concerning its mistake.

There was something in the Adamic Race that could respond to such counsel as was given. Here I would say to you, though to some it may seem a strange thing to say, that the capacity in a Soul to hear such a warning with the Understanding, and to require such a warning, revealed great ages of growth and ascension of Being. For the warning was not concerned with the ordinary acts of life such as are associated with the outward manifestations; it concerned itself with the misappropriation and consequent misuse of the power that came to the Being as the result of growth through appropriating the Tree of Life itself. It was a warning to guard the Soul against the use of the power so acquired, for other than Divine purposes.

Here we are face to face with the great temptation that assailed others in high places to seek power for its own sake, and the use of it for false ambition's ends; and caused those who fell to make an excursion to this world with a view to establishing a materialized system; conduct which resulted in the bringing down of this world from its one-time high estate, filling its directors with the love of place, the love of power, and the love of dominion. The fall of this

The Love and Misuse of Power

world was not through any simple and most natural harmless mistakes made upon the outer planes. *The great Descent was the result of the wrong use of the central will of the Being on the part of those who at one time had access to the Tree of Life.* Therefore, it is said, in the further part of the story, that the Tree of Life had to be guarded lest anyone, even a member of the Adamic Race after that Race had become involved in the great declension that took place, should be induced to enter into a state of evil thought and purpose, evil vision and feeling and desire for power, and under such conditions should seek to appropriate the most sacred Mystery of the Tree of Life. For remember this, that in the measure in which the Tree of Life is partaken of, the Soul acquires the knowledge of the Divine Mysteries. That is the meaning of the Mystery. In the measure in which a Soul ascends in state it acquires power to appropriate Divine Things; and this growth is through the appropriation of the Tree of Life. It expands and deepens in the consciousness of the Divine Mysteries. It comes to know how those Mysteries are operative in the Universe of Being, in the various systems, and even at the heart of this world.

Now, herein lies the reason for guarding the Tree of Life. Those who brought this world down did know something of the Divine Mystery which gave to it its motion, its magnetic status, and its fourfold atmospheria. And it was through the misdirection of these ruling ones that the world came down to be a materialized system. When you know that this world was once clothed in what I may call its own magnetic light through the solar action upon its magnetic poles, and that light was not communicated to it as light has to be communicated to-day, but through the Sun's action upon the Planet's magnetic poles, then you understand how different the world is that now fills the vision. In those days to which I am thinking back, there was no photosphere of the Sun such as there is to-day. Where the photosphere now is, glorious spheres encircled the sun. These were the Solar Angelic Heavens. That was before HE Who is our FATHER-MOTHER had to make "a tent for the Sun to dwell in." The Tent or Tabernacle was the photosphere through which the Sun under the changed conditions could minister unto the fallen estate of the Planet-Soul Judah, and other members who were affected. You see how great the Mysteries are lying behind these things! For those who brought this world down changed the magnetic streams of the Earth so greatly that it lost the power to become clothed with magnetic light through Solar action upon its magnetic poles. On its outer planes the Earth does not rotate on these poles. As you know, its poles of rotation are more than twenty-three degrees inclined towards the ecliptic. That is also the distance of the magnetic poles from the poles of rotation.

Greatness in State and Lowliness

Now, the counsel given to the Adamic Race was this; they were not to seek power and dominion as those did who brought the world down. For remember, those who wrote those wonderful stories, knew this Mystery. The story veils the depth of the tragedy even whilst it indicates. It veils the mystery at the heart of it, though it implies that such and such dramatic situations arose, and that such a tragedy befell the world. Therefore the Adamic Race was warned against partaking of the Tree called the Tree of Knowledge. In other words, they were counselled not to use the knowledge of Good for purposes that were evil.

The Adamic Race will, therefore, be seen to have been a most advanced race in that they could be counselled not to seek powers to bring down the Heavens—the Heavens within themselves, and the Heavens of the system to which they had been sent. They had been warned ever to be humble, ever to walk with GOD in the cool of the day. Even such a writer as Emmanuel Swedenborg, who wrote in the third quarter of the past naros, affirmed that he had come to the knowledge that the members of the first race, the Adamic Race, were noble in state, and that even the human children were pure and beautiful and lovely in their embodiment, that they lived on what were then exquisite productions of the vegetable kingdom, the herbs and the lower fruits, and the more advanced on the higher fruits.

In occult philosophy that time is spoken of as "the Golden Age." There are many who think the Golden Age was a vain dream of the imagination of poets and mystics, and not a reality at all. But it was no vain dream. We have lived, even in this life in the consciousness of our Being, back in those days. This message can affirm with an unfaltering proclamation, that all the works of the FATHER-MOTHER are glorious; that this world was once most glorious; that its children were lovely, not only in the hidden centre of their Being, but also in the manifestation of their life. And they were educated in the lesser Mysteries by members of the Adamic Race. The Messenger named Adam, came to those who belonged to his race. He brought back the Mysteries to them. They were interpreters of these to the children of

109

this world. They interpreted the Breaths of Nature, the atmospheres, the various orders of life, the trees, flowers, and fruits, and Planetary motion. They were the Divine expositors of Love and Wisdom.

Therefore the Adamic Race was a great, noble congregation of Souls who walked with GOD in the measure in which they had attained to the realization of HIM. For we can walk with GOD only through our consciousness. We apprehend HIM through becoming conscious of HIS ensphering of us, then HIS overshadowing of us, and then the interfusing of our Being. We walk with HIM as a Soul at one with HIM; as one in HIM; as one whose life is a suspension from the Heavens on to the earth. Such a Soul is all HIS own. Life is upheld by HIM, nourished from HIM, enriched by HIM, illumined within the Sanctuary of Being through the glory shed as the result of Divine magnetic action upon the Soul's magnetic centre. *That Life is His Indwelling realized.*

Ages are gathered up into that part of the story which represents "the Fall." Great Planetary changes of a disastrous order were effected long before the Adamic Race fell. Ages before it yielded to the subtle breaths, the children of this world had been taken far down below the beautiful ideal Life unto which they had attained. Through those ages the Adamic Race struggled against the materializing influences which were so persistent and powerful that they became dominating, and at last some even of them succumbed. Those are spoken of in the language of later days as the House of Ephraim. Those who brought this Planet down sought to dominate not only this world, but the Divine Purpose itself to such an extent, that they thought a materialized world was better than a wholly spiritual world. A manifest world of God is one whose spiritual substances are never fixed. That does not mean they are never solid. Do not confound fixity with solidity. You can have a spiritual solid whose magnetic elements are not fixed. And you can know that they are not fixed in this way, that magnetically they can respond at once to the Divine Law operating within their realm. But when they become fixed they cannot respond. That is the difference between what science thinks of and describes as matter, and what is true spiritual substance. Real spiritual substance is never fixed in its magnetic elements. When it becomes fixed it becomes matter. It has lost the power to respond to the Law operating within its kingdom of magnetic attraction. Its volitive magnetic elements are in bondage. It has, therefore, no power to respond to the magnetic action that would have attracted it. The result is that on the outer planes great and most drastic changes have to be effected very gradually and with great caution. And this will have still to be for some ages, in order to so change the elements that they may at last find their own realm and get back to that magnetic state wherein they can respond to the magnetic law of the realm to which they belong.

Results of that Fall to the Race

Now, when the Adamic Race was at last brought down, it was as the result of the conditions which had obtained and prevailed for ages. Their fall might truly be said to have been the effect of the subtle influences upon them of the materializing serpent, that betraying and satanic spirit which had caused to take place the changed polarity in the Planet. The whole race was brought down in some degree, though some members fell farther than others. But all of them through the fall lost Eden. And Eden has been behind them ever since. For note this, that Eden does not represent a geographical situation, nor an ordinary chapter in the history of such a Race. Eden represented for the Adamic Race, a Life of high realization wherein each member could walk with GOD, and the power of clairaudience to hear HIS voice; and to have such experiences not simply in an hour of devotion, but at all times. They could so walk with HIM that they were ever in the consciousness of HIM, feeling HIS touch through the motion of HIS Being within, and beholding HIS glory. For their vision was obtained by means of the inshining of that glory into the sanctuary of their Being. It is quite true that in all the ages there have been saints, and not only in the Christian era, though the Church of the latter has specially claimed the saints. The children of GOD have been saints in all the ages; for they are the saints who have the capacity and willinghood to travail. And travail is produced through deep Divine motion in the Being. Such motion can be realized only by those who have been able to receive greatly of the Divine magnetic streams which flow into the very Sanctuary of their Being. The measure of a Soul's Divine capacity is also commensurate with its power to travail—that is, to endure, to bear burdens, to unfurl the Divine Cross even in the midst of burden-bearing, to stand immovable upon the Earth amid the awful physical and spiritual cataclysms resulting from it being shaken to its foundations. Only Divine Souls can so stand and travail. All Souls are potentially Divine; but the only Souls who have realized the great things of

III

their Divinity, are those who have endured that which only the Gods could endure, and those who are of them. So, the measure of a Soul's power to bear burden, is the measure of its Divine capacity; and it is the testimony of its past heritage.

In this sense the Adamic Race in this world has been the race of Divine travaillers, knowing inherently in the centre of their Being the glorious Mysteries, and seeking after them. Ephraim has been seeking them so much through the higher mind; but the inner tribes of Israel have been seeking them through the realization of the Being. The full understanding of the Mysteries cannot come through the mind. You may gather knowledge concerning them, but you cannot thus understand them. The understanding of the Mystery of GOD is through realization, and not through knowledge gathered from without. The knowledge about the Mysteries gathered from without is not to be despised. But such knowledge is to be transmuted into dynamic force by which the life is raised to higher planes of consciousness, to grow and evolute and to ascend into the realm where realization becomes for the Soul. That is the realm of the Soul's high and glorious experience. *God is known in consciousness through realization. The Mysteries of God are thus wise known in realization.* The Saints of GOD through the ages have been seeking after those Mysteries, desiring to regain them. The real spiritual travaillers in this world have been seeking after HIM Whose vision they lost. Is not that the meaning of all beautiful spiritual literature and liturgy wherein there is true Soul motion? It is the desire to get back to that state wherein the members of the Adamic Race walked with GOD. Oh, think of it and all that it means to walk with GOD! It is not simply believing HE is a Presence Who is near. It is more than having passing sensations as if HE must, through ministries, be influencing you. It is to walk with HIM in the daily rounds of Life and in the inner world of consciousness for ever. It is the eternally great experience of living in HIM, moving in HIM, deriving from HIM, serving for HIM, having no Life apart from HIS, and consequently no purpose that is not HIS own, no service HE does not bless, no thought HE cannot illumine, nor desire other than HIS own creating.

In these days we are in the midst of Adamic travail, or the travail of the Sons of GOD. Adam was a Son of GOD. The whole Adamic Race were the Sons of GOD; and the members of that great Race are arising again to-day. In our vision we have been back to the ages when they ministered upon the Earth amidst unfallen conditions, and interpreted and revealed the Divine Love and Wisdom. In the fulness of the consecration of their powers they were as giants upon the Earth, not merely in outward stature, but giants in their vision, in the passion of their Being, in their power to take burdens and bear them upon GOD'S Cross within them. They were great in their giving, and in their administrations they were as minor Gods in this world. We have looked back through the ages that have risen and set since the fall. We have witnessed the streams of influence which have flowed through them. We have looked on the ebb and flow of ages, the calm and the tumultuous motion of the tides of experience. And now to-day we stand upon the threshold of the new era, the birth of a new race. Many people are looking for a new race. Some think it will arise in America, expecially in California; others look to Australia, and some to other countries. Such are looking for a new race of the Human order which will be finer physically. But that is not what is meant.

It is to be the arising of the Sons of GOD. These will come through all the great races. There is a congregating of them in these isles to-day, greater than there has been for great ages. These Souls are here for one great purpose. They are coming back to make Divine Life manifest. They have again to recover their consciousness of the Divine Presence and understand in clarity of vision what brought about the great declension even amongst themselves. They are coming back to be once more restored to their ancient Inheritance. Their powers of vision and remembrance are to be regained; for they must again remember how the Divine Love was betrayed through those who loved place and power, ambitious spirits desiring to be great before men, and to be equal with the Gods, desiring to have power to control and command the elements and direct them at will, desiring to have the power to say that this shall be done and that that shall not be done, and thus to challenge the Divine Wisdom.

Why, even that part of the story which has relation to the temptation of Eve, is full of Soulic significance. It is the temptation of the most subtle kind to that exquisite Mystery in the Soul—*the desire nature*. Most people not understanding the Mystery would think of the term simply as it is applied to the body. But the desire nature is not physical, though the body may have its desire. The desire nature

The Travail of the Adamic Race

I

*The Earth's
Tragic
Betrayal*

is of the Will. It is related to the Inner Cross, which is the Tree of Life at the centre of the Being in the midst of the Garden. A Soul can greatly desire to be great. It can desire in its ambition to have power to dominate others and rule over them; to direct and control the elements; to be so filled with power that it may be able to impose its will as a God in this world.

Beloved ones, the Sons of GOD in the Heavens of the Divine World are great Souls. They are glorious embodiments of the Eternal Mystery of Universal Being. The Sons of GOD who are dwellers and workers in the Celestial Realms through all the systems, are great Beings. But they are all humble. They are lowly. They know they are dependent upon the Eternal Mystery for all their attributes; for all their power of vision in apprehension and comprehension; and for all realization. It is only when such power is affected in them, as became the case with a few, that the Divine Love is betrayed. Very few, comparatively speaking, have ever left the Presence of the Divine LORD to go forth and found a system of their own as an experiment. It is only too sadly true that some did do this, believing that what they thought was better than what the Divine World had purposed to accomplish through the Celestial Hierarchies. These decided to come to this system. They so betrayed members of the Hierarchy that the Earth became a fixed system. Although the Earth rotates on its axis and revolves round the Sun, yet its outer planes are fixed. When these latter have to be moved and changed, they have to be shaken up by earthquakes. Many theories of earthquakes have been given, none of which touch the real secret of them. They are always accounted for by physical causes. They are a part of the Divine activities at the heart of the Planet wherein its inner planes are intensified in their motion through the Solar magnetic action upon and through the magnetic poles. Herein you will see the Mystery of the Planetary constitution, state and needs, deepens. Those inner planes are intensified in their action producing the Earth tremors, and even forcing to the surface by means of volcanic action, the elements which are in the wrong place.

These are thoughts by the way. Bye and bye you will understand more of this great and most sacred Mystery when it may be unveiled.

We are on the threshold, as I said, of the new race. The new race will express itself even into the physical form. This is quite true; for the life will be noble and the form will be most beautiful; for all the woundings of the ages will be healed. There will be as manifold distinctions of form and feature and countenance as are found to-day, but there will be nothing imperfect. Just as the trees even in the fallen state of the world are exquisitely beautiful in their form, each order differing from the other, and each tree in the same order differing from one another; and also the flowers though having something in common yet all differing from each other in the degree of their manifestation and in the degree of the beauty of their form; and as these are all beautiful and all have capacity to contribute to the economic life of the Planet, so, even as these all differ one from another, whilst yet they have the one life, so shall the members and tribes of the new race differ. Upon the outer planes of manifestation, even as within the inner realms of their experience, shall these differ. Yet everyone will be clothed with the like glory. The glory will be the resultant of the magnetic action at the centre of the Being. That glory will reveal itself in their Aura. It will be unaffected by inimical conditions, and be able to express itself everywhere and at all times.

Every life will be like a sweet scented flower. The fragrance of their lives will be as incense poured forth from sacred censers to heal the atmospheric conditions of this distraught land of Judah—the Planet-Soul.

The new race that is coming is said to be coming through the second Adam. Who is the second Adam? Christ is so named. It is simply the restoration of the Adamic state through the Christhood. The first great Christhood manifestation upon this Planet was through the Adamic Race. There are glints and gleamings of this in the history of the Sons of GOD when they became known as Israel and the children of Zion. All the ages were gathered up into the manifestation amidst the Galilean hills and planes of Judæa and Samaria. That Manifestation was made unto and for the Adamic Race. The second Adam is simply so designated because it was a re-manifesting of that which the Adamic Race knew. Therefore the whole purpose of the Message of the Manifestation days was to find the Adamic Race known as ancient Israel. The Sons of GOD became known as ancient Israel in the later ages of their history. To find the Sons of GOD who alone could respond to the vision of GOD, the Master came to Israel. Though every human Soul is a Son of GOD potentially, yet a child cannot know what the vision of GOD means to the Soul until

The Master and the Adamic Race

it has grown and evoluted through great ages, and through expansion and ascension attained to that estate wherein it knows empirically what the vision of GOD means. Therefore no one can respond to this Message who has not known something of the vision of GOD in the ancient times. That is why it is said the Master came unto His own. He came to seek His own. Who were His own but the children of the Adamic Race? Who were His own but His brethren over whom He had been made shepherd, overseer, interpreter for the great FATHER-MOTHER? He had been Messenger unto them through many of the ages during which they have sojourned upon the planes of this Earth. Nevertheless, the second Adam is not to be thought of personally, nor even individually. Remember, the glory of the Message of one sent is not in the Messenger himself. It could not be. The Message must fill his Being. How could he proclaim it if it did not? It must be as his very Life. How could he know it if its magnetic streams were not coursing through all the arterial system of his Being, and expressing itself in every pulse of his Life? For the knowledge of the Divine is not knowledge gathered from without, nor knowledge gathered in the schools. It is knowledge gathered in the realms of realization at the Feet of HIM Who is ever the Presence within the same Sanctuary of our Being. *The Messenger is the Lord Himself.* HE is the Message, not the Servant. The Servant tells it because he knows it, realizes it, lives in the very atmosphere of it, and is sent to tell it. The Servant feels the motion of it because it is the motion of HIS LORD in him. But the Servant must not be confounded with HIS LORD, nor the mere utterance by the Servant with the innermost significance of the Message.

Thus is it with this Message. The Servant of the LORD is sent to proclaim it unto the healing of all Israel and the restoration of the Adamic Race. For the new Race is to be the Adamic Race restored by means of the second Adam. The second Adam is Christ. But Christ is a Principle and a Divine Estate. The coming of Christ is in the Message restored. In the Adamic age all died. All went down through the betrayal. There died in them the consciousness of their high heritage. Through the agelong oppression resulting from the conditions which had grown up and prevailed upon this world, the realization of Christ died in them. The consciousness of their ancient Christhood; the consciousness of the Divine potencies for service;

116

the consciousness of the Eternal Vision in them; the consciousness of His Voice speaking to them; the vibratory motion of His ministries unto them which were at one time Elohistic; these losses constituted the dying of Christ in them. But now that is all to be changed with the coming of the second Adam in the restoration of the cosmic Christhood. That is what this Message has to declare and unveil. It is impersonal. Multitudes ofttimes follow a man or a woman and confound the man or the woman with the Divine Message. That has never saved the world. It is said Messengers have appeared from time to time. So they did. They brought some Message. But very soon the Message became confounded with the Messenger, with the resultant that the power of the Message became utterly lost. Thus has it been through great ages; and the Messengers have seen and known that this would be after their departure. The message has remained simply as occult knowledge. That is where the Christianity taught by the Master landed in the western world. That world has been and still is great in its beliefs; but it is sadly lacking in its realization of the things it believes.

Now the new Race has begun. It is not coming merely through human generation, although through human generation members of that race will come into the life of manifestation. For they must have a true and pure parenthood in those through whom they come, in order that they may be born as Jesus is said to have been—that is, a life surrounded by the atmosphere of the pure and beautiful Jesus estate. But the real coming Race is Soulic. It is the Race of the Christs. It is the race of the Sons of GOD. It is the return of the Race of the Divine Ancients who knew GOD in consciousness. These shall know HIM again. They shall have the willinghood to know HIM as HE is.

Beloved Friends, have you that willinghood? Are you willing to give up everything absolutely, and to be nothing? To be and have nothing apart from HIM, and yet, in being so, have everything? What would you be but a vessel for your LORD? There is no self exaltation in HIM. HE is at once the most majestic and the most lowly and concrete exposition of Being in all the Universe. And to know HIM is surely to be like HIM!

The Adamic Race has come. It is the time when the second Adam should become manifest. Through the second Adam those in whom

Christ died are to be made alive again. They are to hear this Message. Is not that so now? Is not your recognition of the Message the revelation of the awakening of the perceptions of Christ who is in you, and of your own ancient Christhood estate? To perceive the Divine significance of the Message is to recognize its Origin, its Source, its Call. And although you may not have found yourself able to respond to the fulness of its call, yet you are responding in the measure in which you are able to do and are desirous and willing to respond more and still more. And because of this willinghood and deep desire in so many, there shall be such an arising of the Sons of GOD as shall speedily change the whole theatre of the activity of this world, that its drama shall be the one of pure, beautiful, majestic, yet lowly life; a life mighty yet humble; yea, almighty, because of the Omnipotent ONE in HIS children, yet gentle as the love of the tenderest woman in the hour of her heart's deepest emotion. And thus the mystery of the Adamic Race shall be known through the restoration of the new Race, by means of this Message which is pre-eminently associated with the second Adam. As in the Adamic Age all died because all went down; so in the Christ Age all shall be made alive. Yes, even those in whom Jesus fell asleep, who did not attain to the Christ-consciousness in high degree before the betrayal, but were on the threshold of Spiritual Christhood, and who lived the beautiful Jesus Life—even such shall hear HIS Voice. They will recognize the true way and follow it unto the making of HIM manifest in the degree in which they have capacity, and come on in their growth and evolution as the elder children who were in ancient times known as the Children of the Adoption, but who also became involved in the great Descent. These Souls were partakers with Israel in the glory of the Sanctuary; for they were taught by Israel in the later as well as in the earlier ages, the glorious Mysteries of the Divine Love and Wisdom. These were those "who fell asleep in Jesus." This saying is always thought to relate to those who died believing in the Master. What a calamity that would have been for the millions who never heard anything about Him! Oh no! Those who died in Jesus, whether in this country or any other country, whether they worship under the shadow of the Sanctuaries and the nomenclature of Christianity, or before the altars in other lands and through other forms of vision and service, but who have lived the beautiful life—all shall come, they are coming; for these are they in whom the Jesus Life died. The graves are yielding up those who so died; and delivering up also very specially those in whom Christ died. For the dead in Christ must rise first.

Look at the significance of this Saying! The dead in Christ must rise first. Those who knew Christ should be the first to recognize the Message brought back to them, and to become members of the rehabilitated communal Christhood manifestation. The Heavens are depending upon it. They are anticipating it. They are rejoicing in every Soul who returns. Ah, there is a greater meaning in those Sayings attributed to the Master which were not quite correctly presented, "There is joy in the Angels of GOD over one sinner that repented." True, there is joy in the Angels of GOD over one of the ancient Sons who recognizes this Message as it recalls the Divine Vision to the Soul. As the Message finds that Divine something within the Being, it feels moved and drawn; for it knows within itself that this Message is true. And great is the joy in the Heavens. The Heavens are awaiting the arising of all the members of the ancient Adamic Race, known in later days through the prophetic messages as ancient Israel. And there is joy in the Presence of the FATHER-MOTHER over the return of such. The Angels rejoice. The Archangels rejoice. Yes! And the beloved ones who have passed over, whom we have known and loved, and who are with us this morning, they also rejoice. For this Message, remember, is flashed far and wide wherever the members of the Household of Israel are, though there are seemingly so few present in this Sanctuary to hear it. The proclamation of the Message within the little centres is but the active service in the generating station through which the flash-light is sent far and wide. Many in distant parts respond in strange ways. They write saying how they have just touched the Message in libraries, or through a friend, and that it is the Message they have been waiting for all their lives. There are many such instances showing how the Divine World through the Angelic World, is ministering in this day.

This will reveal to you how the ministry of this School, this "Holy Convocation," is infinitely greater than merely ministry unto you all who are assembled here. Your own thought can even flash its image into distant parts of the world. And, if that be so, you will the better understand how it is possible for the Angelic World to convey the Message as this Message is unveiled to you in this Sanctuary and in other Sanctuaries. Here you get back to the cosmic element in the

119

Yielding up the Kingdom

Message itself; and how in the Return, and through all the ministries rendered wherever a real Son of God is, or one who was once in that estate of consciousness, the influence of such a gathering goes forth to strengthen Divine Life in the World and give to those who are seeking their way back, streams of encouragement. Thus in Christ shall all be made alive. And, in the full arising of each, then there shall be a yielding up of the Kingdom unto the FATHER-MOTHER. That saying is pregnant with meaning. It is the yielding up on the part of every child of the FATHER-MOTHER who was once of the Adamic Race, HIS Kingdom established within themselves; so that HE may have regnancy over it. You will thus see the very language is full of Divine significance. When you can say, O my FATHER-MOTHER! My prayer is just to be ruled by THEE in everything! Then shall the distraught world be healed and the children of Judah know the joy of HIS salvation. Then shall there be a practical application of real spiritual atmosphere and power unto the healing of all Souls; unto the healing of all the social and national conditions, and the restoration of the elements to spiritual states. Then shall the Earth again yield her increase and become responsive to the magnetic streams from the Divine World, till every sphere expresses HIM Who is the Perfect ONE, and the All Glorious ONE.

I never feel so inadequate as when I have to speak of HIM; HE is so wonderful in HIS Love, so glorious in HIS Wisdom, so tender in HIS approach, so exquisitely lowly that HE never makes you feel HE is stooping to you; and so gentle in HIS methods that HE can exalt you even until you are able to stand before HIS High Altar, and endure the outflowing of the magnetic streams of HIS Mystery, thus sharing in the majesty of HIS glory. May this hour have brought you nearer HIM in this way. May it have brought HIM more clearly to your vision. May this hour have given you a divine urge, an increase of energy, unto the great Realization of all that your Being yearns for.

O Holy and Most Blessed and most glorious One.
May this hour be verily the rehabilitation of the Household of Thine Ancient Children, the restoration of the Adamic Race of Thy Sons who came forth from Thee unto the manifestation of Thee! May their manifestation now be unto the accomplishment of this world's healing! Amen and Amen.

120

D

THE OBLATION
IN RELATION TO
VICARIOUS BURDEN-BEARING

THE QUESTION AND ANSWER

THE SERVANT A VEHICLE

THE VICARIOUS BURDEN OF ISRAEL

THE OBLATION VICARIOUS
    FOR THE PLANET AND HER CHILDREN
    FOR LUCIFER
    FOR PLANETARY HIERARCHY
    FOR THE HOUSE OF ISRAEL

THE PASSION WAS OF GOD
    THE SERVANT WAS HIS VEHICLE

THE OBLATION
IN RELATION TO
VICARIOUS BURDEN-BEARING

QUESTION—SOME OF US ARE NOT QUITE CLEAR AS TO THE MEANING OF VICARIOUS BURDEN-BEARING.

WE KNOW THAT KARMA FOR EACH ONE OF US REPRESENTS THE OUT-WORKING OF OUR OWN HISTORY, AND THAT THOSE WHO WERE OF ISRAEL KNEW WHAT MIGHT BE CALLED VICARIOUS BURDEN-BEARING, IN THE SENSE THAT THEY WOULD NEVER HAVE BECOME IDENTIFIED WITH THE EVIL IN THIS WORLD HAD THEY NOT IN THEIR LOVE FOLLOWED THE CHILDREN OF JUDAH IN THEIR DESCENT; THAT IS, THEY FOLLOWED THEM, THINKING THEY MIGHT BE ABLE FURTHER TO HELP THEM. BUT ARE WE TO UNDERSTAND THAT, OTHER THAN THIS ASPECT, NOT ONE OF THE CHILDREN OF ISRAEL COULD BE SAID TO HAVE BEEN, NOR BE, THE VEHICLE OF VICARIOUS BURDEN-BEARING, NOR IN ANY SENSE CO-WORKER IN THE LIVES OF THE OBLATION WITH HIM WHO BORE IT, NOR IN THESE PRESENT DAYS CO-WORKER WITH THE SERVANT WHO HAS RECOVERED THE MESSAGE, GIVEN IN THESE DAYS, OF THE MANIFESTA-TION; WE MEAN, CO-WORKER IN THE SENSE OF A DUAL MANIFESTATION, SPECIALLY IN CONNECTION WITH THE MESSENGER AND HIS REVELATION?

IF YOU FEEL YOU COULD MAKE THIS POINT QUITE CLEAR TO US, WE FEEL IT WOULD ALSO HELP US TO UNDERSTAND SOME OF TO-DAY'S RELATIONSHIPS AS REGARDS THE ORGANIZATION OF THE WORK AND THE WORKERS, AND WE MIGHT COME TO KNOW JUST WHAT EACH ONE'S OFFICE AND PLACE IS AND HOW A TRUE CO-OPERATION MIGHT BE COME AT BETWEEN EVERY WORKER AND BETWEEN THE WORKERS AND YOURSELF AS FOUNDER OF THE ORDER AND LEADER OF US ALL.

*　　*　　*　　*

I answer this last question because, in the first place, it has been given to me several times of late under different forms by different members and workers. And I answer it also so that there should henceforth be perfect clarity throughout the Order regarding the Manifestation and the Oblation. The answer can only be fragmentary; yet I trust it may be with sufficient clarity to enable you to apprehend the significance of both the Manifestation and the Oblation in relation to the matter raised in the question. And in endeavouring to make

123

such clear to you, I would plead with you, as so often I have pleaded with you, and if it were possible I would accentuate and intensify the motion of my Being in that pleading, that you should transcend the personal realm in general, and transcend the personal equation and even the individual equation in particular, in relation to Servants and Messengers. For, although in the Divine administrations individuals are used as the vehicles of the Divine Love and Wisdom, and when ministries have to be rendered upon the outer planes of a world like this, what we have to regard as the personal has also to be used as the vehicle of the individual who is the vehicle of the sublime Love and Wisdom, yet the personal and individual aspects of the Servant and Messenger must be transcended. They must never be accentuated. They must be lost in the Message. Therefore, whatsoever I may have to say to you in this hour that might seem to have relation in any degree to the personal and individual, you will at once understand that there is no personal allusion either concerning myself or concerning others. I will think always of these as vehicles, as I ever think of myself as the vehicle of my LORD. Of myself I would say that I am a man amongst you, an individual member of HIS Children, a brother amongst brethren. But I am HIS, and I am HIS Servant. Yet I have no personal claim, nor individual claim. I want to disabuse your mind of all its Pauline conceptions and traditions of the Master and His ministry in the Manifestation Days. I would save you and the Message from the Pauline conceptions of the Master that are creeping into the interpretation of the sacred Mysteries I have had to unveil to you, having been privileged and honoured of the Heavens to have such ministry. There must never be any more Pauline betrayal of the Message by any claim on the part of anyone such as Paul made. The Message is not mine. Even the Passion was of no man. I am just HIS Servant. Whatsoever there is of love in me is HIS own Love, and I have no claim to it in any personal or individual way. It is mine only because it is first HIS, to make it manifest through the individual, and through the personal, and thus reveal HIS glorious Mystery. With this understanding on your part, and clarity of your vision, I will endeavour to briefly unveil the profound matters raised in the question.

* * * *

All the Sons of Israel have travailed. They all travail to-day on these planes; and some travail more deeply than others. The burdens

of some appear greater than the burdens of others. So was it in the
days of ancient Israel for every Soul, according to the degree of its
capacity and the nature of the ministry it was called upon to render
for the Divine Love unto the children of this world. That the
Children of Israel accumulated what is known as karma, though not
in the world's sense at all, is also true. Yet it is true only in this way:
their going down in ministry on behalf of the children of this world,
led them to become involved in the conditions which obtained and
prevailed for ages, so that the beautiful garments of their Christhood
became shadowed, and then defiled as they were bespattered by the
sensuous mud of this world (I am using these terms mystically).
All of them were deeply affected, and their priestly robes became
changed.

These and similar conditions have been with them through the
great ages. From time to time they have been partially cleansed
and sufficiently healed to enable them to enjoy again something
of their childhood to the FATHER-MOTHER. But the joyful sound
of the perfect salvation and the full return into the consciousness
of the Presence, they have not known; and so they have travailed.
Karma has followed them.

This latter will become clearer when you think of Souls returning
to the consciousness of the Great Love. The path by which a Soul
goes out is the path by which it must return. All Israel went out,
and so Israel has to return. Each one returns burdened with the
burden that the path of their going imposed upon them. For they
have to carry that burden along the path of their return, until it is
quite blotted out. It is not, however, karma in the world's sense;
of that I may speak later. It is rather the burden of their heritage
which they have accumulated during their ministry in this world in
contrast to the glorious heritage of the Christhood which once was
theirs. It is because of such travail that those wonderful old songs
were written concerning the Soul's yearning after the Divine—

"When shall I come and appear before GOD?" "Why hast THOU
forsaken me O LORD?" "Hast THOU cast me off for ever?" Only
the Soul who had known, and who had the consciousness of having
known that Presence, could have so prayed. You do not miss what
you never possessed. It is not as something lost. You may desire
something you have never had, or you think you would like to have
now, and you might miss the acquisition of such. But to feel the loss

*The Travail
of the
Sons of
God*

125

of something means you have had it before; it has been your possession.

Thus in the burden-bearing all travailed; but all were not alike. Some walked through shallower waters. Others had to make their way through tumultuous deeps. I may not permit myself to unveil this to you in the history of your own past, for it would carry me through great ages. But I want to make it clear that all did not carry the same burdens, nor in equal degree; but all travailed. The Divine Love and Wisdom alone knows the measure of any individual Soul's burden, and the depth of that Soul's passion. And thus, no one can know what the travail of Israel was, individually or collectively, unless it be revealed unto such an one from the Divine.

All the children of Israel who were sent to this world have shared in this burden bearing. And for them it was vicarious. Now vicarious burden-bearing may mean one of two things, or both, namely, that you bear something for yourself vicariously, or you bear it for another. There are things which cannot be borne for us by others; these we must bear for ourselves. Even the Divine cannot bear certain things for us except by bearing them in us. We must bear them for ourselves even though it is the Divine Travail in us. There are things which the Divine alone could accomplish for this world in the changing of its karma; for the spiritual impoverishment which befell the world was great. The Divine Love did that in the accomplishment of the Oblation which could not otherwise be done, even by the Planet's Hierarchy.

So, vicarious sacrifice is the burden-bearing by a Soul unto the blotting out of its karmic burden. Indeed, it is the only way; for there is no hypothetical redemption anywhere, such as the Church still believes in. Redemption is practical; and every Soul must bear its redemptive burden. But it is the Divine Who travails in the Soul, and in the degree in which the Soul yearns to be like the Divine. Therefore, you can bear vicariously for yourself. And you do so. The travail of every Soul is vicarious.

You may also share the travail of others and vicariously carry part of their burden. There are burdens which cannot be transferred, but there are some which may be; at least, in part. Such you may take upon yourselves in order to help them in the vicarious burden of their travail back to the realization of the Divine Love and

Wisdom. Was it not that which Israel sought to do in this world for those to whom they ministered? And that is the reason why all the members of Israel are so full of travail in this day. They sought vicariously to carry the world's burden of misdirected passion, and that burden took many of them down into the realm of that misdirection, and caused great suffering to them.

For whom the Oblation was Borne

From all this you will understand the real meaning of a vicarious sacrifice. It is the offering of yourselves in blessed willinghood to bear unto the blotting out of the burden of any accumulated effects of travail within yourselves and upon yourselves; and to bear such unto the uttermost. And that which causes the burden-bearing in you is the motion of HIS Holy Spirit; for it is the outworking of HIS own glorious purpose to refashion you and bring you back once more into the fashion of HIMSELF that you may again radiate HIM, through being clothed with the resplendence of HIS radiance.

*   *   *   *

Was the Oblation a vicarious burden-bearing for Souls indirectly? Was it the burden that Souls were carrying at the time that made the Oblation? Oh no! It was what certain Souls had wrought within the Planetary Heavens ages before, that necessitated the Oblation. The Burden was of a Planetary nature. It was a burden of a World order, written upon the Planetary Heavens by the Planet's children as they were all affected by the materializing influences which had been brought to bear upon the whole, at one time, beautiful Spiritual estate of Ierusalem, the Holy City and Household of Judah, and the Kingdom of Ya-akob-El, the Planet's Angel and Divine Vicegerent.

Though the Oblation was a vicarious burden-bearing, yet it was not instead of individuals, except indirectly. It was not a bearing of the burden which individuals must carry for themselves and heal and transmute; it was the accomplishing of such a change in the elemental conditions of the Planetary Heavens as would make it possible for the individual and the race to carry their burden unto the blotting out of the effects of their sin. For if you do wrong, the only way to blot it out is to do the right and be healed; there is no other way of being healed. If you have done wrong to anyone, you will never be healed until you do the right thing that will rectify the wrong. You cannot escape from this law of Divine rectitude and justice. For rectitude and justice form the Balance of Life. And

127

it is of the very nature of the Divine Law of perfect rectitude and equity, that a Soul must restore all its life to the balance. Of course, the karma of Israel was not accumulated through their seeking to sin against the Divine Law, nor desiring after those things which caused them to sin; though they became heavily involved. Their karma was incurred in service. But notwithstanding this they have to carry the burden. Yet it is the Divine Love that travails in them and bears them up.

You could not endure this age with its great outpouring of Divine magnetic streams; you could not endure the vibrations of such an avataric encompassing, if you had not been of those who travailed through the ages with the world burden in you as well as upon you, and if you had not known in some degree that other glorious heritage which was the possession of ancient Israel.

The Oblation was a vicarious burden-bearing in this sense—it was for the Planet. It was wrought out within the Planetary constitution and not apart from it. And it was on behalf of all the children of this world indirectly; on behalf of the Planetary constitution most directly; on behalf of the lower Hierarchies in the Planetary constitution—those who operated on the lower Planetary spheres—most directly; and, therefore, it was on behalf of the sphere of Lucifer, the Angel of the seventh Planetary sphere, and even of the Kingdom of Ya-akob-El.

The burden which necessitated the Oblation was in the Planetary Heavens. The Divine burden-bearing had to be within those Heavens. For the states obtaining there were evil; and these had to be changed by contacting them, and entering into conflict with them, effecting their overthrow by a process of purification. The vicarious nature of it was comprised in the Divine Love and Wisdom having to stoop to such states to affect them unto their blotting out.

I hope the day will come soon for you, when you will behold in its true light what the Divine Love did. Can you think of that Love stooping to do those things which filled it with scorching pain continually? It is well that the Children of Israel should know. I have often tried to impress upon you, and I cannot cease to impress upon you, that you should not think of this stupendous work of Divine Burden-bearing in relation to the Servant who was the vehicle; but to think only of the LORD of Love in HIS Passion for the

VICARIOUS BURDEN-BEARING

children who had been carried down; and for all Israel; and for the Planetary Household, the Hierarchies included; and even for the once glorious Kingdom of Ya-akob-El. No man or servant could have done it. No individual, however great, could have accomplished such a thing. It was of the FATHER-MOTHER in HIS Divine Passion, for all HIS children. And it was vicarious to that Love. It was the LORD's vicarious Burden.

A Voice Heard in Ramah

The Church is quite right in thinking it was a vicarious sacrifice; but its interpretation is quite at fault. It has failed to understand the nature of it. It was the Divine Love stooping to enter realms that were absolutely Hells; to extinguish the fires of passion which were operative even in the Planetary Heavens. Because of what had been done upon the Earth's planes by the enemy, the children's bodies were filled with misdirected passion. Their desire nature had been changed in its motion and turned from true polarity. When they passed from these planes they carried all their changed feelings, yearnings and purposes with them. They changed the Planetary Heavens until these became as pandemonium. They made of those Heavens a Hadean world of darkness. They even changed one realm of the Planetary Heavens and made of it the Greek Tartarean world.

Bear with me. I cannot speak of HIS Love in its sacred Passion and unveil the vicarious burden-bearing of it, without being moved to the very depths of my Being. It was HIS own Sacrifice. The burden of suffering was HIS. HE accomplished it vicariously. The Heavens were full of sorrow. Have you ever heard the weeping in Ramah? It is said that Rachael wept for her children. Ramah was the Kingdom of Ra. It was the Divine World of the Eternal Light. Rachael was the Angelic World. The Angelic World ministered to the Children through the Planetary Heavens. The Angelic World was heard weeping for her children. That was the Divine Love, through the Angelic states, sorrowing over this World.

A voice was heard in Ramah, Rachael weeping for her children, and would not be comforted because they were not. Where were the children? Lost amid the awful conditions that arose after the Betrayal. These were not only the children of this world. The whole of Israel had become involved in it. Over them the Heavens wept. Some people think that an Angel could not weep. But an Angel's power to sorrow is the measure of its Godlikeness. An Angel's

K

The
Servant
The
Vehicle
of His
Lord

power to enter into the Mystery of the Divine Sorrow is commensurate with the realization of the Divine Mystery within itself. Is not all Love in its burden-bearing of the Divine? Love itself is Divine. It is the FATHER-MOTHER Principle in us.

Now the burden-bearing of the Oblation was borne by the LORD of Love through HIS Servant, and there was none other with the Servant as sharer of the Planetary karmic burden. I have to emphasize this that there may be clarity of understanding. Some suffering of a collateral nature took place on the part of others in the way of burden-bearing. But it was not of the Passion. The Great Love saved them from such. Indeed, many who might have considered themselves equal to bear that burden, and who might have been willing in themselves to respond to a call without knowing the full nature of it, would either have had to be recalled or they would have gone down beyond recall. The Oblation could not have been accomplished by other than the Divine Love.

I keep urging you not to think personally about anyone in relation to this great Mystery. The One who was the vehicle was only HIS Servant. We are all HIS Servants. Of myself I ever think that I am only HIS Servant, and all I have been able to give you in the other Schools and in this School concerning HIS Holy Passion, I am able to give you because of HIS Love for you. And I am able to unveil to you only what HE permits me to give. You have had to receive here a little and there a little. As the revelations of HIM proceed, HIS Love's Mystery deepens and expands in the visions, as you ascend in state. But the ministry is of HIM; you will understand. Though HE accomplished it through HIS Servant, it was HIS own vicarious Burden. And it was through the one chosen Servant only that the Burden was borne.

But that Servant had brethren. There were those who stood in intimate relation to him to whom he ministered great ages ago. He knew them in the unfallen days. He had ministered to them, before those days, upon the Bethlehem. He ministered to them during many ages after the fallen world-state. He ministered unto some of them during the days of the Manifestation. What was more natural than that the Divine Love, in HIS exquisitely beautiful way, should choose a few of these? The seven special fishermen of Galilee who toiled, it is said, all night and caught nothing until the dawn of the fourth watch or fourth Naronic cycle, were of those HE chose to meet the Servant on the way.

Certain conditions had to be provided to make possible the Oblation. Whilst he would be involved through the ministries he had to render in many directions, they were appointed to be the special friends who would provide conditions for him to enable him to do the work. They had even to betray him. He could love them with a love he himself could not understand, and which moved him profoundly. They were so constituted as to be irresistible to him, and he was irresistible to them. And it was arranged that through the change in him they should not know him, and he should not know them. It was in this way that they unconsciously provided the conditions. Within themselves, and amidst their own circumstances and ministries in life, they provided those conditions which were necessary for him, and amid which he could accomplish the Oblation. By means of magnetic attraction, absorption of the fluidic images, transmutation of those elemental states within his Lifestream, followed by the elimination of the elements absorbed and transmuted—for he could not make use of them—the work was done.

Such was the part played by some of his intimates whom the Divine Love appointed to thus aid him. But though He chose them to do such work, He did not impose on them the Planetary Burden. Let this be understood once for all.

Some of those dear to him were with him in more than one of his Lives; some were present factors in a number of the Lives; and one most intimate friend in nearly half of the Lives. But there were others also; for the Fellowship of the Saints is great. The fellowship of his Brethren was considerable; and of these quite a number were appointed to minister to him on the way. They had their extremes in experience. They comforted him; yet they often betrayed him. They felt lonely oft-times, as he felt lonely amidst the travail; but in him it was a loneliness begotten of absence from the consciousness of GOD; as one afar off, though the Being was always craving to realize HIM. So they also travailed during the Oblation. As those who were appointed to be his helpers, they shared something of the sorrow of the travail, though not of the Planetary Burden. And surely, in passing hours of recovered blessedness, something of the joy of ministering unto him became theirs. They did not know the nature of the ministry they were rendering for the Great Love on behalf of the Planet in their

*The Great
are always
Lowly*

ministry to him. But they were of his Brethren. He was their Brother; indeed he was their Elder Brother, had they known it. Yet he did not claim so to be. Even in the earth sense, a wise elder brother never thinks himself as older and better than his brethren. In wisdom that could not be. For age of Being is in realization. To attain to realization of high degree a Soul must have lived through countless ages. But it does not think greatly of itself because it has lived through those ages. Even when it is called to look into and through those ages, it is never burdened with the consciousness of being old and great. There is no thought of self-importance.

Beloved ones of the FATHER-MOTHER, I would have you be at all times as little children. Even in the majesty of your love and in the might of your power for service, I would have you always remember that in HIS Presence you must be as little children. Never get inflated in the world's sense. Never get lifted up and grow vain. Never boast of yourself. It is not the way of the children of the FATHER-MOTHER. To know HIM is to know the sublimest lowliness before HIS majesty, and gentleness in the midst of HIS almightiness, which is HIS Omnipotency. Therefore, little children (for so I may address you, being myself a little child of the FATHER-MOTHER), Love ye one another. Where Love is triumphant there is no false ambition; there is no pride; there is no self exaltation; there is no consciousness of superiority; there is no love of dominion; there is no desire to dominate and rule over others.

Little children, love ye one another!

In the opening words of this unveiling, I said we must surely see to it that the spirit of the Pauline motion never has the least influence in the Order of the Cross. The most amazing thing in the New Testament is the personality of Paul. How he writes of himself! How he claims even the Logia that were spoken by the Master! How he makes use of some Logia that had relation to Israelitish history and the travail of the Master, as having relation to himself on a portraying of burden-bearing in his own ministry. Paul shall share in the glory of the Kingdom when it is restored. But it will be through his own restoration, and not through any personal ambition to be the chief Apostle; not through an ambition to found Churches; nor pride of place and heritage; nor through any special attributes for government; nor because of any special gifts to carry this Evangel. We are all great in HIM when HE makes us great.

"LORD, THY gentleness hath made me great," is always true. *How to* *become* But I can be great in HIM only. For if I am great, I have not an iota *Servant* of consciousness of it. And if I can minister for HIM, it is not through *of All* any consciousness of greatness in myself. It is quite otherwise. Bear with me if I seem to lay much emphasis upon this truth. But I must cast the evil out that would seem to be throwing its shadow on the restoration of the Message. If ye be as little children, myself one with you whilst I am here, it shall be well. If there be any difficulties anywhere, they will all melt away. Love ye one another. Even as I have loved you, love ye one another. Yet I would have you do something far, far greater than that. I would have ye love one another, even as HE has loved you, ànd does ever love you, Who is my LORD and your LORD, my FATHER-MOTHER and your FATHER-MOTHER.

Now the questioner will see, and the others who have sent similar questions to me will see, and understand. In the application of this subject-matter there is no need to go into details, so far as I am concerned; for in the application of what I have asked of you, all things will become beautiful. Let him and let her who would become greatest amongst you, be the servant of all. For so shall he and so shall she, be likest the LORD of all Who is Servant of all. Be great in your love. It is lovely to have the privilege of loving. It is good for us to have objects to love. It is blessed to feel the streams of love flowing to us, and to have the capacity to reciprocate those streams. It is a great and sacred privilege to let people know you love them. You cannot bottle up love. It is the wine that bursts all old bottles; it will out and reveal itself. But if you tell anyone that you love them, and yet you do not show it, you are deluded; you have deceived yourself. If GOD said to us; if HE in this very hour could substantially stand before you so that you would know it was HIM-SELF, and you heard HIM say that HE loved you, and yet HIS Love did not flow out in living streams to you touching all your Being, you would go away saying, I have not felt it though the pronounce-ment was made. HE cannot love me. But, GOD never says what HE does not mean. Our LORD loves HIS children unto the uttermost. If HE did not, do you think for a moment that that Love, without saying that it was stooping, would have caused its magnetic streams to flow down from the Divine Kingdom through certain Celestial systems, and then through the Angelic Kingdom that belonged to the Solar Body, and then through that into the Encompassing Hosts who had to dwell near enough the earth, to keep spiritual life alive within the Souls of the children, and reach unto the Planetary Heavens, there to endure unspeakable things?

If I have spoken familiarly to you, dear ones, and as if I somehow knew HIM, it is indeed because I do know that Love. Would that I could reveal it in its perfection. Would that I could translate it in all its sweet yet mighty, dynamic force. Would that I could radiate its glory. Would that I could show to you Love Himself. Assuredly you would never forget the vision again!

Come back then, and be HIS lovely children. Let no one assume to be greater than another, in any earthly sense, nor in a heavenly sense. All are different with different ministries. There is some ministry for each one. Some are to be overseers. Some are to be Interpreters. All are to be Revealers in some degree. Some are to be Priests before HIS Altar. Others are appointed to minister amid the courts of the Gentiles in the more outward spheres of life. And all are blest of HIM.

There should be no difficulty in the future administration of the work, none. If you love divinely, you will be falling over each other to serve HIM perfectly, and to reveal to one another that you are the children of HIS Love. If I have accentuated your travail in any way, you will, I am sure, bear with me. I have not meant to do so, though the travail always reveals to me the Divine Sorrow that obtained for ages, and the aftermath of which still lies athwart the threshold of the Inner Worlds, and must needs be so until all the children are restored. And you are all to share in that restoration.

I have had to speak to you intimately of that which must seem to you through apprehending the Message, the travail associated with the Return in my own Being. But, oh, my beloved friends, think impersonally. If ye did otherwise it would hurt me greatly. The Passion was borne by my LORD. It was HIS sorrow reflected into me. I feel it profoundly. I could not but sorrow with HIS sorrow. But you have great cause for rejoicing in this day. It is this joy I would bring to you. It is the joy of HIS approach to you; HIS becoming with you and in you; the joy of your Return; the joy of the overcoming of your travail; the joy of the accomplishment of the restoration of the Christhood; the joy of being sharers with HIM in HIS travail, in some small degree; the joy of being called to-day to be a son, a daughter, for HIM; the joy of being asked to be once more the vehicle of the passion of HIS Love that HIS magnetic streams might flow through you to touch unto healing all other Souls. That is the joy I would bring to you. With it I would fill your cup unto overflow.

A Prayer for Israel

O my FATHER-MOTHER. May all THY children know verily how THOU dost love them, how THOU hast travailed for them, and how THOU dost encompass them in this hour, and Overshadow them; how THOU seekest to heal them unto the uttermost; how THOU desirest to clothe them in priestly garments again, that in their daily ministries, as well as in the ministries of the Sanctuary, they may be THY beautiful ones, THINE Angelic ones upon the earth-planes; THY revealers; THY interpreters; the manifestors of THEE, to bring back joy to this sorrowing and distraught Earth.

May we all thus ever bless THEE that THOU hast so honoured us in calling us to be THY Children, and also to be THY Servants, bearing the Cross for THEE that the Resplendence of THY Love may come back again to all THY Children and turn the night of the World into the Glory of THY perfect Day.

O AMEN AND AMEN!

135

E

THE SECRETS OF GOD

THE SECRETS OF GOD

A number of questions have been asked which are related to things Celestial and Divine, and also of a Planetary nature. Rather than attempt to answer each question with the fulness that the questioner might desire, I will gather most of them up into one theme which I hope will touch the great mysteries sufficiently to give, not only to those who sent the questions, but to all of you, glimpses into the Secrets of GOD. Herein I will have to speak of the Naros; of Planetary and Celestial creation and generation; of the relationship of Abraham to this Planetary system; and, should it be that the Heavens will it, something of the intimate relationship between Israel, Ya-akob-El, and the House of Ioseph. In so far as it may be possible, I will tread that path, and I will ask you to accompany me.

There are Divine Secrets that may only be unveiled to those who are in a state to receive them. That is no reflection upon those who cannot receive them. What is meant is this; there are certain aspects of the Mystery of Life, Universal Being, Planetary, Solar, and Celestial motion and ministries, which have to be guarded, and which may only be unveiled as the Will of the Heavens permits. The Secret of GOD is with those in whom is HIS Holy Awe. That means more than is apparent. But the writer of the ninety-first Psalm, who stated it, knew that only he who abideth in the secret place where there is known in consciousness the Secret of the Most High, doth dwell beneath HIS Overshadowing. That one lives in the consciousness of the Omniscient Presence. The writer of the Psalm knew there was a Secret at the heart of the Universe, and that only the Divine Presence HIMSELF might unveil that Secret to the Soul. And such an unveiling to the Soul would be irrespective of whether the Soul had come up through a Planetary evolution of Human estate, or an Angelic evolution of Celestial estate, or Solar evolution of Divine estate.

One of the great secrets held by ancient Israel was that of the Naros. When the secret passed out of the hands of the real teachers in ancient Israel and became the possession of the occult schools, it was made a secret knowledge held by the priesthood in occult centres, and communicated only to those who swore fealty to the priesthood and to the

139

*A Day of
Celestial
Significance*

occult brotherhoods; and **by** the violation of their vow—in some instances during sad and barbaric times when the spirit that dominated the mind of the ancient priesthoods as well as the occult schools, was oppressive and cruel—those who divulged the secret had to yield up their lives.

The Naros is a secret associated with an inter-Planetary-Lunar-Solar motion. It was the Prophetic Day. It is a Planetary-Lunar-Solar day in combination. The Moon has its day. This Planet has its day. The Sun has its day. But then we are not thinking of the twenty-four hours of this Planet, nor the nigh twenty-eight days of the Moon's day as it rotates on its axes, for its day is about equal to its earth revolution, that is, its revolution around the Earth, of which, as you know, there are almost thirteen, for all practical purposes, in the year, each one in some respects differing from the other. If you could see the orbit, not in the sense of the circle around the Earth, but that which the Moon makes in its revoluting round the Earth, you would be deeply interested. But those things we cannot speak of now, beyond naming them, to show you the inter-relationship not only of Souls, but of all worlds, as we shall see.

The Naros was a period covering fully six hundred years. It formed an inter-Planetary-Lunar-Solar day. Supposing for the moment, that on the day in which the Sun enters Aries, the 21st of March, there was a new moon in one of the parts of the Heavens, if the time were chronicled, and if one lived all through the intervening years until the next new moon came at the close of the period of six hundred years in identically the same place, it would form a Naros. For the Moon never appears in the same place, as the new moon, until six hundred years have passed.

Now this was used as a Planetary-Lunar-Solar day, and was related to the unveiling of the Celestial Hierarchies in their ministry to this world. When the prophets were speaking of the Inner Worlds, they were measuring time, not by the Earth's day or the Moon's month or the Solar year, but by the Planetary-Lunar-Solar day.

The word Naros is a sacred term. It was related to the Messengers. It is in this way that the occult schools came to believe that at every Naros a Messenger appeared. And it was so, though not necessarily after the order that the occult schools anticipated, proclaimed, and have taught through the ages. It was a great solar period wherein new ministries could be rendered to the Earth. When that day dawned which heralded the new Naros, there were celestial situations suited to the appearing of a Messenger. This is expressed in the phrase, "the fulness of time," although there is a yet larger and fuller Divine significance in that expression. It had a celestial significance, and was applied, for instance, to the coming of the Master, when GOD in "the fulness of time" purposed to heal this world by means of a Redeemer. The Master as Redeemer came in "the fulness of time."

The Naros in Relation to Prophecy

What was the fulness of time? It was the period when the celestial situation enabled Him to appear to make such a Manifestation for the Divine World as was to be given to Israel. He came with the dawn of a Naros. The word had, all through the ages, a Messianic character; for every Messenger is Messianic, whether the Messenger comes through and on to the Kingdom of the Human estate, or is retained within the spheres of the Angelic World (as had to be the case during great ages unto Israel) or remains within the sphere of the Solar World.

Here are just glints and gleamings to you of the stupendous nature of the Divine ministry, and how it is not to be circumscribed by what is called the appearing of the Messengers, nor with the coming of a Messenger in the Human estate to interpret the Divine Will. The Naros, therefore, was a secret sacredly guarded in the prophetic schools in order to defend the One who would have to appear when his day of manifestation came. The secret had to be held so that those who were enemies to the Christhood should not know when the real Naros was about to begin, that they might not be able to send their emissaries to oppose themselves to the work the Messenger was sent to accomplish. It is true, through the betrayal of the sacred Mysteries, the knowledge did occasionally leak out, with the result that false Christs arose. This has been repeated even since the days of the Manifestation. Christhood is not to be circumscribed by the persona of a man; nor even by his individual equation. Christhood is a state of the Being. And when Christ appeareth through a Servant, the latter doth not make any claim to be Christ. That has never been so. Herein you may distinguish the real Messengers from those who are influenced from other realms than the Divine, though in themselves individually and personally for the time being, perhaps, unconscious of the nature of the influence brought to bear upon them, and who

141

arise to hinder, if not altogether to defeat, the purpose of the appearing of GOD's Messengers.

Thus the Naros spoke of the Messenger. When used by a Prophet it foretold Messianic ministry. It was also made use of for a day of new Solar action. It spoke likewise of Planetary conditions, indicating that they were of an order that needed the appearing of GOD's Messenger. It was the day or period associated with the purpose of the FATHER-MOTHER in relation to the sending of the Messengers for revelatory and redemptive purposes, and "the fulness of time" for the realization of these.

The Naros, therefore, was one of the Celestial and Divine secrets, held sacred in the Celestial World because of the significance of it in relation to the Divine ministry to this world and other members of the System.

You may think I have veiled much from you. There is much that it is still necessary to withhold. But bye and bye ye shall know more, if ye seek unto the real knowing of the truth through the embodiment of it.

The Naros was also associated in the early ages of this world's evolution and ministries, with the ascension of Souls. It applied to the individual, the community, the tribe, the nation, and the race. For, with the appearing of each Messenger even, though only so far as the Messenger was concerned from the direct Solar World, there was, in the unfallen days, a new ascension of Souls. Those were the Souls who were able to rise into a higher estate of spiritual consciousness. You will, therefore, see the vastness of the mystery couched in the Naros, though it came to be occultly considered as something related only or chiefly to a Planetary-Lunar-Solar constitution with other members of the Solar Celestial Hierarchies.

This leads me now to speak to you of another mystery associated with the Divine. It is that of *The Mystery of creation and generation.*

Creation and Generation are not the same.

Generation is related to the law of growth and evolution. It is the means by which growth and evolution take place within a Human Soul.

Generation is related to manifestation. All that is generated for a Soul after it has been created, is unto the end that it may grow and make manifest the Mystery within it; and continue to grow in the degree of its manifestation and evolution by taking its ascensions ever more fully into the realms of the Higher Breaths.

Creation is the mystery which can only be known to a Soul when it reaches the Divine Kingdom. The secret must be guarded. But it may be (indeed it is) permitted me to say so to you, that the creation of a Human Soul is by a process that I might express in such scientific terms as magnetic action, then spiral motion, followed by conglomeration, by means of which latter there is the process of ingathering, and then the process of the polarization of the things ingathered and conglomerated, followed by the bringing of them into unity: then the Divine active Principle accomplishes all the rest.

Creation of Souls

The elements out of which the Soul is built up and amidst which the motion takes place, are those of which I have spoken at various times to you, and in tentative ways written of for you. They are in the midst of the Divine Ætheria.

Now the Divine Ætheria is related to the Great Mystery of Universal Being. All worlds are formed from it. All Solar embodiments are the exposition of its mystery. It is related most intimately to the Mystery of GOD Who is HIMSELF Universal Being; and it contains within itself the Divine Omnipotence and the Divine Omniscience.

It is because of this that a Soul can grow to Divine Consciousness through the realization of the Divine Omnipotency, and ascend through all the arcs of the Planetary stations, the Angelic stations, and the Celestial stations, until it can dwell in the consciousness of Omnisciency. It does not become Omniscient in the absolute sense. No embodiment is that. That is a secret which must needs be guarded. There is but one GOD, and HE is LORD of all. HE is LORD of all Lords above. HE is GOD of all the Gods. The Gods are the celestial and divine expositions of HIMSELF in the degree in which they have realized the Sacred Mystery of HIS Universal Being, and in such realization been appointed Divine Vicegerents over a system, to represent the Presence and the Regnancy of the Sacred Mystery in some concrete embodiment.

Therefore, the creation of a Soul is by Divine action. Planetary evolution is not the creation of Souls; it is the generation of the vehicles for Souls who have been created out of the Divine Ætheria. Perhaps that will help you.

Generation proceeds throughout the Universe. It is related to growth even in the Celestial realms; and to evolution. The ordinary conception of evolution you will doubtless now recognize as being wrong. That which the mystic Church should have known and held

The Origin and Growth of Souls

sacred has been permitted to be dealt with by those who are seeking to understand the secrets of GOD in nature's manifestations through what is known as scientific processes. And because the elements of the Earth, which originally were full of Divine vitality, can still generate, notwithstanding their present fallen conditions, material scientists imagine that Human Origins and evolution have come that way. The Earth now generates many forms that are altogether evil, as the result of the influences of astral and occult conditions upon those elements. Indeed, the influences of thought and desire and will of an inverted order, are manifest. Thus the elements are made to produce forms which are evil. Such elemental creations are not inherent in the constitution of the Earth; nor are they in accordance with the holy purpose of our FATHER-MOTHER. All evil things in the world are the result of the evil thought, desire, and action, resulting from wrong purpose and inverted polarity of the will.

There is no such manifestation of real evolution upon the earth-planes as material science affirms, though there is the evidence of the generation of forms. Of course, material science would not recognize this, because it is outside of the field of scientific study and beyond the range of scientific knowledge on the outer planes, with all that can be gathered from the Darwinian theory, glorified in some respects by Wallace and others who have followed since Darwin wrote his "Descent of Man" and "Origin of Species," and by the most modern apologists. All that can be gathered is that there does seem to have been an endeavour on the part of some spirit in the Earth to reproduce something which, in the Human estate, we name man, and that the path of the evolving process is through the creatures beneath the Human Kingdom. Through the study of human embryology and the embryo of creatures, there has been found to be such an apparent likeness between the two orders, that physical scientists have come to the conclusion that the principle is the same throughout all nature.

But that is entirely a misconception of the facts. Even embryology is a testimony to the dignity of the Soul of man. Where the human embryo is said to be like the embryo of certain creatures for the first three months, the likeness is only apparent; for when the human embryo is three months old great changes take place. The embryo takes upon itself the fashion of the human appearance. What changes it? Simply the channel of the motherhood? Is it the result of the human nature of the motherhood? That might relate to form, but there is something far more than that in the miracle that is accomplished. The fashioning of the human Soul-form with its elegance, its exquisite attributes, such attributes and such potencies as gradually meet to reside within it, is such that the child, in a comparatively few years, can so expand that there becomes *that* within it which can seek (as we have known even in little children) to be touched from the higher realms. And herein there is a clear indication of the relationship of the child to the realm whose touch it seeks.

The Divine Nature of Souls

Bear with me for having brought these things before your notice in this fashion; but I have been led to do so of very necessity in the exposition of this most sacred mystery. It is the secret of GOD in relation to generation. But in a much more closely veiled way in relation to creation, it is GOD'S secret. Man has the power to generate; but only the Gods have the power to create for GOD. And this latter service is rendered only as directed from the Divine World.

By creation every Soul is Divine; consequently, the fulness of a Soul is its realization of Divinity. After it realizes its Divinity there are other degrees of fulness it proceeds to enter into. You yourselves will realize your Divinity long before you realize the Divine Omnipotency and Omnisciency. That does not mean that you know yourself to be Divine. You will know yourself to be from the Divine, sustained by the Divine, enriched through nourishment from the Divine, illumined through the ministries from the Divine. To realize your Divinity is to realize the nobility of your childhood to the FATHER-MOTHER in fulness, and then to proceed to know HIM still more and more.

Creation is the direct work of the Elohistic ministry amidst the Divine Ætheria. Every Soul is created in the likeness of Elohim. Having been formed into a little world in itself, with all the potencies of a universe in the sense of capacity to receive the magnetic streams of the Universe into itself, the Soul is sent forth on its journey, and its journey is taken up with generation. And the law of generation pursues it all through its journey. Every form is generated for it that it has to enter, pass through, minister in and through, until it attains that estate wherein, in an ordinary human sense, generation ceases. But that would only apply to its Earth's evolution. For generation may have to play a part in its further history, if ministries are given it to render wherein the law of generation must become operative again for its manifestation and ministry.

L

145

*Evolution
and
Hierarchies*

*Bless the Great Love for permitting in this hour so much to be unveiled
of His own Holy Secrets.*

In this connection I would now speak of the evolution of Hierarchies.
The question has been asked:—

"Do the members of the Hierarchy proceed directly from the
Elohim, or do they ascend in similar fashion to Human Souls?"

As I have indicated, there are various orders of evolution. There is
growth and evolution within the Celestial spheres. For you will note,
from what has been unveiled to you, that all Solar embodiments are
embodiments of Souls who have not only known the Divine creation
in realization, but who have passed through great cycles of ages of
growth, evolution, and ascension of consciousness. The glory of the
real Sun is the sum of the glory of all the Souls who fill it. But its
glory is more. Through the unification of all those Souls, and the
outflow of the magnetic stream of each, and the polarization of these
in all the Solar spheres, the resplendence of the real Sun becomes
greater even than the sum of all the individuals whose home and
sphere of ministry it is. In like manner is your own auric glory greater
than the sum of all the beautiful Divine, Celestial, and Spiritual
potencies and substances which are full of the Angelic cells of which
your Being is built up; because those cells move in obedience to the
central magnetic principle, which is the Divine pole of your Being;
and as the Divine approach affects that pole, every cell is affected;
then, when they all act in combination, their glory becomes greater
than the glory of the sum of all the individual cells put together.

I will try to make this clearer to you by illustrating from the outer
estate. It is said that every cell of our body has latent consciousness
and memory, and such a statement is now accepted. There are, it is
affirmed by material scientists, not only hundreds of thousands, but
millions of cells in our body. Many say that the human body contains
billions of cells. But here figures are most difficult to express the truth.
They are difficult and often very inadequate vehicles. There is so
much guess work in all such scientific statement. But we will suppose
it to be true that there are millions of cells in the body, each one of
which has within itself a life-principle, and is so magnetically constituted that, when obedient to the central will, and the central will
is obedient to that One Who Overshadows it, then every cell becomes
unified with the centre. Each cell has consciousness. Yet you are not

conscious that your hand is full of cells. If any one hurt you, you would be conscious something had happened. The cells would immediately communicate to the centre. For real feeling is not in the body, but in that which vitalizes it. And there is no real feeling, general or local, apart from consciousness. In a regenerate Soul there is not even an astral body to act as an intermediary between the spiritual Being in its Divine garment and the vehicle through which it manifests. Consequently, in this latter case, every hurt to the body is felt at the centre of the Being by that one more acutely than through the astral body by the unregenerate individual.

Consciousness and Memory

Now, if every cell has latent consciousness and memory, the personal consciousness and the personal historic memory must have relationship to the cells of the body when they are upgathered into a polarized unit, so that physical consciousness, as it might be called, is related to the consciousness in every cell and also to the historic memory. For the memory in every cell is gathered up into the centre of the vehicle of manifestation, and polarized.

Now you will be able to apprehend how this law operates in relation to a Soul. You can suspend the consciousness latent in all the cells of the body, and the memory which they possess, by an anæsthetic, but in doing so you only suspend the consciousness which is latent in the cells in their relation to the individual to whom the vehicle belongs. But in your inner consciousness, however, which is your real consciousness—the consciousness which operates in you in this hour as you rise in your thought, emotion, and purpose before the Divine—you transcend all merely personal consciousness. In your spiritual state you gather it up. You can come back again to the centre. You can transcend the circumference of your outer life. But in doing so you do not lose it. At will you come back to it. Your consciousness rises beyond your outer life, beyond your mind's activities, beyond your heart's emotions, beyond your understanding. You rise to that apex of your Being where you become conscious of a light streaming from afar and breaking itself upon your magnetic apex or radiant centre, producing the very radiance, in some degree, of the holy spectrum begotten of the action of the Elohim upon you.

You may thus apprehend how much vaster is the consciousness than that of the personal equation; and the time will come when your consciousness will be so much vaster than your individual equation. And by this latter more is meant than is apparent. For, though you

THE LIGHT WITHIN US

*The Soul's
Divine
Equation*

are an individual Soul, recognizing yourself as an individual child of the FATHER-MOTHER, yet you can transcend the realm of the individual until you attain to a realm wherein you will feel as if you were not separate from the Eternal Mystery. You become conscious that HE is everything, and that you are nothing. And yet you become everything in HIM. You give your all. You receive all that you are able to receive out of HIS fulness.

Yet what you receive will be exactly in the measure in which you have given all. The measure of your giving and receiving will also be in the measure of your growth and evolution, your descension and your ascension. And then when your Soul-consciousness reaches the Divine World and enters into it, your individual created Will also realizes Universal Being, and you become henceforth one in HIM. You are no more a man, no more a woman, though you will have the man form or the woman form for ministry on the outer planes. No more in consciousness will you remain merely an individual child of a Planetary constitution like this: you will know yourself to be a member of a greater system. Even a child of the Solar Body ceases to be only such when once Divine consciousness is attained. The Soul ceases even to have any consciousness of belonging to any System. It attains the state of HIS All Pervading Holy One; dwells in Nirvana and is one with HIM. Such is the Being's Divine Equation.

Now you may perceive how the Gods grow to be Gods; and how their Godlikeness is in the measure in which the cells of their Being have been upgathered and polarized after having been influenced through great ages from the Divine Centre. For all their potencies are in Divine Estate. And through the polarization those potencies of GOD become expressed, revealed, and manifested in embodiment, and interpreted in the ministry.

That is the explanation, and in part the exposition, of the growth of those we name the Gods. A Soul can rise from degree to degree until it takes in the three hundred and sixty degrees of the circle of its manifestation upon the world, and within the realm to which it belongs. Having accomplished so much it begins a new arc within the circle upon a yet higher realm of manifestation until it acquires Divine power by means of passing through all the degrees belonging to that system wherein it is manifesting and serving. And when it has accomplished that circle of its growth and evolution, it becomes capable of being evoluted or polarized in its consciousness, on to yet another and higher kingdom where it begins the same order of experience and ministry, but in higher degree. Thus it is ever growing from being a child upon each Sphere into which it is evolved, towards the realization of the fulness of its Divine Life. For it always begins as a child new to that realm, but having the capacity to take into itself all that is within that realm, and grow as a result. Its childhood may be of Celestial Estate; yet it grows.

Even the Gods have attained their Estate

Thus have the Gods attained. Thus do the Gods attain. And thus, also, do Souls rise even to know the Gods after like manner, and to dwell with them, not only in the Planetary degree, nor in the degree of other members of a system, but even in the Solar degree. And Souls can grow to know HIM Who is the All and in All, with a fulness which may be expressed as Nirvana, not only in a Planetary sense, nor in a Solar sense, but in Divine Estate. For in a high Celestial degree the Soul may dwell in the consciousness of HIM. HE becomes everything to it. It knows nothing apart from HIM. It cannot have a ministry asked of it, a ministry of unveiling, of revealing, of manifestation, without its attributes becoming at once loosed. The gateways of the Being are opened to and for the Divine.

But here once more, we enter the realms of yet greater mystery. Here you may attain to the knowledge of things appertaining to Divine action in the Celestial Spheres. You may attain the knowledge of the Divine Mysteries contained in and expressed through the motions, the embodiments, and the ministries of a Celestial system. But in such an exalted state of consciousness you will know without being conscious of such a knowledge. It will be with you as if you knew not, until the Divine commands you to bring forth that knowledge. In that hour the treasure-house of your Being is opened, and the Divine permits to be brought forth from that treasure-house whatsoever may be given unto others to whom you minister. And in such an hour you will understand how it comes to pass that, however great you may become in your experience, even to the attainment of that estate which will entitle you to be a dweller amongst the Gods, and be even as one of the Gods, yet you will remain in mind and heart as a little child, ever waiting to hear the Divine Voice, and upon hearing it, to respond to it with Divine spontaneity, living not for yourself in any sense whatsoever, but only for GOD and HIS service.

Such a presentation of the great Celestial Mystery will enable me now to make clear one of the questions concerning the mystery of

The Divine Justice and Equity

karma in relation to the Planetary Hierarchies and the realm of the Gods.

Karma is an Eastern term. It has come to be associated in philosophy with the resultant of the accumulated effects upon a Soul of the lives which it has lived. If the karma be good, then the Soul gathers of the good up into itself at the close of each life, and more especially at the consummation of every cycle. Certain names are given to cycles and celestial periods; but these are often written and spoken of without a true understanding of their meaning. For, as indicated to you elsewhere, there are evolutions associated with tribes, greater families of tribes, out of which peoples grow until they become nations within the same race. Then there are Celestial Kalpas. These are great epochs, and are related to the growth and evolution of races. You will begin to see—especially those of you who have read the philosophies in which these things are casually stated, and sometimes greatly emphasized, but mostly misunderstood and misinterpreted—the inner significance of things.

Evil karma is that which a Soul gradually eliminates from itself by the process of adjustment. If it has done wrong to anyone, it must put things right. It must restore the balance. It may not be able to put right what it did of wrong, in the next life, because it may not appear at the same time as the one it has hurt. Therefore, it may take many lives before the opportunity will come. It is like the Planetary cycles; it has to wait the opportunity to right the wrong it did. That is accounted evil karma, though it is only the burden of the wrong one has done pursuing the Soul life after life, as if determined that the Soul shall bear it until it blots it out by its own carrying away of the burden.

The Principle of justice is of the FATHER-MOTHER. HE is the Just ONE. So beautiful is HIS justice that there is no pursuing of HIS children with judgments of affliction in the sense of a judge who is determined to get out of them the full resultant of all their mistakes. That is not the way of the Divine Love and Wisdom. It is not the way even of human love. And surely human love is but a phase, an individual reflection, of the Eternal Mystery we name the FATHER-MOTHER. HE is just. The true balance of any life expresses HIS equity. HE must be just to each child. Because HE is just, HE must have each life in perfect balance. If a Soul has done wrong to another on the earth-planes, inadvertently, and therefore quite unintentionally, it is not held against that one. It does not become a pursuing karma; and opportunity for blessing the one who has been hurt will be given quite early on in that Soul's experience. But if it has *willed* to hurt another, then it will have to endure until it learns how to will good to that one. For where Souls will to hurt each other, there is some old history of opposition begotten of the tragedies of the Earth. Such Souls have to learn how to desire only good for each one. And herein may be witnessed how the Divine justice steps in so exquisitely beautifully. As soon as the Soul desires to put right any wrong it has done, healing has begun in that Soul. The shadow that was lying athwart the threshold of that one in the inner planes, disappears. And it gradually disappears also upon the outer planes. The willing-hood to put the thing right gives the Divine Love opportunity to so direct that Soul that it shall have a concrete opportunity for bringing blessing to the one who has been hurt, either on these planes or on the other realms. We minister to one another all through the ages. There is no end to it, whether here or there.

How Karma is changed

Now, we do not think of this law as applicable to the Gods, for we do not think of the Gods as Beings who have fallen. In the mind of the questioner there is undoubtedly present the story of those who went out from the Divine Presence in anger, and who sought to found a materialized system. Such fallen ones came to this one time glorious Planet which was the kingdom of Ya-akob-El. By their action they wrought disaster to the whole Planetary manifestation, and thus imposed great suffering. The karma they accumulated through their great mistake must needs be borne unto perfect healing. And they themselves must share in the work of restoration. In willing good, a Soul, a Race, a Hierarchy, or a System comes into harmony with the Divine Will Who always wills good. And in the case of those who are called *fallen angels*—one-time ministrants of a Celestial and Angelic order who went astray—they have had as their karma to bear most sadly, and tragically in the case of some of them, the resultant of their mistake. By their action they affected a large celestial area for a time. Some of those spirits who became most rebellious and would not hearken to counsel, are in the prison-houses. They could not restore the Planet-Soul Judah to the estate from which they brought her down by their action. They could not give back to Ya-akob-El his kingdom in the perfectionment in which they found it. They could

151

not restore Israel to their glorious ancient Christhood. They could not bring back the children of Judah to the estate of unfallen Ierusa- lem. But, in order that they might find healing, they have had limitations imposed upon them, whilst they have also had ministries given them to render to those whom they smote, by serving these in the land where they had been smitten. And although their ministries are not obvious, nor they themselves known to be such fallen spirits, yet they are known to the Divine World. And as such they are being specially ministered unto.

And now, in concluding this unveiling I would say to you, that *the karma of Lucifer*, the one-time star of the Morning, is now a karma of sorrow. So likewise is the karma of Ya-akob-El one of sorrow that his kingdom should have been so smitten through the part played by Lucifer in the great betrayal when he listened to those who came unto him purporting to have a message from the Divine World, and by doing so, sold his inheritance for a mess of pottage. That is a simile, a metaphorical expression, a cryptic statement, yet burdened with tragic history, as you will find set forth in the story of Ya-akob-El.

But Lucifer now rejoices to see this day; for in it, his karmic burden is being lifted and healed. He rejoices in the true spiritual movements, for by means of them he is being liberated. And as the arising of Israel very specially proceeds, so is he being the more fully liberated. He can now take a more real part in the administration of what are, at present, the upper elemental kingdoms and those associated with human generation. He is rejoiced where the children of the FATHER-MOTHER upon the earth-planes arise to live the beautiful life; for every beautiful life that arises, contributes to his liberation, and to the restoration of his sphere within the Kingdom of Ya-akob-El.

Now, I would have you also understand this mystery concerning the kingdom of Ya-akob-El. To be a Planetary Angel is to be a minor God. For the Planetary Angel, understood metaphorically, sits upon the throne of regnancy in the Planetary constitution. He has a Celestial Hierarchy with him. That Hierarchy through its individual members, represents ELOHIM as the Elohistic ministries appertain to the Planetary evolution. It was of that Hierarchy that Lucifer was the seventh Angel, or the Director of the seventh or outer sphere, counting from the Within.

But in addition to the chief Hierarchy there are many in the minor Orders operative within the various spheres. It might be quite correctly stated that each great sphere has a Hierarchy within itself for administration. A world like this even, though small in comparison with the System, requires great overshadowing from the Divine World, and majestic and tremendous operations from that World through the One who represents the Divine Presence in the Planetary administration, and is GOD's Vicegerent. From Him directions are given unto and sent through the various Hierarchies, first through the Chief or Celestial Hierarchy, and then through the lower Oligarchies—though these latter are lower only in the degree of ministry and estate.

Abraham and Ya-akob-El

Now this brings me to the sphere wherein I may answer the question concerning Abraham, wherein he was related to this world. You will note this, that Ya-akob, in the old Scripture, is represented as being the grandson of Abraham; for the triplicity is named Abraham, Isaac, and Jacob. THESE ARE DIVINE NAMES. Abraham is related to a yet higher sphere than Ya-akob-El. He is Ya-akob-El's patriarch or high priest. He is not only the mystic individualization of the Planetary constitution in its Divine Estate, but, as was known and taught in the ancient Mysteries, he was and is a Divine Patriarch or member of the Divine Royal Arch. He was the Friend of GOD. He was regarded as one who was in the estate of a God. For a Soul who was A-Brahm, is one who was Brahm in embodiment within a system. He was also in his degree of estate and ministry, Ab-Ra-Mah. He was, therefore, a Patriarch of a higher order than Ya-akob-El, one to whom Ya-akob-El is most intimately related.

There is a depth of significance in those sayings which you find in the Logia concerning the children of Abraham. You will remember that the Jews were always relating themselves to Father Abraham, thinking of him as an earthly patriarch. But the Master had to say to some of them in an hour of deep questioning, *If ye had known Abraham, ye would have recognized whence I came.* In this saying there is just a glimpse of the marvellous relationship which must have existed between Abraham and the Beloved One.

Herein the Overshadowing ONE is showing you the grandeur of the Mysteries of the FATHER-MOTHER. HE has been unveiling these to

153

Ya-akob-El
and the
House of
Ioseph

you; for it is HIS purpose that you should know these sacred things in the degree in which HE considers it well you should know again at this present time of your Return into the Kingdom. Those who are of Abraham are the children who knew the Divine in high estate; not necessarily in Universal Being or LORD-consciousness, yet in high estate. Divine Life is one. The Eternal Life is one. It is one in its quality, though it is infinitely manifold in its quantity. HIS Life is one in all the children who can commune with the Divine World; but the quantitative degree is dependent upon the Soul's own opening out unto and reception from, the Divine.

Thus, in some measure, you are all related to Abraham, Isaac, and Ya-akob-El. Israel is related to Ya-akob-El chiefly through the ministry of the Christhood unto this world. Was Ya-akob-El of the House of Ioseph, one has inquired? That mystery we must, for the present, leave. But Ya-akob-El was the father of the House of Ioseph on the Earth's planes. In every Planetary constitution, the various Houses are repeated in some degree according to the nature of the manifestation. In this system there is to be a House of Ioseph. That House will be formed of those who attain to certain degrees of the Life signified by the Sign of the Cross. Though not in universal consciousness, yet, in manifestation, these will be Children of the Cross. For the children of Judah will also belong to the House of Ioseph when they become Children of the Cross. When the sacred mystery of the Cross in the Principle of their Being, has been so fully unfolded in their growth and evolution, then they will be GOD'S Cross-bearing children in this world. They will be members of the House of Ioseph, and become united to the system of which it speaks. Having attained to so much they will be ready to ascend, to be taken up higher, and to enter into a yet fuller consciousness of the great Marriage Feast of the LORD of Being within the Soul.

And now I would say to you in closing this unveiling, that whatsoever there may have been for you of Divine Light in all the revealings, remember it is of HIM. The Gift is HIS; the Blessing has been from HIM. Whatsoever there has been in it of interpretation that will help you to understand the Mystery of HIMSELF within you, it has been begotten of the motion of HIS own Love and Wisdom. And in whatsoever measure there has been heard within you of HIS call to come up higher, and to be once more the Children of Abraham, it is of HIMSELF. He is not only Brahm in the sacred Mystery of Being, and Brahma in the glorious manifestation of HIS Mystery, but HE is also Ab-Ra-Mah in the outflow from HIMSELF of HIS sacred Mystery to fill you, and through filling you to clothe you, according to your degree, in HIS holy auric Light, the most glorious of priestly garments for the mediation of HIS sacred Mystery.

With me bless HIS Name for HIS loving kindness, HIS great goodness, HIS loveliness unto us, HIS majestic condescension, HIS sublime stooping to meet us where we are, and to help us up into the state and service where HE desires we shall be once more, as the radiant children of HIS Holy One, and the ministrants upon this world of HIS most Holy Love and Wisdom.

O most Adorable One, how may we even essay to thank Thee and bless Thee for Thy great goodness unto us?

But Thou readest our very Being. Thou knowest that all its motion is unto Thee.

F

THE WORSHIP OF THE MOST HIGH ONE

CEREMONIAL MINUS OF WORSHIP

WORSHIPFUL CEREMONIAL IN THE HEAVENS

PREPARATION FOR WORSHIP

THE APPROACH TO THE HIGH ALTAR

THE INNER MOTION OF WORSHIP

THE GREAT ADORATION

THE HOLY EUCHARIST

THE DIVINE MASS IN THE HEAVENS

THE WORSHIP OF THE MOST HIGH ONE

The worship of the MOST HIGH ONE, next to the cognition by ourselves of HIS sublime Mystery which HE has unveiled to us, is the supremest theme. After reaching a certain stage of growth and evolution in the Ascension of Life, the Soul enters a realm where further growth and evoluting carries it into the higher degrees of conscious realization of the glorious Presence, where it gradually acquires, through that realization, the interior knowledge of all things associated with HIS sacred Mystery Who is the LORD of Being as that Mystery is made manifest in the Heavens. And worship is the path by which the Soul attains to this high Estate.

To worship HIM is no perfunctory service. It is no formal gesticulating before HIM, some acquired action and posture revealed in the singing of songs and the recital of prayers, or in the acclamations of HIM in forms of belief, or in and through symbol. All these things may fall far short of worship. All these things are done in Worship. We may have taken part in such services. We may have shared in them with others in the outer Sanctuary. But they are often done without worshipping; though they are spoken of by many as worship or essential parts of it. To indicate an extreme case of the lack of the real worship even where the greatest ceremonial was and is observed, I would name instances. I have witnessed the greatest irreverence where the greatest ritual worship, ostensibly offered unto our FATHER-MOTHER, was observed, in Milan, Naples, Florence, and Rome. Even our own worship, which is oft-time sadly lacking in the ceremonial and ritual part of true worship, but which is not to be circumscribed by the limited circle of hymn singing or psalm singing, and offering audible prayer, individual or collective, but has its fuller motion in the inner Sanctuary, is something greater, intenser, and more spiritual, with truer angelic atmosphere, than anything witnessed in the great Cathedral Churches of those Cities.

I would ask you to accompany me in this hour, for I would take you with me to other realms than these outer planes, that you may witness what worship is in the Heavens, even amid the Celestial

*Ceremonial
and Ritual
in the
Heavens*

Hierarchies and the Divine World. The reflections of such worship should verily fall upon the threshold of the Sanctuaries of Zion. And surely as the Regeneration proceeds many concrete expositions of such worship will find manifestation upon the Earth as reflections of the glorious Light shed by the worship of the FATHER-MOTHER in the Heavens. As they bear upon this transcendent theme, I would in this unveiling answer some questions sent in concerning the place ritual had in the ancient days of Israel, and what place ritual occupied in the worship rendered in the Heavens. And in relation to these I have been requested to speak yet more fully on the mystery of Prayer. Therefore these will be gathered up into this sublime theme.

*   *   *   *   *

You must have been arrested in reading the old Scriptures, even as they stand in their imperfect presentation of Truth, with the frequency of worshipful expressions. The Psalms are full of them. And when you come to the transcendent visions, such as "The Call of the Servant," set forth in the sixth chapter of Isaiah, you must have been impressed, not only with the transcendent glory unveiled in that partial revealing of a great mystery and a great consecration; but you must have been impressed surely by the ritual of the Seraphic worship where they call to each other, alternately affirming the holiness of the Mystery they name the LORD GOD of Sabaoth, the Universal LORD of Being, the LORD of all the Heavenly Hosts, the FATHER-MOTHER. Then when you turn to the Apocalypse even as it stands in the New Testament, you must have been arrested by the grandeur and order of the worship of the Eternal Mystery set forth there in a tentative and veiled way; and how there was not only individual song, but likewise communal song and prayer. It is said that the great multitude around the Throne with one voice proclaimed the glory of HIM Who reigned; and that the Elders and the Four Living Creatures —the Four Eternities and the innermost vehicles of the active ministry of the FATHER-MOTHER—made ascriptions unto HIM. In their exalted state they were not above worshipping HIM. They were not beyond ascribing to HIM all power, all the glory of Love, all goodness and majesty, all honour and dominion and regnancy. Then, towards the close of the Apocalyptic visions as set forth in the New Testament, and given in somewhat changed but truer form in the Logia, the multitudes of Angels and Archangels rose up with exceeding great joy, and proclaimed in the presence of the sacred Mystery, "Now are the kingdoms of this world become the kingdoms of Our LORD and HIS Christ; and HE shall reign forever and ever."

I would love you to be able to recall to remembrance, in such degree as you yourselves have known in past ages those transcendent visions and experiences. The purpose of my ministry to-day is not only to break again unto you the Wisdom of GOD and to unveil HIS secrets, and thereby to recall to your remembrance such as you may be able to recover, and to unveil many other things concerning yourselves which could be restored to you only through being so unveiled; but in addition to these, I would have you in your vision back in those realms into which surely you look at times. My own vision is ever there, and I would have yours there also. And I would have you understand this glorious Message in its fulness; and also, that, whilst there are ministries to be rendered through the Altar and before the Altar, my ministry unto you is from the Altar. It is not that I turn my back to HIS Altar; that could not be. HIS High Altar is ever before me. I am always looking at it. It is only to the symbolic Altar that I have to turn my back whilst mediating unto you. *My Being is ever before His High Altar.*

Beloved ones, these things could not otherwise be broken unto you. The purpose of this hour is to help you back to such a vision of the worship you once rendered HIM; and that ye may recall the manner of it. It is the worship you are again to render HIM, and the order and degree of its mediation. That worship will be restored within the communities of Israel in the coming days; but it can only be restored through the Children of Israel who are receiving these Teachings, becoming filled with the vision of all that such a restoration will mean.

* * * * *

Come now with me, even into the Inner Heavens; for I would help you to see what takes place there. And what you witness be sure to relate also to yourself; because the Heavens are reflected within you. Relate to your own life what you see and hear, for that which proceeds there is intimately connected with yourself. Indeed what you witness must also proceed within you. You will share in the Divine Processional. Come, let us worship and bow down before our LORD!

M

THE PREPARATION

Now there are glorious embodiments in the Heavens, and there are powers that are fleet of feet and fleet of wing. There are most glorious ministrants rendering transcendent ministries. In their ministries they worship HIM; for perfect service is worship. When there is a call for an Assembly to Worship, and there is given a communal service unto HIM, there is no rushing in an unprepared way. Even the Gods would prepare themselves to approach HIS Presence, as that Presence is concretely embodied in their various realms. In such an hour of transcendent worship there would be further unveiling of the Divine Mystery within the Divine Kingdom. There are times when great numbers of Celestial systems can unite in the adoration of HIM. And in the Celestial Processional, the sacred Mystery which is always veiled within the Divine World, would be more fully unveiled even to the Gods at given periods.

That means, that in the hour of such revelation and such transcendent worship, there is revealed in fulness of splendour, the Glory of the Eternal Mystery. The Eternal Light unveils HIMSELF from realm to realm.

This will help you to understand the meaning of such sayings —"Let all the angels bow down before HIM." They are not all in one place; they are not all in one world, nor in one sphere, nor upon one system; yet they can be called. They hear and obey the Divine World command: "Let all the angels worship HIM."

*   *   *   *

So must it ever be with us when we worship GOD. There must be preparation. What does preparation imply? It has to take place within. Our attributes must be got ready and marshalled. They must have the right motion and be in a state of balance. They should be recalled from all outer activity, and become in harmony with the motion of the central pole of our Being. For thus only can we be ready to approach HIM. There can be no true approach without such reverent soulic preparation. No one can rush into the Divine Presence. The approach must be of regal quality.

It is said of the Four Living Ones, that they had three pairs of wings. These represented the powers of Divine attributes. With twain they covered their face, symbolizing in both the centrifugal and centripetal

motion of Being, absolute reverence. The action is Cherubic. It
expresses the absolute reverence of the Being before HIM.

With twain they covered their feet. There is nothing obvious
concerning their ministry of approach to HIM. Even in their most
important ministry, though so great, all is covered. There is an
absence of individual obtrusion.

With twain they did fly and soar. They had Divine power to move
before HIM. The motion of flight unto HIM and from HIM, when
commanded by HIM to serve, is expressed as Divine fleetness. In
their action they worship HIM. When the Voice commands that all
the Angels worship HIM, then there is Divine commotion. But there is
no Earth-sense rush. It is the commotion of the flight of the Spirit
within the Being of each one. It is the cherubic and seraphic motion of
preparation; for they all prepare for their worship of HIM.

You have expressed this state and motion in some degree in a
marvellous way. In the preparation of this sanctuary which had not
been built for such a service; in your approach to and coming into the
sanctuary; in the beautiful motion of your Being in prayer, meditation,
exultation, and blessing. You must understand these things, since
you have done them in some degree. You should, therefore, be able
to interpret what is done in the Heavens in a greater degree. How
different it is for the one who mediates, to come into a sanctuary
breathing the very atmosphere of the prayers of the children of GOD,
from going into a hall where the mediator has to begin to create an
atmosphere for the worship, either by changing the elemental conditions present, or, if they will not change, by the special ministry of
Divine Involution driving those conditions out of the door. One has
had to do such things to find even a solitary Israelite amidst the
company that assembled to hear such a measure of the Message as
then could be broken.

This is told to you not that you may think of all or of any of the
difficulties that may have presented themselves to the Servant in the
past years; it is spoken simply to illustrate to you the wonderful
helpfulness of a real preparation, and the changing of a room or hall
into a real Sanctuary. Therefore, you will understand the motion of
my own Being, as I have visited the Groups of Students of the Message,
and found that the children everywhere have not had beautiful
Sanctuaries consecrated to this wonderful ministry, where they could

meet, commune, and aspire; where they could leave their atmosphere to find it when they came back again, because it had so saturated the seats, the wood and the stone, that on their return there was still present the sweet fragrance of the incense of their outpouring when last they met, awaiting to greet them on the threshold. This is an experience that can be intensified. And if you will think from the Earth to the Heavens you will understand how the whole Heavens are far flung with the incense of the prayers of the Saints, the aspirations of GOD'S Christs who are there, and who travail in their ministry for HIM unto the children who need special mediation.

That is true preparation. And I am rejoiced as I look into your faces and behold the motion of the Divine Heart in you, as that motion causes the radiance of HIS Light to shine within you and through you. I am rejoiced that this consciousness of preparation for approach unto the Divine has laid so great a hold of you, and that there is such a deepening of consciousness, not only of its need, but of all that it will bring of blessing and strength, of enrichment and realization.

AFTER THE PREPARATION THERE IS THE APPROACH

It may interest you to know that in the Heavens there are Processionals; but they never become formal. There is nothing perfunctory, materialistic, and formal in heavenly processionals. There is such a natural falling into place, a vibrant and harmonious way of doing the things that are most natural to the Angelic World and to the various Celestial systems according to their degree of manifestation and realization of the Mystery of the FATHER-MOTHER, that formality such as the Earth witnesses has no place. There is nothing stereotyped in the creation of the FATHER-MOTHER. You know that in nature there are not two trees alike of the same order. You know that no two leaves on the same tree are quite equal. Variety is infinite. And so it is in the ministries of the Angelic, Celestial, and even Divine Realms. The danger on the outer planes is where the thoughts of the children have been inclined materialistically, and to give fixity to those things which should ever remain volatile, and in this way to make formal the elements of worship which should ever be the spontaneous outcome and outflow of the Being's motion. Even where there is formulated Ascription, Adoration, and Prayer, and these become the communal exposition of the heart's motion and the Being's adoration in the Heavens, they remain volatile.

164

Now, in our approach to the Divine, what should we do? What should we feel? How should we become like HIS true children in our approach? You need not tell HIM you are coming; for HE knows. When you really essay to approach HIM in your Being, you telegraph a message to the Angelic World, and through it to such Celestial estate as will correspond to the state within you in your approach. Thus the Divine World knows.

In our approach our prayer should contain such expressions as are potential and subjunctive. If I may, I would approach yet nearer THEE, that more fully THOU mayest bless me. I would be THINE wholly. But I know I can only fully realize THEE as the measure of my capacity expands and deepens before THEE. As I grow in consciousness before THEE I ascend THY Hills, and climb THY heights from Mount to Mount, and on the way I behold more and more the glory of THY Lebanon. LORD, if it may be so, I would come to THEE in this hour, aye, in this moment. I would come to the High Altar of THY Sanctuary, even where THY Presence is within my Being. LORD Thou knowest I am coming, for THOU knowest all things.

You need not tell HIM anything: HE knows everything. But you may ask for all that you feel you need, if you ask it in the way that HIS child should. For that is the real meaning of the saying, "If it be THY Will." It is always HIS Will to bless. It is always HIS Will to enrich. It is always HIS Will to chase shadows away. It is always HIS Will to raise HIS children out of the stony places and quench the fires begotten of their travail. But HE can only do those things in the measure in which the petitioners can receive and endure HIS ministry. Therefore, the approach itself becomes *a prayer*. It is prayer expressing our desire to be near HIM in state. Prayer is usually thought of as asking for something. To ask of HIM is not wrong. Hitherto you may have asked but little. Ask great things of HIM. But always be sure of this, HE will give you only what you are able to receive. HE will not withhold what you are able to receive. HE never withholds what you are able to receive, if ye ask HIM in rightness of mind, heart, and spirit. Why does HE not give it without your asking? HE cannot. Remember that your asking of HIM is the motion of your Being. It is the approach of your Being in purpose. Your desire to get near HIM, to be blessed of HIM, is an asking of HIM. And if ye ask thus ye shall receive.

The Soul's Processional within the Sanctuary

Prayer is, therefore, the Being's motion in its approach to HIM. Prayer is the ascending motion of the Being unto HIM. Prayer is the yearning of the Being for the realization of HIM. Prayer is not simply a requesting in human terms; it is asking in such terms as express the motion of your Being.

Surely the thoughtful must wonder when they seriously look out upon all the religious communities, and reflect on the multitudinous prayers offered daily throughout Christendom, morning, noon, and night, that in answer to such continual praying, the Great Love would change this world and save HIS children who are caught in its turmoil, and turn the world's impoverishment into Divine enrichment! And many must be amazed that such does not take place. They must inquire how it comes to pass that the world does not change.

The lack is not in God. He ever answers true prayer.

True prayer is not simply asking GOD in a formal way for something; nor in a moment of great need, telling HIM you do need this or that blessing, and that you must have it. Prayer is first a humble and purifying preparation to approach HIM; and then that motion which is the flight of the Spirit to HIM. When you thus come before HIM, just come as HIS child and not as a beggar. However needy you may be, HE never indicates that you are a beggar. It would be an unhallowed thought to apply to HIM. I ask of THEE, O LORD, that THOU wouldst bless me. For this I come to THEE. My prayer is that THOU wouldst help and enrich me to grow more like THEE.

Even the angels thus pray. Perhaps you think they need nothing. But they need all that is associated with their life.

Even the Gods pray. Surely, surely, you say, they are without need of blessing. Why, all the members of the Hierarchies are dependent upon the Eternal Mystery for their strength, for their power of administration, for the Light that fills them, for the Regal status they hold. They are dependent upon the central Source of all for the sustenance and enrichment of the Mystery of their own Being, and so they have their prayer and their approach and their worship. They gather strength as we gather strength, though their degree may seem in their realization, greater and fuller, the measure being that of their capacity to receive of HIS sacred Mystery. Do you think the Planetary Angel, Ya-akob-El, never prays? Do you think he has never wondered why the Divine World was so long in reaching out to him? In the

166

very book to which I referred this morning, that of the Divine
Messenger named the Prophet Isaiah, we find these words:—

"'Why sayest thou, O Ya-akob-El?

'My way is hidden from the LORD'
And my GOD hath forgotten me?'"

Here, even the great administrator of a world like this, in the hours
of his travail, is revealed as feeling as you yourselves have oft-times
felt in past ages, and as you have not infrequently felt in these days of
the Return, when you have grown almost desperate because of the
conditions that are inimical to you, not understanding the cause and
meaning of your travail have called out, "Hath the LORD forgotten to
be gracious? Hath HE in some strange way shut up HIS tender mercy?"

This will help you to understand the oneness of prayer throughout the Universe; how all are dependent upon the central Mystery;
how all derive the Blessing from that central Mystery according to
their need; and how each Son of GOD, Angel and Archangel, the
greater Gods and the Gods of the greater systems, those who are
Divine Administrators as well as those who might be termed the
minor Gods, such as those who rule over worlds like this, all pray.
And is it not a lovely thought that in the Universe of the FATHER-
MOTHER there is such Divine Unity? That they are not all working on
their own, as separated units? That they are not all administrators
working in their own sphere as if they were separated from and
independent of the central body? That they are all one with the
Divine World? That they also pray in the approach of their Being
unto the FATHER-MOTHER?

Herein you may perceive that it is in the very constitution of the
Human Soul, of a Planetary Soul, of a Solar-Soul, and of a Celestial
Soul in the sense of a glorious stellar embodiment, to pray unto the
FATHER-MOTHER; *that prayer is an essential part of the worship of
Him with them as it is with us.*

Here suffer me to say this word to you. When you pray, remember
HE knows exactly your state. Therefore, do not use language which
implies things that are not true concerning yourselves. To do so
would immediately cause a veil to come between you and the Divine
World. You must be true. You must be correct in your approach
to GOD, and righteous in your prayer to HIM. HE knows your

Sincerity in Prayer and Worship

downsitting and uprising. HE knows you from the Cup of your Divine Spiral to the feet of the Standard of HIS Mystery wherein you stand in the midst of the Great Deep. To tell HIM you are a great sinner when you do not believe such of yourself, is to bring the darkness around you. To tell HIM that you want to divinely love everyone, when you know you do not desire to manifest love to some you know, is to be untrue, and to prevent the Blessing. Do not tell HIM you want to love everyone when in your heart you have no such intention, for that would hurt you; rather ask HIM in HIS own way, in HIS own wondrous ministry, even if HE makes you travail in your Being, to consume within you the elements which prevent you from loving everyone. For these elements are in yourself. There may be elements which in their manifestation in another, are not very beautiful; but you must learn not to emphasise those frailties. you must see the Being. You must learn to love all the children divinely. They are to be reckoned as GOD's beautiful Divine Children, notwithstanding the shadows that may lie upon their garments. HIS radiance is in them, and it is greater than any shadows you may see. Look for HIS own radiance within them. Recognize their Divinity, even as you would have your own recognized. The same Divine Mystery that is in you is in them. They share with you the Auric splendour of HIS indwelling.

Thus in this hour I would impress upon you the need for reality so that your prayer, when you approach HIM, may be absolutely sincere.

Lord, Thou knowest my downsitting and mine uprising. Thou also knowest the obstacles in my way, obstacles some of which I see and some I do not see; and perhaps, Lord, some I have not desired to see. If that be so with me, Lord, reveal to me everything that is hindering me from approaching Thee, and give me strength to put every obstacle out of the path of my approach to Thee. I come to be blest. I come to realize Thy Blessing. I come to be healed. Thou art my Healer, the great Blesser, the enricher of my Being. Through Thine enrichment alone can I come unto the realization of Thee and Thy glorious Mystery within me, and grow more like Thee. I come that I may learn how to worship Thee, and become fully consecrated.

★　　★　　★　　★

THE WORSHIP

After such a prayer comes the worship. The worship, in its degree, is the effect of the approach and the resultant of the prayer. Do many

168

understand what it is to worship HIM? Apparently not. For the true worship of HIM is nothing less than to acknowledge HIM in everything; to see everything in relation to the resplendence of HIS Being, the glory of HIS Love, and the wealth of HIS Wisdom. To acknowledge HIM fully and truly in everything, is to come to the great Realization that *He is all and in all*—an expression more easily uttered than understood, and the depth of whose meaning is of the very vitals of our Being, and of the Eternities themselves. To acknowledge that HE is all and in all in our own Being, is also to come to the understanding of HIS Mystery in the Universe of Being. It is easier for men and women to think of HIM in an indefinite way as the ONE who fills the Universe of Being, than it is for them to understand definitely and divinely what it means to acknowledge HIM as the ONE Who fills the universe of their own Being. For it is easier to think about HIM as filling all systems in a general way, than it is to bring that great truth home, and recognize that HE is the ONE Who must fill all the realm of the Soul, all its spheres and all its planes; that HE is the ONE Who must vitalize all its potencies; the ONE Who alone can clothe the attributes with the glory of HIS Own Mystery; that HE is the First and the Last, the Alpha and Principle of our Being, and also the Omega, or the perfect fulfilment of our Life; that HE is not only the Arche—the Mysterious magnetic Centre of our Life, but that HE is also the Amen—the sublime circumference or fulness of our Life.

Jehovah is our Arche and Amen

For Israel surely, if not to-day, yet in the days that are drawing near, HE shall be not only recognized as the Arche, but HE shall likewise be the Amen in its sevenfoldness—that is, JEHOVAH, the LORD GOD OF THE SEVENFOLD PERFECTIONMENT, THE REALIZATION OF HIS INDWELLING PRESENCE AS ELOHIM, THE SEVENFOLD SPIRIT. To worship HIM is not simply to tell HIM you love HIM; that you praise HIM and trust HIM for redemption; that you hope in the days that are to come, to realize more perfectly HIS own Life. To worship HIM now is to acknowledge HIM to be the LORD of Love, the LORD of all Lords above and beneath, the Regnant ONE Who is all and in all in your Life, from its centre to its circumference, from its Divine Cup to its heavenly Understanding, from the Apex of the Sacred Spiral of your Being, to the foundations and the standards of GOD upon which you rest as you move amidst the Great Deep of HIS Mystery.

Many lustily sing that they worship GOD and adore HIM in all HIS

True Ritual is of the Soul and the Heavens

ways. But how few discover that to sing thus of HIM is not necessarily to worship. *Do you adore all His ways concerning yourself? Then that is worship.* When you come before HIS High Altar, having prepared yourself and, through the preparation, having essayed to approach HIM, and then having realized your approach through the opening out of your Being by means of your prayer, then you worship HIM.

Lord, Thou art everything to me. I cannot live without Thee. I cannot be happy if Thou be absent; but Lord, I can be happy even in the midst of world unhappiness, if Thou be near me. O my Lord, I can be full of joy to the overflow of my cup, even whilst the world pours into that cup its waters of bitter sorrow. For what Thou dost pour in of joy transmutes what the world pours in of bitter sorrow begotten of the Earth's Sinim, until my whole life becomes full of the joy of Thee; the joy of knowing Thee and of being honoured to approach Thee; the joy of the vision of Thee, and the joy of hearing Thy Voice.

Such worship is Angelic: it is Celestial: it is Divine. It is the Cherubic motion of worship. It is the inward motion of the Being in the adoration of HIM. There is also the Seraphic motion of worshipping. For even the Seraphim who sing one to another of HIM, and sing to HIM, can also move outward in blessing. For Divine worship is service. But it is a service lit up with the Light of the consciousness of HIS Presence, as that is realized in the Worship through the inward or Cherubic motion of the Being. For our service in life to be a real worship of HIM, a testimony of HIS goodness and Love and HIS Presence with us, must take on the radiance of that which we have acquired in HIS Sanctuary through our approach to HIM by means of our prayer, and the opening out of our Being unto the acknowledgement of HIM.

"Bless the LORD, Oh my Soul, and all that is within me bless HIS Holy Name." That is the way of worship. When you worship GOD, bless HIM. And here I would repeat and emphasize; in your worship of HIM, do not say things you do not mean. For HE is not a man or a woman to be pleased with foolish expressions, or expressions which though in themselves beautiful, are yet not quite correct and true. Just be your beautiful, natural self always before HIM. HE is lovely. You need not fear or dread to come before HIM, except in the sense of being filled with the Holy Fear, which is the Divine Awe of HIS Presence.

170

Now, in all this you will recognize the obvious fact that the Soul has its own Ritual for its individual self. When Souls meet together they have what might be called a multiple Ritual. In a Fellowship such as this, there are times when we repeat together the LORD's Prayer; and I always feel you pray in its recital. I have heard it so recited that it has filled my Being with unutterable pain. There is no prayer more rapidly recited in all the Liturgy of the churches, than that Prayer; and yet, every phrase of it is burdened with Divine meaning; and should lift up the whole Being and fill it with spiritual exultation and Divine Realization. The Prayer should bear the one who prays it to the very footstool of GOD, the threshold of the Divine World.

The Divine Te Deum and Tu Adore

Now, I have shown to you that in the Inner Worlds there are forms of song for the individual, and also communal song and ritual of adoration. Every realm is resonant with the Divine Te Deum. We praise Thee, O GOD: We adore THEE; We bless THEE: We acknowledge THEE to be the LORD of All: such praise may be heard in all Kingdoms. All Realms share in the Adoration of the LORD of Being. For as worship is the recognition of HIM as the LORD Who is all and in all, in and through the acknowledgment they all become full of the joy of HIS Presence.

And thus is it with ourselves in our Heavens. Then we turn to the outer spheres and we think of our service in Life, and go forth to touch every part of Life and everything in Life with the glory we have beheld and seen and felt. For that glory has filled our Heavens with its own magnetic Power, and enriched us for service also upon the Earth. Henceforth, whatsoever we touch in every sphere of our experience, we make the action a worship of HIM, a living reflection of that which we have received in the hour of blessing before HIS High Altar. It is thus that all our service—those acts which would be accounted the lowliest service as well as those which would be accounted of the higher service, the more outward as well as the most inward ministry—can become true service for HIM, most sacred because most consecrated, most full of healing power and redemptive ministry.

To worship HIM, beloved ones, is the acme of Life. It is the Crown of Life. It may be you think of the Crown of Life as the highest realization of HIM, and that is the highest experience of it. But you cannot get anywhere in realization without the worship of HIM; because through worship realization comes; and it comes increasingly until it actually becomes in you.

But such worship leads to The Adoration.

Here I would say to you who have passed through the Church where the service of the Holy Eucharist is offered, and especially where the Mass is its chief service, that the arrangements or order of the Mass, with two exceptions, is originally from a Divine Order, from the Approach to the Divine Act of Adoration of the Most Sacred Mystery. For the Adoration of the Host in High Mass, which is accentuated in Pontifical Mass, is nothing less than the bringing down into a materialized exposition, the most Sacred Mystery of the Adoration that takes place within the Angelic, the Celestial, and the Divine Realms. For the same Mass is offered in varying degrees within each of those Realms. That which is adored in the minds and hearts of the multitudes who enter those sanctuaries where the Mass is celebrated, is the unseen Presence of the LORD of Being. HE is invisible to the worshippers, though some few may be so impressed as to feel HIM near. But all such experience is empirical. Alas! the worshippers, through the false teachings given to them, believe HIM to be specially present in the Elements.

But why adore the Elements? The word Pope means the archfather. If, therefore, the Pope or Chief Patriarch celebrated Mass, why do not the people adore the Celebrant? For surely he is something more and higher than the Elements upon the elemental kingdom which may be used to symbolize the dual Sacred Mystery? Why not adore the Celebrant since the Divine Mystery is in him? That Mystery is in him as a living Principle. As the Eternal dual Principle, it is represented by the Bread and the Wine, the Substance and Lifestream of his Being: then why should the Elements, which are only inanimate symbols, be adored when an actual living, moving, revealing Being is before the Altar? Because to adore the man would be considered idolatry. And it would be idolatry. But it is surely a worse form of idolatry to adore the Elements.

The meaning is, however, there all the same, though it is lost in the changed materialized form. The Holy Eucharist, offered in symbolic action, signifies the offering up unto the LORD of the Mass of the Soul. The Presence of the LORD is in the Being. It is within the Celebrant. It is in all the worshippers. The Mass is the symbol in process of the offering of the Being. Just as you would offer a flower of love to a beloved one as the token of your love, so you may, through the Holy Eucharist, express what you are endeavouring to offer through yourself unto the LORD of Being.

But in the celebration of it, adore the LORD of Being only and not the Elements. Worship GOD alone. Never adore the mere symbols you use. They are only aids, not realities.

Throughout all the true glorious Scriptures, only the LORD of Being is worshipped. Even when it is said that the Lamb upon the Throne is worshipped by Angels and Archangels, it is a mystical expression signifying the Divine Passion. The Divine Love is ever regnant upon the Throne of the Sacred Mystery. The Lamb of GOD is the Love of GOD as Divine Passion. It has been wounded with many wounds throughout the history of Divine Travail for this system. In the adoration of the Lamb upon the Throne, it is always the LORD Who is worshipped. All the Angels bow before HIM. They greet one another before the Altars where they worship. They are ever full of the Divine Awe. They have their cherubic and seraphic motion, and in these they worship HIM alone. The Ritual of their worship expresses Preparation, Approach, Confession, Blessing, Service, Praise, Adoration, Exaltation, Transformation, Transfiguration, Atonement, and the Great Benediction.

In its truest form the Ritual of the Mass is an endeavour to give an earthly expression of the Ritual of the Adoration of the HOST in the Heavens. And when all Israel is healed and restored to the ancient cosmic manifestation of Christhood, and all the members who once shared in that transcendent worship in the degree in which they were able to, and in the realm whence they came, are exalted in their state to the Christhood, then will they be able to restore upon these earth-planes such a Soul Ritual as will reveal to those who seek to unite themselves unto them, the real meaning of Divine Approach, of Prayer unto the Divine, of the Worship of the Divine, and of the Glory of the Adoration of the Divine.

Adoration, like worship, is dual; it has its Cherubic and its Seraphic motion. Its Cherubic motion is when the Being is caught up through the vision and enters into the atmosphere resulting from the Spiral Breath of HIS holy motion. In such an hour the whole Being is

173

Ensphered within those Realms and adores HIM. To be bowed down
—as it is said the Angels are bowed down before HIM, and even veil
their faces in the worship of HIM—does not mean simply outward
gesture. It signifies the posture of the Being for the Adoration and
the Praise.

Praise is expressed in the Soul's motion. It is harmonious action.
It is Divine rhythmic mediation.

Adoration is the motion of the Being. And to be caught up of HIS
vision, and borne into the Spiral Breath of HIS encompassing
Presence, is for the whole Being to become one with HIM. That
verily is to bow before HIM. For herein the entire Being—elements,
potencies, and attributes—is transfused with HIS magnetic stream,
and thus it is glorified. And it is of the very nature and constitution
of our Divine Fashion that we should so bow before HIM.

*O my Father-Mother! How shall I manifest Thee? If I express Thee
truly, then surely all my motion is Thine own motion through me! For
only the Spirit of Thyself within me could understand how to adore
Thee, Thou Who art the Lord of all Lords, and the God who is embodied
in all the Gods. O Adorable One! I bless Thee that Thou hast revealed
unto me that Thou art the glorious Jehovah!*

*   *   *   *

I have loved to take flight with you there. You get into the realm of
Vision for fleeting moments. And when you do, I love you, if that
were possible, yet the more. All self is lost in the glory of HIS Radiance.
In such events we scarcely know we are individual Beings, or that we
are merely units; for we feel so much to be part of HIMSELF, one with
HIMSELF, each unit adoring HIM. Unto this end the Adoration
expressed in and through the service of the Mass, must come back to
Israel. Israel must restore the real Adoration. To do so the motion
of the individual must be the Adoration of HIM; all symbols be the
language only through which HE is to be expressed and interpreted,
and never mistaken for HIM. To adore HIM, having once seen HIS
vision and been wrapped in the very atmosphere of HIS Spiral Breath,
is to go forth unto the perfect embodiment of HIM in the Service of
Life. To adore GOD is to embody HIM. What would be the good of
my adoring HIM through the motion of my Being, if I were not also
going to embody HIM unto the revelation of HIS Love and Wisdom
through my Being?

174

Herein is seen the dual aspect of the Adoration. There is the Cherubic, which motion is inward. Through it we are borne to the High Altar to look upon the vision of HIS glory, and share in the transcendent and ineffable atmosphere of HIS sublime Mystery. But with that there also comes the Seraphic motion. For you would note, that the Seraphim, though they adored the Eternal Mystery, had also outward motion wherein they ministered of HIM *from* the High Altar. *The Sacred Stone of Fire from off the Altar is the Eternal Host.* To receive it is to become in HIS fashion and be evermore one with HIM.

That is what you are called to do and be.

★　　★　　★　　★

Oh, for the day to come wherein even the world children can turn and say, "Who are these men and women who so strangely love one another; who interpret Life so differently from others, and who are so noble in their bearing and holy in their outlook; who are willing always to take the burdens of others and bear them beautifully; who are full of a Joy of Life which is not evanescent like the joy that seems to fleet across the sky of our experience, and then like the passing meteors, go out; for their joy seems to leave no bitterness behind it, to bring no bitterness with it, and to be from a source we have not yet tapped?" Oh, for the day when the children of this world can say this, and ask that they may learn of such Life and the Joy of it! Oh, for the day to come when Judah's Children will see that the Children of Israel have come amongst them again, and have made the land of Judah resound with real songs of gladness! And what a yet greater day it will be when, as an outcome of Israel's manifestation of the Christhood, all the Children of Judah, like Ruth of old time in her approach to Naomi, shall say to the Children of Zion, "Your GOD shall be our GOD. Whither ye go we shall seek to follow. The GOD of your vision and worship whom ye make manifest unto us, shall henceforth be our GOD. We also would be of HIS people. Where ye dwell we would also dwell and make our habitation with you."

Judah's Children must share in the glory of GOD made manifest through Israel. What a time it will be when the whole Earth shall turn, through its people, its nations, its races, and say, "Your God shall be henceforth our GOD; for the glory of HIS Love is so real within you that we behold its radiance through you, and feel its magnetic potency." Yes, in that day, even those who cannot see far into the inner mystery of Life, will verily know you in your manifestation as the embodiment of that most ancient prophecy, wherein it is said, "Said I not unto you, 'Ye shall be as Gods for me.'" For by that is meant the embodying of the sacred Mystery of GOD, and the revealing of it unto the children of men, in so far as they can receive of such a sublime revelation from you.

Beloved Ones! The purpose of this hour and this unveiling shall verily be realized if such a Worship comes back to Israel through the Liturgy and the Divine Ceremonial of the individual Being, and through the true Ceremonial and beautiful Liturgy of the communal Life wherein the very Host of GOD shall be revealed and unveiled to all who are able to receive of so great a Mystery.

O Adorable One! How glorious Thou art! What wealth of Love Thou bestowest upon Thy Children, great and small in the stature of their Being! How majestic Thou art in the manifestation of Thy Glory when Thou leanest down to the estate of each one that not one should go unblest!

Unto Thine Israel, the transcendency of Thy Love and the resplendence of Thy Wisdom Thou bestowest, that all the Tribes may be glorified in Thee, and mediate from Thy High Altar of Thy Most Sacred Host, and thus make Thee gloriously manifest!

G

THE GIRDLE

ITS MONASTIC ASSOCIATIONS

ITS USES FOR ADORNMENT

THE GARMENTS AND GIRDLES OF ANGELS

HOW THESE REVEAL ATTAINMENT AND OFFICE

THE GIRDLE OF ADONAI

THE APPEARANCES OF THE ELOHIM

THE GIRDLES OF ARCHANGELS

HOW THE SOUL ATTAINS THE GIRDLE

SOLILOQUIES OF THE SOUL

THE GIRDLE*

The Ruby at the Girdle, so far as it is expressed in the Hymn, is a poetic expression with mystical significance; but the meaning of it will be in the degree in which the writer realized it. As a keynote I would take the expression from *The Logia*, read this morning:—

Primarily Mystical and Spiritual

> "HE was clothed in a garment of glorious light, which covered
> HIS feet;
> And it was girdled at the breast with a golden cord."

The girdle, primarily of innermost significance, has come to have, also, an outer expression, in some instances with considerable meaning. In some degree that meaning is consciously recognized; but in some of the uses to which the girdle is put, it is worn without any feeling that there is something mystical, and even Divine, expressed in the girdle. It is worn oft-times as a matter of adornment; sometimes to give grace to the garment or to the person wearing it; sometimes, perhaps, for mere outward effect; but sometimes also worn out of real love for it, and with a latent sensing after that which it must signify elsewhere than on these planes.

Some girdles, according to the estate and the consciousness of the wearer, are perfectly simple; some are multiple in their fashioning; and some, as in ancient times, more especially when adorned with precious stones, have one stone in the front where the two ends of the girdle meet. Such apparently earthly and human aspects are full of mystical and Divine significance.

In addition to the girdle being an adornment, and a thing of service in fastening a garment, it was made use of in ancient times for carrying things which had to be hidden from the view of others. In very difficult and dangerous times, it was used for the bearing of script containing secret messages. Others who had no way of carrying their earthly possessions, changed their treasures into gems and used the inside of the girdle. But the girdle has also been, for great ages, a symbol of humiliation. Slaves were oft-times girdled. A leathern girdle was the sign of bondage. It was in this way that the humiliating aspects of the girdle came to be applied mystically as the symbol of

---

*In answer to a question.

179

mourning. In the Old Scriptures are many such expressions. "*Gird
yourselves in sackcloth unto mourning.*" But the girdle was also the
symbol of consecration. The monastics had their robes girdled;
and the girdle was in harmony with the habit they wore. And in the
times of a pure monasticism, when many things were understood,
the girdle worn signified the degree of office filled.

From the innermost realms all things high and beautiful have come
forth. The girdles of the priesthood had a mystical signification. The
girdles spoken of in the Old Scriptures, which were of different orders
and colours, were originally descriptions of things that were spiritual
and Divine, but brought forth in the language of symbology into the
priestly services of the Sanctuary.

But the real mystical significance of the girdle has to do with life's
service before the Divine. Thus we have such scriptural expressions
as these:—"Put on the girdle of righteousness." "Let your loins be
girt with truth and your reins with righteousness." Or, as it should
be, *Let your loins be girt with righteousness and your reins with His
purity.* Because the loins represent the balancing of life and the venue
of certain service in the outflow of magnetic streams, as some day I
shall be able more effectually to unveil to you, when it will be possible
to say many things to you in the full assurance that they will not be
misunderstood, misinterpreted, and misapplied. To girdle the reins
as distinct from the loins, with His purity and truth, was to make sure
that the whole of the creative forces, not only in the outer vehicle,
but also in the inner planes of the Being, were consecrated for pure
service, with pure motive, and real sacrificial ministry unto HIM Who
is the FATHER-MOTHER.

The girdle, therefore, has a Divine and most inward significance
in relation to the Soul's constitution; and the Soul's growth; and the
Soul's realization. For it also expresses mystically the Encompassing
Presence, the assurance of being girt about by HIM Who is our life,
Who is the atmosphere of our life, Who is the potency of our life,
Who is the Energizer of our life, Who is the Upholder of our life, and
Who is the Administrator unto us and within us—the real Administrator through all our real service. The girdle HE gives to us with
which to gird our loins and our reins, will speak of the degree of the
life unto which we have attained. It will indicate the degree realized
by us of HIMSELF, the ministries unto which HE has called us and
appointed us.

Such is the meaning lying behind the expressions found scattered through the Scriptures about girding our loins and our reins with righteousness for HIS service.

It is said in the allegory of the Feet-washing that, when the Master taught the disciples how to lay down their lives for the Divine, *He laid aside His garments and girt Himself with a towel.* Though the allegory had a special meaning in relation to the Oblation, yet it was also illustrative of how the life might have to be girdled for special service. It is thus that John the Baptist, concerning whose ministry I have spoken elsewhere, is said to have been girt with a leathern girdle about the loins. The leathern girdle was the symbol of humiliation and bondage, so that even in details those beautiful Scriptures are full of meaning. It was a part of the ministry of John the Baptist, not in proclaiming the ways of purity in life, but as a shadowing forth of that girdle which would have to be placed upon the loins of the One who was to become the Servant of the LORD's Passion for the accomplishment of the Oblation. In the days of the Manifestation, the Master naturally wore a girdle, because the garments themselves which He wore demanded one. But these were worn by Him with an understanding of their mystical significance.

*   *   *   *

Now I would ask you to come with me to the realm where all Truth obtains and becomes manifest in its purity, and in its radiant fashion. Come with me into the Angelic World.

The garments of the Angels are fashioned out of diaphanous elements, of great translucency; and through these there is a revelation of the radiant Presence, as HE is made manifest within the Angelic World. The garments are fashioned out of the exquisitely pure elements of the Angelic Atmospheres; but the degree of both radiance and colour is dependent upon the magnetic state of each Angel. For an Angel's robe is generated according to its estate. And each one is girdled at the loins with the girdle that expresses the estate of the Angel, and the service unto which it has been appointed.

The old-fashioned earthly upper loin girdle is more expressive of what obtains in the Angelic World. The lower girdle is expressive of the girding of the reins, and thus the veiling of the creative forces. And this is done, not simply in relation to what you would think of as its associations in relation to the human body; but it obtains in the

Angelic World in relation to the creative forces of every Angel. You do not think that the Angels are almost nonentities, except that they are beautiful in their fashion and their special motion? They are creative agencies and centres of creative forces for the ministry of the Divine World. Herein, as I have indicated to you tentatively in some of the Teachings, is a great mystery, more fully to be unveiled bye and bye, should the Divine Love permit it.

Now the girdles worn by the Angels have their adornment uses also; and the adornment speaks of the gifts and the graces which have been attained unto and acquired by those who are ministering. Thus you will see that the earthly girdle adorned with precious stones, is but an earthly reflection of great spiritual and Divine things. If in the Angelic World you should meet Angels by the way, you would see them all differently adorned. They would be robed according to their estate and the intensity of their Life. Many would be wearing the same coloured garment; yet no two would be alike. Many might be wearing girdles of similar pattern; yet there would not be two alike. Because, like the garment, the girdle would be expressive of the Angelic estates, the realm to which they belonged and the ministry they had been sent to render. The profound significance of this will become yet clearer.

Come with me a little further into the realms of which the vision of ADONAI spake wherein HE was beheld girt with a golden cord. In the Celestial realms where the Gods have their ministries, their estates are expressed through raiment and radiance; and the girdles which they wear denote their qualities—not only the inherent properties of their constitution, but those estates into which they have entered in their Divine Evolution. The Powers they have attained unto and acquired, are expressed in their adornment, the quality of their garments, and in the degrees of their girdles. The girdle worn by each becomes to them a badge of their office and the insignia of their estate; and it reveals the degree of their relation to the ELOHIM and to the embodiment of the Sacred Mystery.

Thus each one is adorned like a royal personage enrobed in the garments of state, and girt with the insignia of regality and regnancy. The garments and the girdle together express the office and the estate; the nature of the regnancy and the degree of the individual ministrant's realization; and also the quality of the ministry that has to be rendered within the sphere unto which that one is appointed, is in harmony with Divine Law and administration.

This will help you to understand that the garmenting of the outer vehicle had originally a spiritual significance. And when you all come back to the fulness of vision, according to the degree in which you can apprehend that vision; when you are all awakened to the realization of that which the vision conveys; when you all come up out of the darkness, out of the long shadows, and you have shed from your personality and your individuality (whose magnetic centres have gathered out of the darkness and drawn into the treasure-house of your mind, your emotion, and even into your intuition where you have your age-long memories;) all the things that are not beautiful, which do not belong to the Angelic World nor to the Celestial realms—for such things could not have been begotten in you of GOD—then you will understand more fully the real significance of garmenting the body rightly, even upon the earth planes, and how it comes to pass that the Angelic World is a realm of such exquisite beauty. You always think of Angels with diaphanous garments. To the artist's imagination they are always perfect in their colour, even in the most delicate tints. That being so, you will realize that they express Spiritual, Celestial, and Divine qualities.

When Israel was sent to this world, as members of the Christhood community, they came through the Angelic World, clad in the garments of their different orders and several estates, ready for the ministries which the Great Love had appointed them. And each Soul was girdled after its order, estate and office. The girdle also bore the insignia of the tribe to which that one belonged. This latter will help you to appreciate more fully what I would now unveil to you.

Within the Divine World itself garments expressive of order, estate, and office obtain. And these are interpretive of the ministries to be rendered. And the girdle signifies the priestly office. In the vision of ADONAI He was beheld garmented in Light, and girt about the paps with the golden cord. No language could describe that girdle. In the Celestial realms where the Divine World is embodied for manifestation and transcendent staral ministries, each one represents the Seven Sacred Tinctures of ELOHIM in the degree in which that member of the Hierarchy of the Gods has realized the transcendent Mystery, and, likewise, the degree in which that one has

183

The Girdle of the Adonai

to express and make manifest the Mystery in and through ministry. In the Inner Worlds, whither we have been carried in our vision, we look upon the ADONAI girt with the golden cord. The vision is full of Divine revelation. The golden girdle is the Eternal revelation in concrete fashion of the Love with which ADONAI is ever girt. HIS mysterious garments of Light ineffable are girdled with the encompassing Fire of HIS Sacred Mystery. HIS Face and Hair are of the Radiance of White Light. It is the Eternal Radiance that is there in HIS hair. It is luminosity begotten of the magnetic activity in the centre of HIS own sacred, mysterious Being. And the Glory becomes manifest as it sheds itself unto HIS feet. Such is the Mystery contained in HIS girdle. It is the golden cord of HIS Love. With Divine Love HE is girt round about. HIS loins represent the Divine Balance. The Divine Balance reveals the perfectionment of the Eternal Love. HIS girdle also represents the purity and the perfection of the ministries of that Love in all its creative outflow. The majesty of its action is most revealing as it calls unto the individual Soul, and fills its Chalice with Divine potency for the manifestation of ADONAI in some concrete exposition. Though in the vision there is no description of all the other colours—the ruby and the sardius, the topaz and the emerald, the sapphire and the sapphiric purple-amethyst, and then the amethyst; yet they are all there; the Seven Tinctures are present, the Seven Lamps are lit; the Seven Flames burn and have motion. And they are all in HIS girdle. The Golden Girdle is not the Golden Lamp itself. It is rather the unifying Principle that holds all the Lamps lit up with the Tinctures of the Sevenfold sacred Mystery. The Girdle holds them all in its Mystery of Love.

Thus it comes to pass that others also must reveal those Seven Sacred Tinctures of HIS ELOHIM. And so the Seven great Archangels of the Innermost Sphere become the vehicles for the revelation of the Mystery. Every Sphere has its Angels and Archangels. Every staral embodiment has its Angels and Archangels. Our own Sun has its thousands and tens of thousands of Angels; and it has also its Archangels in the Innermost Realm. All that is expressed in the Celestial and Angelic Realms is up-gathered. Though we speak of the Seven intimate or divinely near Archangels as these are set forth in "The Divine Renaissance," where there is given an Angelic and Celestial interpretation of those glorious Beings in their relation to the

184

ELOHIM, there is a yet more inward Mystery related to them in their office, and their relation to the ELOHIM, and the ELOHIM to the LORD of Being.

Thus, in those Seven Archangels we may witness the Mystery; for they are containers of the Seven Sacred Lights.*

Oriphiel is as the pure Ruby Light. That precious Tincture like a glowing stone is beheld in the Girdle when the ELOHIM have to be made manifest to and within certain of the Celestial Angelic Spheres. *The Ruby thus revealed is the Spirit of the Life-Eternal.*

Anael is as the ancient Sardius Light. The Sacred Tincture is revelatory and interpretive of the Divine Wisdom embodied and manifested amid the Spheres through the operations of the Second Elohe.

Salamiel is as the pure Topaz which is the sacred Tincture of the Third Elohe, whose ministry unveils the auric splendour of the third Heaven, whence proceeds unto manifestation the golden glory of Divine Atmosphere. That speaks of the Realm of Worship, the motion of the Breaths.

Raphael is as the pure Emerald. His realm is that wherein the Fourth Elohe maketh manifest the Balm of Gilead. It is the fourth Heaven, where the atmosphere is composed of the Breaths begotten of the motion of the Spirit of Love. The sacred Tincture expresses the Divine Mystery of Compassion and Pity.

Zachariel is in the realm of Sapphiric Light. It is the Tincture of the Fifth Elohe, and the realm that represents the Spirit of Devotion, absolute and complete. Within this Heaven the Elohe of Sapphiric Tincture makes manifest the Adoration that is perfect Sacrifice.

Michael is the Archangel of the Sixth Elohe and in Tincture is the Sapphire Purple. Here the Potency is of the inner Mystery of GOD, and the atmosphere is flooded with the intense Radiance which flows from the Divine Centre of the Cross wherein are focussed all the Potencies of the Mystery Presence. Here, the full meaning of Righteousness and Equity is realized.

Uriel has as his Tincture the pure Amethyst. It is the Ray that merges into the Great Mystery of the White Light, and fills the seventh Heaven with the most sacred Atmosphere of the Divine Awe. It is the realm of the Seventh Elohe. Within this realm there is up-gathered all that is expressed in the other Heavens; and the sacred

---

*See Divine Renaissance, Vol. II.

Tinctures are all unified through mergence into the great White Crystal Sea of the Eternal Mystery.

Now, as each Archangel is enrobed from the Divine, so is each endowed with the Girdle. It is the badge of their Office. And in their Girdle the sacred Tincture of the Elohe for whom they are the vehicle, is represented. Through the most precious gem in the Girdle would the illumined know who the Archangel was, and the order of his ministry; and also the Heaven entered.

It is in this way that the Soul apprehends the LORD in manifestation in various degrees upon the seven Heavens, through the Girdle worn, and the precious Tincture revealed as one of the seven sacred Gems. And in like manner also does it realize the presence of one of the ELOHE as HE is revealed in the Girdle of the corresponding Archangel; and likewise the realm and service of the latter. For the vision of ADONAI upon and within the Heavens is according to the degree attained unto by the Soul, of vision, power and realization. Thus one Soul may see the Ruby in HIS Girdle; another behold the Golden Sardius; whilst another sees the Topaz. HE is aspected in each. But when the Soul fully realizes the Presence, and is equal to looking into all the Heavens, ADONAI is beheld as wearing all the Gems; for all the Tinctures are gathered up into HIM. HE beareth in HIS right hand the Seven Stars.

Thus the Soul may see the Ruby only at HIS Girdle, and through the vision come into the consciousness of the Mystery of Life. Another may see at the Girdle the sacred Sardius Light, and come to the vision of HIS Radiant Countenance and know the glory of HIS Wisdom. Another may behold HIM girdled in that Golden Light associated, in its more delicate colours, with the deep Topaz, and know that HE is also the Lord of Counsel; for that is the Colour you would behold if you went into HIS Counsel Chamber for instruction from HIM concerning the Mysteries which you might be permitted, and indeed asked, to convey Celestially and Angelically to the children who are needing the unveiling of HIM upon the earth-planes. Those who are moved by the great passion of Love, not only to desire to be counselled by HIM, to have the Light of HIS Wisdom shining within them, and the inspiring power of the motion of HIS Spirit of Life in a high and great degree, but to be made sharers of HIS Passion in a yet fuller sense; in their approach to the Inner Worlds, these, having passed through the realm of the wearer of the Girdle with its Ruby, and then the realm of the wearer of the Girdle with the Sardius Light, and pressed still farther forward through the realm of the Divine Counsel Chamber into that of the Emerald Sphere, where HIS Girdle is as the living Crystal that speaks of HIS Divine Love in the Passion. For the Souls who enter that realm come to drink yet more fully of the Cup of HIS Passion. They come to understand more fully the Mystery of HIS Love in its magnetic outflow. They would witness the embodiment of ADONAI as the glorious Emerald flashing its Light and realize that they were in the Crystal Sea of pure substance that took on the radiant Tincture of the Emerald, and signified the Presence of that Love Whose compassion is so great that none of HIS children are shut out of the blessing of its motion, even those whose dwelling is upon the circumference, and Whose pity or tenderness is supremely manifest unto all little ones; and that even the creatures share in HIS Love as the Divine Pity in its most majestic embodiment and outflow, is mediated unto them.

Thus would you behold HIM, if you were such a Soul—not with the Ruby burning at HIS Girdle, for you would have passed through the Gates where such vision came; nor with the Topaz, the sacred Tincture which represent the Elohe Who has that glorious Radiance; for you would have come to the Kingdom of the Green, whose miracle of splendour is indescribable. HIS own Sacred Mystery you would have beheld in the embodiment of the LORD of Compassion and Pity, the all-fulness of Love in its Eternal quality.

And if you would go farther (and I ask you to accompany me without fear, but full of reverence; without the fear that is dread, but with that Soul fear which reveals itself in exquisite lowliness and reverence of HIM) you will behold HIM with Fire flashing in HIS Girdle, more intense than the Fire of a Ruby; greater in its Flame than the Fire of the Sardius; greater than the Flame of the Topaz and the Emerald together. You will behold HIS Girdle aflame with the Sapphire. What is the Sapphire the revealer of? Complete and absolute Devotion—a Devotion concerning which there is no limitation in its giving nor in its sacrifice. The Devotion of the Eternal is expressed in HIS creative manifestations. GOD'S Devotion, if we could use such an expression concerning HIM, is revealed in HIS glorious embodiments. These express HIS Love. HIS Love is signified in the Emerald. It is the everlasting Green of HIS Compassion unto all HIS children. To understand the Divine Devotion, the living Sapphire of the Love that gives unto the uttermost and serves unto the uttermost, and Whose Altars are Altars of living sacrifice—that is a Divine quest and great attainment. To be able to receive that Love as HIS Revelation, and to know it in its magnetic intensity, the Soul beholding it, enduring it, is also to become absolutely one with it. For the Soul can only endure in the Divine Realm that which it would become absolutely one with. You can only look upon the Ruby and all that the realization of it stands for on HIS Girdle, by becoming one with that Life. If you were not fully one with it in spirit and the motion of your Being, and in the holy purpose of your will, though you might get a passing glimpse of the Ruby, it would be nothing more, because you could not endure the outflow of that Sacred Mystery into your Being. It would upset the balance of all your planes. For, to endure the full vision, you must be balanced perfectly upon all your planes. Therefore, when you see the Sapphire in HIS Girdle burning, you are called to absolute Devotion. You are Divinely commanded to a Life that gives everything absolutely for your LORD. That does not mean squandering your potency. It does not mean diffuseness in the use of energy and gifts; but it does mean the perfect consecration of all the Being to HIM.

O my Lord, I thank Thee ever! The Ruby Thou hast given me, and I have drunk of its Red Wine: the Sardius Thou hast given me, for Thou hast Overshadowed me and thus given in the Cup on the standard of my Being, the luminosity that becomes the Eternal Light, Thine own Radiance within the Sanctuary of my Being; Thou hast given to me Thy Topaz, that exquisitely balanced radiant Spirit of Life that instructs unto the consciousness of receiving perfect Counsel from Thee: Thou hast given to me Thy Emerald that I might know Thy Passion in the glorious fulness of its outflow, and understand the measure of Thy Compassion and the circumference of Thy Pity; for such exalted gifts I bless Thee. But I would know also how it is all done. And if I may not know the secret of it, I would, nevertheless, know, through vision and realization, something more of Thy Perfection, and the outflow of Thy Love expressed as Devotion in Sacrifice. For Thou art revealing to me that there is no perfect Devotion without Sacrifice, and there is no sacrifice worthy of the name that is not the revelation of the Being's Devotion.

So within that realm I would have you see in this hour the Sapphire of the Elohe, that HE may lead you to the Altar of absolute Devotion.

Lord, Thou hast given me Thy Life. I have drunk of Thy Wine. Thou hast given me to share in Thy Radiance. Through the cup of my Being Thou hast filled my Sanctuary from Thy fulness. Thou hast given to me Thy Holy Elohe to be my Counsellor, that I might minister for Thee in the outflow of Thy Love unto all Thy children whom I meet in the way within the realms where Thou dost command me for ministry. And whilst I would know of these, even unto perfection, I would know Thee in the sublimity of Thy sacrificial motion wherein Thou becomest the Lamb of God. I would be as one whose Life is Divine Love in sacrificial ministry.

You drink the Wine from HIS Ruby as HE pours it forth from the precious Chalice at HIS Girdle. You drink of HIS Light; of HIS Counsel; and of HIS Love's Passion, from the Chalice of HIS Being in HIS absolute giving we name Devotion. It is only then that you are able to pass through the Gate and then the Portière of the next Realm to behold HIM in the Girdle with the Sapphire-Amethyst. The Elohe Who represents HIM has that most precious mysterious Gem in its primary state of first water. What does it signify? It represents *the secret of all creation*, founded in Righteousness. It is the Mystery of GOD'S Righteousness—HIS Uprightness and HIS Equity. To understand GOD'S Righteousness the Soul must have drunk of Life and been illumined. It must have had the heavenly Counsel to understand the Divine Purpose. It must be filled, even until it is Divinely impassioned, with the Passion of the Gods, aye, of the Elohe Who represents the Divine Mystery of that Passion. And then, having known these, the Soul must have drunk so deeply of the Spirit of perfect Devotion, that there is no shrinking from any service the Being is called upon to render. The Soul of such an one will naturally say,

Lord, dost Thou call me to so great a ministry as this? Yet if Thou be with me, then Thou canst accomplish it through me. And my Being is Thine to be the vehicle of it, if Thou so commandest me.

It is only then that the Soul may be let into the Secret of Creation. To see this have I led you. For only then may you know, really know, the Divine Secrets. For, do not imagine because they have been partially unveiled to you, that you know them. You have had instruction concerning them; you have glints and gleamings of the resplendence of them; but you can only know them in consciousness. I hope this is now made clear to you. So, when you see that Sapphire-Amethyst at HIS Girdle as an intense Flamè, then you are in the Gateway, and looking through the Portals into the realm where the Secrets of GOD are not only interpreted, but where those Secrets are realized.

And then, with all those qualities gifted from HIMSELF—and, of course, there is nothing apart from HIM of Spiritual and Celestial and Divine quality—you see HIM next full of HIS Mystery. And as HE unveils the Mystery, the gem at HIS Girdle becomes pure Amethyst, the Heliotrope that speaks of absolute Divine Awe. And the Being cries out in poignant ecstasy.

O my Lord! Who am I that Thou shouldst so endow me? Who am I that I should be privileged and honoured to behold Thy Glory so expressed, first as the Ruby, then as the Sardius, then as the Topaz, then as the Emerald, then as the Sapphire, and then in the mysterious depth of the Sapphire-Amethyst? Who am I that I should now look upon Thee in this revealing of Thyself through Thy Girdle as the Divine Awe? Life, Wisdom, Counsel, Love, Devotion, Righteousness, and Awe—Thou hast revealed Thyself unto me as these.

It is after that glorious realization that the Sacred Mystery becomes the ADONAI garmented in Light, girdled at the Breast with the Golden Cord. For all the Light of the gems is in that vision. They are Elohistic expressions of HIS glorious Radiance. HIS Face and HIS Hair, the Radiance ensphering HIS Countenance, are white Light, Light white as snow. And the Glory streams through HIS garments to HIS feet. There it reveals HIS Splendour in HIS ways.

Let this be your prayer through the realization of Life yet more fully:—
Lord! I see the Ruby at Thy Girdle burning. But I would also share its Mystery. For I would share Thy Mystery in Life. I would see Thy Countenance again radiant as the Sun. At present it has to be veiled to me as with a Jasper Veil, and unveiled only as Thou knowest I am able to endure the vision of Thy glory. I would know Thy Wisdom in its exquisite resplendence, that it may fill me, to flow through me also as one of the Streams of my Being. I would know Thee in that seemingly quiescent estate represented by the precious Topaz, whose activity is so inward that it is not manifest objectively, but in the midst of which I am learning to know Thee more and more as my Counsellor and Instructor in the Mystery of Thy Radiance and Thy Life.

190

O my Lord! I would know Thee yet more fully in Thy Love, and behold the Emerald at Thy Girdle flashing forth the Fire of the Passion of Thy Love, that it may fill me, hold me there, enabling me to endure until I can be filled unto all the fulness of my Being with Thy Passion for service. For I would be absolutely Thine, a man in the fashion of Thee filled with Thy Love; a man full of Thy Compassion and Pity even as a Son of the Gods, to be bye and bye a Son of God if Thou deemest me worthy of so great an honour. I would be the vehicle of Thy Holy Passion for Redemption, or for Revelation, or for Administration, or for Regnancy, unto whatsoever Thou mayest call me. I would reveal Thee on the earth-planes through such venues as Thou commandest through my hand— through my general Art, fine Art, Sculpture, my Musical gift, my formative Colouring gift in the home or in the world, my Revealing gift through the quietude of my life or the outflow of Thy great Love in me; I would be filled with Thy Passion unto the revealing in every estate of Thee; counting it worthy to do the humblest service; counting it an honour to be commanded of Thee to do that which would be accounted as stooping, though there is no consciousness of stooping in Love; for Thy Love gives itself wheresoever it is needed, even unto the lowliest degrees, without any feeling that it is beneath the dignity of its nature, its secret, its mystery, its regnancy, to be even as God unto the little child as well as unto the Gods the embodiment of Thee.

I would be Thy child full of Devotion so that when Thou askest me to do anything I shall never hesitate for a moment as to whether I should obey Thy command, or whether the service Thou commandest of me is such that my devotion should be called forth to testify of itself in the rendering of that service.

I would be like Thee. I would have my sacrifice complete and absolute. Thus alone would I come to know Thee in Thy Secrets, because it would be safe then to know. Thus would I enter into the realm where the majesty of Thy glorious Mystery is manifest everywhere, and be strengthened from Thee, girdled in my loins with Thy Righteousness, by which I should be held in perfect balance amidst the tremendous forces of a manifest Universe; and in my reins, so that all my creative forces (which are on the earth-planes, even in the most perfect form, and which dimly shadow forth the Divine Mystery of the creative forces in the Heavens) may be let loose by Thee in the innermost realms of my Being through the revealing of Thyself as the Ruby, the Sardius, the Topaz, the Emerald, the Sapphire, and the Sapphire-Amethyst. For I would that all my creative

The Soul's Aspiration unto the Perfect Life

forces might be so girdled, that they would be for Thee and for Thee alone. For all the potencies in me are Thine, all my power to use them is Thine, all my attributes are Thine, all the Mystery of Thy Being realized in me is of Thee and from Thee, and I would have such realization for Thee. I would be accounted worthy to look out upon Thy Universe as it is reflected within the spiral of my Being, and written on the Girdle with which I am girt. I would be wholly Thine. In the midst of such Secrets I would be filled with Thine Awe. I would realize more and more that Thou art ever, not only the Alpha and the Omega, and the Arche and the Amen, but that Thou art also in me the most holy Mystery of the I Am That I Am. For I would be Thine in the absoluteness of my Being, to be ever in Thee as Thy child, and to function from Thee in the consciousness of that childhood and my union with Thee. I would be ever from Thee, as one dependant amidst the spheres from Thine own Sacred magnetic Mystery.

I would be for Thee in the measure that Thou livest in me unto manifestation of Thy Love, and through me unto the revealing of Thy Glory. I would see all Thy Sacred Tinctures evermore as the Seven Sacred Lamps of Thine Elohim in Thy Girdle as I behold them before Thine Altar and upon it. I would look upon these even in my lesser childhood, though Thou accountest it great enough to endure the revelations of Thyself. I would perfectly embody and interpret Thee, and through the embodiment reveal Thee, and through Thy Radiance with which Thou fillest all the Sanctuary of my Being, I would show forth Thy Glory. I would thus be Thine.

O my Father-Mother! How wonderful Thou art! How glorious! How tremendous is Thy majesty! How Almighty in Thy Potency! And yet how exquisitely beautiful in the lowliness with which Thou dost reveal Thyself unto Thy children! For Thou stoopest to touch each one, to bless each one, to call each one, to endow each one, to ensphere each one, to involute unto and through each one, even until each one comes in fulness to realize Thee and to be Thy vehicle, in lowly estate, to know what it is to be with Thee as Thou callest unto the high estate of Sonship. For Thou callest all Thy children to have part in the glorious Mystery of Thy Universe, embodying and manifesting, interpreting, revealing, and in the motion of the Being to become just one with Thee, for evermore. Amen and Amen.

Beloved ones! May you have glimpsed the Ruby at HIS Girdle burning, and more, much more in this sacred hour!

H

THE BLESSING OF ISRAEL

VALUABLE LOGIA OF ISRAEL
MOSES THE MESSENGER
AARON THE MEDIATOR
BEHOLDING THE LORD GOD
REALIZATION AND DIVINE KNOWING
ENTERING THE CLOUD OF RADIANCE
ADDRESSING THE INEFFABLE

THE BLESSING OF ISRAEL

I would read to you the few verses in which in the Old Scriptures that Blessing is expressed. In one of the volumes of the Logia of Israel it will be presented to you as it should be; but it is wonderful even as found at the close of the sixth chapter of the Book of Numbers. Of course, these gems are so mixed up with much that is merely outward, that the reality of their most inward and Divine significance is not easily beheld and realized.

Valuable Logia of Israel

"And the Lord spake unto Moses, saying,
Speak unto Aaron and unto his sons, saying on this wise,
Ye shall bless the children of Israel, saying unto them,
   The LORD bless thee and keep thee. The LORD make HIS face to shine upon thee, and be gracious unto thee. The LORD lift up HIS countenance upon thee, and give thee peace. And they shall put my name upon the children of Israel, and I will bless them."

I would re-read it, giving you a glimpse of the reality, and showing that it is not so outward as it seems; nor is it simply of the relations upon the Earth as it would appear to be, but is related to the inner Being.

And the LORD'S command unto Moses HIS Servant was—
"Speak unto Aaron that he informs Israel of the blessing of the LORD. And thus shall he speak—
The LORD HIMSELF doth bless thee, through having thee in HIS keeping.
The LORD HIMSELF doth unveil HIS Radiance unto thee, and therein reveal HIS grace and graciousness.
The LORD HIMSELF doth lift thee up in the spiral of thy Being into the Spiral Breath of HIS Presence, to fill thee with the Great Peace.
Thus shall HIS Name be written upon thee, even the Secret Name of HIS Mystery."

By song we have been borne into the glory of a redeemed and remantled world. Through the stringed instrument we have been

*Moses the
Servant
of the
Lord*

carried through the ages of that profound motion of Divine Passion which touched this world amidst the darkness and bore it sorrowingly upon its bosom back to the time of hope and new vision, illumination, and the realization that the LORD never forgets HIS children, that however far they may be from HIM, HIS fleeted Love-Messenger of the Mystery of HIS Being can find them all, and effect their restoration unto that estate wherein they can again sing the Songs of Israel.

* * * *

Even within this hour we have all travelled through the ages, and travailed in our journeying. And in this service we would understand yet more fully all that that Blessing of Israel means; for it is with this thought that I would have you go to your homes, and the centres of your activity, and your Groups, and all the ministries that will come to your hand during the coming days. I would have you go in the consciousness of that Blessing, in the sublimity of its Vision, in the transcendency of its Atmosphere, and thus in the glorious reality of its Power to be experienced with an ever increasing fulness by each one of you. And I would approach the unveiling of it in this fashion that you may follow me step by step, and in so following realize the significance of the Blessing.

It is the LORD HIMSELF Who speaks. It is the LORD HIMSELF Who ever speaks to HIS Servant unto the blessing of HIS children. For who was Moses but the Servant of ADONAI? He was a Son of the Gods, though not so represented in the ancient Scriptures. He was clothed in the fashion of a Servant, though he bore a Divine Name, unto the revealing, through manifestation and interpretation, the glory of HIS LORD. For the real Moses was not simply a man. He was a Messenger of the Most High unto Israel. The real story of Moses is soulic, revealing the spiritual history of great ages, expressed in his twice forty years, and then crowned by the third forty years in mediatorial ministry unto Israel. When, looking through the ages, thinking of him we move within realms radiant with the light of the Presence of the FATHER-MOTHER. We find ourselves within a Sanctuary built up by HIS glorious ones. We hear within that Sanctuary the Voice of the LORD GOD of Sabaoth speaking.

Bear this in remembrance that when a Servant hears the Voice of the LORD, He hears that Voice as the resultant of the magnetic effect of the Overshadowing and Indwelling ONE. He hears that Voice as

196

one fleet-footed or golden-winged member of the ELOHIM is sent on a mission for ADONAI unto him, because of such a mission as he has to render unto the LORD's people. He hears that Voice in the Deeps of His Being. As the strings of His Being are played upon magnetically from on High, the Message is conveyed to him through Divine Intonation. Within him Deep calleth unto Deep as that Voice reverberates through all his planes; and he can interpret the motion and intonations, and thus know the Message of His LORD.

Moses the Messenger, Aaron the Priest

I would even have you understand, beloved ones, how a Servant receives His Message from His LORD, that everything in your thought associated with this Message may be exalted to the realm of HIS own glorious Presence Who is your LORD and my LORD, wherein the Mystery of your FATHER-MOTHER and my FATHER-MOTHER becomes unveiled and revealed in degree, and interpreted as each one is able to bear the unveiling and revealing and receive of the interpretation. I would make those Old Divine "sayings" live for you in the coming ages, even as they lived great ages ago before you came to know the darkness that befell this world, and the long night of travail it brought to you.

* * * *

Moses represented the Divine revealing of GOD's Law unto HIS children. He was a Messenger from the Divine Kingdom, in flight through the Angelic World unto the Bethels Israel erected and expressed in a united and unified form as the Bethlehem. And who was Aaron, the brother of Moses, but another service of priestly import personified? For the real meaning of priest is a mediator. But not in the orthodox sense wherein the priest comes between you and GOD, between GOD and you. For the evangelical doctrine of mediation is a helping of GOD to be compassionate, and to make the way possible for you to come near to HIM to receive of HIS compassion. A real priest is one who mediates of HIM, and thus mediates for HIM, and in doing so mediates from HIM. We have nothing that is not HIS, and all we have that is of value in our mediation must be received from HIM. But the mediation is unto the further revealing, manifesting, and interpreting of HIM. Aaron in ministry is the priestly aspect of the Messenger; Moses is the manifesting and revealing aspect of the Messenger.

Speak unto Aaron that he mediates unto Israel of the Blessing of the LORD. Now, it is not simply the blessing of a Servant, nor the

197

Blessing of the LORD through the Servant. There is something profoundly greater. When you give a true blessing, a real heart blessing, the Being's blessing, it is the LORD's blessing. For anything of blessing through you is from HIM. Every good and perfect thing in you came from HIMSELF; and any power in you to transmit the good and the perfect, is the power of transmission received from HIM. That is the meaning of the expression—*Of ourselves we can do no good thing*. That does not mean that we are not equal to doing all the good we would wish; it does not mean we would do evil. It implies that we do good in the measure in which we have realized in ourselves HIS Blessing of good. Our potency is from HIM; our gift is from HIM; the joy of blessing is from HIM.

Now you will see the beauty of the Message. Moses is the revealer of the transcendent Presence; and the Presence in us is the Law of GOD realized; Aaron is the mediator of the Truth. Moses is the Manifestor of the glory of that Presence; Aaron is the interpreter of the Message from that Presence. They can be both in one who is a Messenger of the Most High.

"Speak unto the children of Israel and say unto them, it is the LORD HIMSELF Who doth bless." We think of blessing as the outstretched hand laid upon the head—a beautiful action expressing the transmission of our Love's blessing to another. But there is more than that in this saying, "It is the LORD HIMSELF Who doth bless thee, and keep thee." HE blesses thee through having thee *in* HIS keeping. Herein is seen the beauty of it. Though there doth seem little difference in the form of the expression, yet the difference in the measure of meaning is great. "The LORD HIMSELF doth bless thee and keep thee," is not so rich and full as "The LORD HIMSELF doth bless thee through having thee in his keeping." There is deep significance in this latter form of the saying, if only our language could really express it. If only our tongue could in ample terms reveal the majesty and the fulness of the blessing that is implied here! For the LORD to keep us is to have us in the auric atmosphere of HIS Presence. It is to hold us up as those who are dependant from HIM, to keep us always as those directly supported by HIM. We are all sustained through the inner Principle of our Being. We are magnetically held from the Eternal World. That will be realized more and more as the years and ages go on in which we come more and more fully back into the consciousness of HIMSELF. But in our dependence on HIM, in HIS laying hold of us like stars dependant from the Celestial Spheres, HE encompasses us with an atmosphere that will keep us in the consciousness of that state. So that is the first blessing of the LORD, the GOD of Sabaoth. It is to be ensphered from the ADONAI, most radiant, glorious and ETERNAL ONE, who is the exposition unto us of the most Sacred Mystery of our FATHER-MOTHER. HE Encompasses us. HE Enfolds us. And thus we are upheld.

How the Soul Beholds the Lord God

Now think what that means, even that part of the Blessing for yourselves! Try to realize all that is signified in the experience to walk day by day and hour by hour in the consciousness of HIM! In a mysterious way you doubtless often feel, though you do not understand, like one suspended amidst the universe, one dependant from the Heavens and held only by HIMSELF. It is a blessed experience to walk in the consciousness that HE ever blesses you through having you in HIS ensphering atmosphere. That is how HE keeps you in HIS Blessing. Therefore walk in the consciousness that HE enspheres you.

Yet that is not all that the Blessing contains. It is much, an experience greatly to be desired. Is it not Angelic? Is it not of the very nature of the Gods? Is it not of the Glory of the Love that upholds all things, enspheres all things, holds all the worlds in balance, keeps all the glorious Spheres in perfect motion, so enspheres them that their ministry is continual and perfect, as appointed for service unto HIS children ? Think what it means to walk day by day, hour by hour, night and day continually, in the consciousness of being encompassed by the heavenly hosts, enshrined in an atmosphere that is of HIS own creation, the resultant of HIS own Presence within, the fruitage of HIS glorious mediatorial ministry, the Aaronic mediation within the Being ! I would have you walk as children whose powers are glorified and whose elements are light as air rarefied, the planes of whose Being move in translucent atmosphere though having to walk circumspectly upon these planes, and with a consciousness of the needs for your earthly dwelling and ministries, with sufficient memoria within yourselves that you are accommodated to the Earth's density, even though in your spirit you may take flight into the realms of the Most Glorious Presence. Through this transcendent experience, the Life is prepared for the next degree of the Blessing; for you are called still higher.

199

It is the LORD HIMSELF Who doth show you HIS Countenance as HE doth unveil HIS Radiance to you. Who but HIMSELF could have revealed to you so many things unveiled of late concerning HIMSELF; concerning also HIS glorious Ones, HIS Staral embodiments, HIS Angelic ministries; and likewise concerning yourselves, HIS Mystery in you, and the Mystery of your own age-long and æonial history? It is the LORD HIMSELF Who in this day doth lift upon you the Light of HIS Countenance. It is the LORD HIMSELF Who doth unveil HIS glory within you.

Bear in remembrance this vital fact that, however much may be unveiled to you through the mind, and the light of that unveiling fall upon the threshold of your Sanctuary, it is only through yourselves entering more fully into that realm of realization that you can understand what this Blessing means. Reflect deeply upon what it means to be walking in consciousness as one suspended from the Heavens, only touching the Earth through having sufficient density to hold you to the outer planes; yet in your inner Being full of that lightness which is of the supreme essences of the Divine Ætheria within you, those essences out of which we have all been fashioned, and wherein HE HIMSELF becomes revealed within us; that we are in HIS likeness, and that so walking, we also dwell in the consciousness of HIS Overshadowing. For that is what the second part of the Blessing means. HE not only encompasses us, but HE overshadows us.

Surely you have in some degree entered into the consciousness of HIS Overshadowing? Have you never felt it even in relation to the cup of the spiral of your Being, as expressed in your body in the pineal plexus? When you pray and all your Being aspires to reach HIS Presence; when you yearn to be before HIM in all the fulness of your Life; then your cup is in motion; your pineal is affected. For although this latter is closed of necessity in the manifest life on the outer planes, it is ever open to those streams which are not intercepted by walls, or flesh, or bone, or by any vehicle, providing the Being is in the attitude to receive of such a Blessing. It is the LORD HIMSELF Who doth cause HIS Radiance to Overshadow you. It is the Cloud of HIS Presence. The Overshadowing realization will not be only within the Sanctuary of the Being; for it is always there; but it will actually come forth to permeate all your consciousness, and be such a power in your Life that you will walk as one realizing continually the Angelic World ensphering like an atmosphere, and HIS sublime Overshadowing.

*Lord, I would thus ever walk with Thee, overshadowed by the cloud of Thy Glory, full of Thy Radiant Presence; so that, at any moment, when I specially need the Light Thy Radiance alone can give, Thou mayest send it into and through the cup of my spiral. As I need Thee continually day by day for the exposition of Thy Life within me and through me, I pray that Thy magnetic streams from out Thy Cloud may descend upon me with ever increasing fulness, until all **the** arterial system of my Soul as well as my bodies, receives from Thee the Divine Pleroma. Thus would my Being walk, even on the outer planes, in the consciousness of the power of Thy Blessing.*

Yet, as if that were not sufficient, there is a further statement. "It is the LORD HIMSELF Who doth lift up the Light of HIS Countenance upon you and give you peace." There is more in this latter part of the blessing than seems conveyed by the expression. It is most profound. *It is the Lord Himself Who doth lift you up into the Cloud of His Radiance.* Not alone does HE overshadow you; but HE lifts you up in your consciousness into the Cloud of HIS Radiance, so that you may dwell evermore in the Realization of HIS Indwelling. From henceforth you are one with HIM; you are in the Sphere of the Son of GOD; you are moving in HIS Sphere. No one could lift you up to that estate but HIMSELF. None other than HIMSELF could unveil that glory to you. Even if it were possible for a Servant to do this through manifestation, you could not through such a manifestation, if that were possible, realize it. He cannot give it you through another. It is of HIMSELF alone. HIS Blessing unto you is to take you, through the ensphering of you, up into the Cloud of HIS Radiance, and cause your Spiral to beat in unison with the motion of HIS own Being. Through such Blessing of you HE gives unto you the consciousness of HIS abiding with you. By this means you will be lifted up in state. The flight of HIS Spirit in you will bear you unto the Cloud of HIS Radiance in your consciousness. This also means for you, that HIS Cloud overshadows you and becomes by the glorious process of Divine Involution, HIS Immanence realized. Henceforth you not only walk with HIM as one ensphered from HIM; walk with HIM as one overshadowed from HIM; but you live for HIM as one interfused by HIS Spirit, and whose whole Being is interpenetrated by HIS own Mystery in the glory of HIS Indwelling.

201

*The Realm
of the
Urim and
Thummim*

"Thus shall I write my secret Name upon thee." What could the writing of that secret Name mean? It is through your entering into the consciousness of the Ensphering and Overshadowing and Indwelling, that HE deeply engraves HIS own secret Mystery upon the substance of your Being, and upon all your attributes. It is the giving to you, through HIS Indwelling, the consciousness of the Secret of how HE enspheres you, overshadows you, and dwells within you. Until ye come into HIS Presence in such exceeding fulness that ye shall know no Life apart from HIM; know no more yourselves as separate units from HIM; this Mystery you could not understand. But when ye realize that ye are of the Body of the LORD, verily ye shall so walk that HE shall dwell in you. And in your walk HE shall make HIMSELF manifest through you. And it shall come to pass that, though in a world like this, accommodated to a great extent to its conditions, substantial and magnetic, ye shall be in all your Being one with HIM. Even the outer vehicle shall be so purified, so equilibrated, so polarized in all its elements, that it will be for you a vehicle of perfect order—that is, as near perfect as can be in the world's present state—for the revealing, the manifesting, and the interpreting of HIM.

Oh, to have HIS Name writ large upon us and within us that we could be HIS perfect embodiments! That men and women might see that Sacred Name engraven upon us and come to understand something of the glory of HIS Love and resplendence of HIS Wisdom! Oh, that it were written so fully within us that it should also be manifesting HIS Mystery through us! Oh that we could all walk as those Who are one in HIM, Ensphered, Overshadowed, and caught up into the Spiral of HIS glorious Mystery!

It is there, and there only, that you will understand the Urim and the Thummim, the dual Mystery of HIS own creative motion; the dual Mystery of HIS Omnisciency wherein HE remembers all HIS children; the dual Mystery wherein HIS Omnipotency finds perfect realization and manifestation.

*   *   *   *

This is HIS Message of Blessing to you with which to crown HIS manifold gifts vouchsafed to you in these days. It is the LORD's Message.

The LORD HIMSELF doth bless you through having you in HIS keeping.

The Soul's Prayer unto the Ineffable

The LORD HIMSELF doth unveil the glory of HIS Countenance unto you, and bring the atmosphere of HIS great Peace.

The LORD HIMSELF, through the Ensphering and Overshadowing of you, doth lift you up and translate you in consciousness into the Cloud of HIS Radiance—the Divine Spiral Breath—and cause HIS Own Life-Streams to flow through all your arterial system, and glorify the shrine of your Being, unto the end that HIS Mystery may be written in every part of you.

Henceforth you may be as the Gods are, manifestors of HIM, mediators for HIM, interpreters of HIM, glorious apostles from HIM for the revealing and interpreting of HIS resplendent Love and Wisdom in the service of Life to which you have been called, through every opportunity that comes for specially interpreting and manifesting HIM, for embodiment, for worship, for praise, wherein there is to be found manifested HIS own continual Blessing.

This is the Message HE has moved me to give you. I know HIM, and I can but repeat that HE is the altogether lovely ONE. And I would have you now come back into the consciousness of HIM. In this Message HE would recall you to that high Estate wherein ye once looked out from the midst of such realization, and went forth from HIM for ministry sublime. However grievous became the experiences that followed that sublime going forth as a result of the new conditions that arose, yet it was a Divine going forth crowned with HIS Blessing. And HE is just the same to you, yesterday, to-day, and forever. He is your LORD, even as HE is my LORD; your FATHER-MOTHER even as HE is my FATHER-MOTHER. Therefore, in response to HIM you *will* come unto the knowing of HIM thus as the Ensphering ONE, the Overshadowing ONE, and the Indwelling ONE.

All praise to HIM! All Blessing from HIM to us, and again through us to HIM evermore!

Resplendent One and most Ineffable! In this most sacred hour we would bless Thy Name, and once more know Thy Blessing in these three great ascending arcs of Thine Overshadowing.

We would be ensphered from Thee that our Life may be one with that of Thy heavenly Hosts, and our service in Life be as theirs is for Thee.

203

We would be the witnesses of Thy Glory, and look upon the Light of Thy Countenance as those who stand upon the Mount of Thy transfiguration.

And we would be uplifted and upborne into the Cloud of Thy Glory, and look upon Thee with unveiled faces until we become fully in Thy Fashion and evermore bear Thy Holy likeness unto manifestation.

Since Thou hast so honoured us in Thy calling of us to come up to Thy Divine Mount and enter into Thy Cloud, we would be Thy Children of sweet response, and thus come to Thee that we may be altogether Thine.

O Amen and Amen!

I

A DIVINE RHAPSODY

A GATHERING OF ANGELS
THE MOTION OF THE HEAVENS
THE CHERUBIC ADORATION
THE SERAPHIC PROCLAMATION
THE VOICE OF THE SEVEN THUNDERS

A DIVINE RHAPSODY

In musical definitions a Rhapsody would be considered something made up of unified scattered elements, all of them breathing great emotion, culminating in what might seem to be an extravaganza of intonation, of rhythm, and of their combination.

The titles given to musical pieces do not always seem to be correct. Certainly the real Rhapsodies, Symphonies, and Sonatas have their origin elsewhere than on the outer planes. A Rhapsody, such as one of the Hungarian compositions with an excess of emotion, might seem at first to be an extravagant presentation of elements, intonation, and rhythm; yet even the Rhapsody that appears to be most emotional, if it be pure, has its origin elsewhere than on the earth-planes.

I would take you with me to other realms, even to those of Divine Origins. I would ask you to accompany me, as I endeavour to unveil those things that are most real to me, and which I would have most real to everyone.

I would outline what I have to say to you, thus:—

1 A Gathering of Angels,
2 The Motion of the Heavens,
3 The Cherubic Adoration,
4 The Seraphic Proclamation,
5 The Voice of the Seven Thunders.

It may be that you have thought of Angelic Song only in a promiscuous way. You may have thought of the Angels simply as ministrants unto worlds like this, and unto communities of Souls and individuals. All which is true in part. It may however be that you have never thought of them in a general way, meeting as we meet ourselves for worship. It may never have occurred to you that even a gathering like this is provided for by the Divine Love and Wisdom; that when a house is specially consecrated to the Divine Service, and there is *real worship* in it—that is, Soul motion in which there is the understanding of what worship means as an expression of the Soul's heavenward flight—the community gathered together is Encompassed from the Divine.

*The Divine
Service of
Music*

It is said that like attracts like. Souls cannot aspire unto the heavenly places without bringing the heavenly places to themselves. This House is full of Angelic presences. As we built up, through the motion of our worship, the conditions for our sacrifice to be offered unto our LORD, and our consecration to be made unto HIM upon the Altar, there was an upbuilding of a Spiritual Sanctuary and Altar through Angelic ministry. This Sanctuary became transformed. It became a part of the great Sanctuary of the Heavens wherein, for the time being, our thought, our desire, and the motion of our Being, have carried us.

That which takes place in such an hour as this, also takes place in the Heavens themselves when there is a gathering of Angels belonging to this sphere, or another sphere, for the purpose of worship. In every sphere there is a representation of the ADONAI. The embodiment of ADONAI is never worshipped instead of the Overshadowing One. The ADONAI is worshipped as the Lord of Being, in and through the motion of the Angelic throng towards the centre of the High Altar of the Sanctuary. This latter is fashioned out of glorious Divine Elements for the purpose of the Worship.

Mozart in his Twelfth Mass, in the hour when he wrote the second main movement, entitled "Gloria in Excelsis," sensed something of Angelic Adoration of the Sublime ONE. Those of you who are familiar with the great works of musicians will remember how he opens The Mass with the Kyrie Eleison and follows with the Gloria. How transcendent the latter is! It is not now often sung; nor is it easy to sing. But how gloriously it can be expressed! You remember the movement that is thus expressed—"Let all Angels bow before HIM, and declare HIS wondrous works"—a movement that fills the Being with the consciousness of the Presence and the Adoration HE should receive from all the Hosts.

When the Angels belonging to a sphere, or to a department of a sphere, are called to worship, they are summoned by means of a tolling of the heavenly bell (even earth-bells are the echoes of heavenly things). Then they come together to worship. They have their vision of the LORD of Being. They are moved by their vision. Their divine emotional nature must express itself. They are magnetically attracted to the centre of their own Being as that is represented in the sphere where they manifest and minister. They are held by the one who represents, for the time being, ADONAI within their sphere. But they know they are only held to that one through the Overshadowing of the LORD of Being. There is no idolatry in the Heavens. Individual Angels, even Archangels, are not worshipped; but HE Who is beheld overshadowing the Head of the Angelic community, is adored. HE is recognized in HIS Overshadowing of the one who has been appointed as the Angelic Director of that sphere.

"Let all the Angels bow before HIM, and declare HIS wondrous works," and that not merely in a universal sense, in the vastness of which the reality might be lost; but specially all the Angels of the community within the sphere; or, all the communities within the spheres, which have gathered together. For the Angels have their Great Days. They have their great Festivals. We could speak of some of those Festivals; and how the Church, getting glints and gleamings, introduced Festivals to be observed through the ages, the meaning of which lies far beyond the outer statement and the oft-times meaningless ceremonial. To attend a Festival in the Angelic World is to be upborne into a state of such transcendent joy, that the song that bursts forth from the Being might well be named "A Divine Rhapsody."

You would observe in the passages read from the Apocalyptic vision that, whilst there is a unifying spirit of thought and motion in them, yet they are quite distinct elements. Though they can all be brought together, and though they all speak of one great theme; yet they are various in their intonations, and their keys change quickly. But in their unity they speak of HIM Who is the Perfect ONE. And they make up into a glorious Divine Rhapsody.

Realize what a Sanctuary on the Earth should mean; how it should be the expression of the Sanctuaries in the Heavens where Angels worship and adore, and in which they praise and bless. You do know that adoration is embodiment: it is the embodiment of HIM. There is no other adoration. For that which we speak of as adoration when in the whole motion of our Being we bow before HIM, is true adoration only in the measure in which our life is the embodiment of HIMSELF. Like our worship, it is in the service. It is in the song. It is in the ascription. It is in the proclamation. To serve truly is to worship; to serve selflessly is to adore.

An Angel can take and give a cup of blessing in ministry, and the act is an act of worship. In like manner is your cup of blessing to another an act of worship. And communal worship should be the unified expression of all that the Souls making up the community have felt and do feel in relation to the LORD of Being. It should be the crowning act of all the service rendered in the hours preceding.

Try also to realize that when you come here for worship, it should be primarily for the worship of GOD, and not simply because of the man or the woman who is mediating before the Altar. If you come merely because of the Mediator, you are coming only to sing songs and to hear what you might consider to be a lecture. You must come in the spirit of worship when you enter the Sanctuary. You must come with your heart as a chalice full of the joy of the opportunity of praising HIM in communal worship. You should come to share the Angelic presences, to join your song with that of the Angels in the adoration of HIM. Let all the Angels on the Earth's planes as well as in the Heavens, bow before HIM. Have your Divine motion before HIM. It will ever be a reverent motion in the acknowledgement of HIM as the LORD of Being. For, to bow before HIM means that you acknowledge HIM to be LORD of all.

I would have your worship of HIM in this Sanctuary to be so real that you would come into a Sanctuary full of the atmospheres of the Heavens, a Sanctuary whose breaths were the Breaths of the Eternities; a Sanctuary where the music was the motion of the Soul, and where the Angels could be recognized through their atmosphere, even as many of you long to recognize them in your vision.

Yet, still more. I would have you be as the Angels. You are already so in the Principle of your Being. But I would have you be so in realization. An Angel is a ministrant. He is a glorified one. He has been transfigured. He is one who is able to enter into the Presence, there to adore. He is one who has the power to go forth from that Presence, adoringly to bless.

Now in those Heavens of which I speak to you, the very Eternities seem to have motion. They are represented by the Four Living Creatures who in their motion proclaim the Eternal Mystery. This is not easily expressed in human terms. Even the Four Living Ones bow before the Glorious Presence. The Four Living Ones represent the Elements of the Four Dimensions. They are Living Elements. They also represent the four great Degrees of the Heavens. They are embodiments of the Sacred Mystery of our FATHER-MOTHER in a Fourfold exposition—the Divine Kingdom, the Celestial Kingdoms, the Angelic Kingdoms, and the Realms of Manifestation.

How Adonai Becomes Revealed

Now, when all the Heavens have their motion, they move towards the Centre of All Things. But that Centre has an embodiment in and through all the spheres. This is a most sacred Mystery. It could easily be misinterpreted. It has been misinterpreted in the past. Therefore it now belongs to the unrevealed Secrets of GOD. But the day is hastening and has even come, when that sacred Mystery may be partially unveiled to those who are accounting themselves the Children of the Kingdom of the Heavens, who are returning in their consciousness to the true vision, and who are endeavouring in their life to embody the estates of Jesus and Christ, and to rise up into the consciousness of the regnancy of their LORD.

The Sacred Mystery is of this order, that even an Angel in high estate, one who has risen to be designated Archangel, becomes, through the Overshadowing Holy ONE, so transfigured before the High Altar within the Divine Sanctuary where host of Angels and Archangels are worshipping, that ADONAI can be revealed in the fashion of that one. In such an hour, those who behold the transfiguration, look not upon the form of the Archangel, but upon the completion of the metempsychosis. They behold the fashion of ADONAI.

The Divine Realities are beyond telling. The splendour of GOD as manifest within the Celestial and Divine Realms, is so transcendent that human speech fails. Yet I would have you sense something of the reality wherein speech cannot interpret, and one's tongue has to be dumb.

Even in this earthly Sanctuary there is, in this hour, such an Overshadowing of the glory of HIS Presence as no tongue or pen could describe. You may behold it. It is of no man. It is of and from HIMSELF as the unveiling of the Message proceeds. There may we witness the opening of the Heavens, and the shedding of HIS glory to fill the Sanctuary of our Being with HIS radiance. There is but one GOD, the FATHER-MOTHER of us all. HE is Universal Being, out from the Bosom of Whom we all proceeded, and Whose Mystery is in us. HE lives in us, and HE manifests through us, in the degree in which we embody HIM. Our very consciousness is of HIM. It is from HIM. In its ascensions it is in HIM and for HIM. If a Soul ever lost its consciousness it would cease to be a Soul, though the

consciousness would not cease. That which produced the consciousness would simply be withdrawn. For consciousness is as Eternal
as is the Sacred Mystery we name the FATHER-MOTHER. And we
are all recipients of the elements which produce consciousness. In
the degree in which we can cherish HIS sacred Mysteries within us,
and allow our consciousness to expand, deepen, and ascend to HIM,
so do we come to know HIM, realize HIM, and become HIS expositions, the miniature revelations of HIS own Mystery.

It is thus it comes to pass that, because HIS Mystery is in the Soul,
the latter can ascend into the heights in consciousness and dwell
amidst the glories of the Celestial and Divine Realms, become the
vehicle of the LORD's transfiguring Presence and the recipient of HIS
outflowing magnetic Streams, unto the embodiment of HIS own
fashion and the interpretation of HIS glory. Though but a miniature
of HIMSELF, the Soul may reveal perfectly HIS fashion and make
manifest the potencies of HIS Mystery in and through embodiment.

We all ascend to HIM through the deepening and expansion and
ascension of our consciousness. And the enlargement of our consciousness is the growth resulting from our appropriation of HIS
streams, the measure of HIS becoming in us, and the degree of our
becoming one in HIM and with HIM.

Now you will understand how it comes to pass that it is possible
in the Solar Body for a glorious embodiment of ADONAI to be the
head of the System (as the Divine Vicegerent) of the transcendent
communities of Angels and Archangels, of Cherubim and Seraphim
who minister there, and yet be but a Child of the Universal Mystery,
a Servant of the LORD of Being; and for such an One, in the hour
when uplifted before the High Altar of HIS Presence, to be so transfigured as to stand in the fashion of ADONAI.

To those who know something of earthly Masonry I would say,
that it is the thought couched in the Masonic Idea of the Divine
Man. For to be a Divine Man is to be one capable of being thus
transfigured. But the LORD of Being can accomplish such metempsychosis in the Soul, only when it has taken its Ascensions. The
power of HIS Streams of glory would overwhelm a Soul if it were not
in that estate wherein it could receive into its chalice, the potencies
of HIS glorious Mystery. The Metempsychosis is also the meaning of
the expression *Ye shall be as Gods*. For the Gods are the embodiments of HIS Mystery, revealers of HIS Majesty, transmitters of HIS

Glory, Vicegerents of HIS regnancy and manifestors of HIS Love and HIS Wisdom.

Surely you may now see that it is a Divine Rhapsody of the Being to be caught up into such an estate? That in the Heavens there are not only Divine Sonatas and Symphonies, Choruses and Chorales, but there are also Rhapsodies? What are some of those wonderful Logia read to you this morning but rhapsodical expressions of Angelic and Archangelic motion? Let all the Angels bow before HIM! Let all the Angels worship HIM!

Oh, the delight in the Heavens in the hours when the worship takes the form of Divine Rhapsody! When the Soul's motion is a song of Divine Joy! When all service is a revelation of Divine Delight! Such a Divine Rhapsody carries the whole Being into its motion, from the crown of the head to the sole of the foot. It is a song of the Being, even though no human words may be spoken through the human lips.

In the Divine Rhapsody we have an expression of the Cherubic Chorale and the Seraphic Song. The Cherubic Hymn is full of the inward motion of the Alleluiah. It is the praise of GOD in the static embodiment. It is the praise of HIM before the High Altar. It is the praise of HIM in the drinking in of the Streams which flow, even to the Angels and the Archangels, out of the heart of the Eternities; for all these live, even as our own Being lives, by means of those Streams. *It is the inward motion.* They look, they behold, they hear, they feel, they cry aloud, they articulate in harmony with the realm where they are.

There is real articulation in the Heavens; though the articulation there is quite different from the articulation on these outer planes. There can be no true comparison; for often here the intonation is metallic. There in the Heavens it is the perfect music of the Spheres. It is the resultant of the Breaths. The reeds and the rushes of the Divine World are set in motion, and they pour forth symphonic song. And the Beings in those realms who share in the motion, oft-times are so upborne, that their motion and their praise can be expressed only in our human terms as composing a Divine Rhapsody.

You must have observed how you were moved inward and upward when you gave the Cherubic note. In the last song we sang it was obvious that you were coming more and more to realize the difference

213

between singing Alleluiah and Halleluiah. The Alleluiah carries you up: it is the Cherubic motion. It would be difficult to shout Alleluiah. You could not do so from the Inner World of your Being. It is entirely an inner motion of the inward Breath to say, Alleluiah! There is the process of in-breathing, even whilst you are breathing out in the Praise of HIM.

Alleluiah! It is Cherubic. It is the Motion begotten of the adoration of HIM Who unveils HIMSELF. The Being gets so filled with the glory of such a revelation that it seeks to share the Seraphic Song. The Seraphim adore with the Cherubim; but their ministry unto the Angelic World is concerned not so much with the Alleluiah, as with the Halleluiah. And thus we have, as it were, the spectacle, Divinely presented, of the Angelic throng turning from the Altar of Vision after they have given their Alleluiahs unto the Presence revealed there, to mediate from that Altar unto other Celestial and Angelic dwellers, of the Praise of HIM. And I did note in the singing of the song how your very Being went out as you sang the Halleluiah! You could not sing the Halleluiah as you sang the Alleluiah! The latter is the proclamation unto HIM, so full of Awe and Adoration; the other is the proclamation unto others concerning HIM. Halleluiah! Praise ye the LORD!

Nay more. The Praise of JEHOVAH Who is the Sacred Mystery of the FATHER-MOTHER, is not only praising HIM in an embodiment, through an embodiment, and in visualizing something of HIS Mystery in and through that glorious embodiment; but it is the praise of HIM as the Eternal Mystery. HE is JEHOVAH, the FATHER-MOTHER. It is therefore the proclamation of the power begotten of the realization of the Tetragrammaton within the Being; for that is HIS unutterable Sacred Mystery. The Cherubim Adore. The Seraphim Adore. The Cherubim are enraptured; but they are full of the rapture of Awe. The Seraphim Adore, and they are also enraptured; but theirs is the rapture expressed in and revealed through the Divine Rhapsody. All Praise the LORD. All the Angels bow down before HIM. They do this in both the Cherubic and Seraphic form. And they call upon all Souls thus to bow down before HIM, and acknowledge HIM, singing the Alleluiah and the Halleluiah.

Then the Seven Thunders utter their Voice. Who are they? They are the individualizations of the Sacred ELOHIM. In their action they become as the impersonations of glorious estates. They are the resultants of Divine Rhapsody. They are the Divine Intonations upon the Seven Divine Planes, within the Divine and Eternal World. They are the Voices of the various Elohe upon the Spheres of the inner ministry. They are the media through which the Seven great Archangels who are the vehicles of the ELOHIM, have their regnancy. When they have motion it is as when it thundereth. It is the magnetic reverberation through all the Kingdoms of the Divine World, produced through the effect upon the Elements of the motion of the Spheres where praise, worship, and adoration are taking place. The Seven Thunders utter their Voice in unison with Cherubim and Seraphim. It is carried to every plane in the Divine World, as it is carried to every plane in the Celestial World, and in the Angelic World. And it is carried to every plane in your own Life when you are caught up and filled to overflow with the motion of the Divine Rhapsody.

The Voice of the Seven Thunders

When Souls are filled from the Divine World, every plane is touched; the Seven Thunders are echoed upon and through all their planes. As it is above, so is it beneath. As it is in the Eternal World, so is it in all the glorious embodiments of that World. As it is in this glorious embodiment, so is it in all the Angelic communities. As it is in the Angelic communities, so is it in the individual Soul. And thus Life can become one in every earthly community, where all the Souls are filled with the rapture of the Divine. Thus may you all become one, and one with the Overshadowing Heavens. For HIS Heavens are within us; and when we respond to the Overshadowing Heavens, we become one with them.

Now, you should be able to understand something of what Handel heard when he was moved to write his Halleluiah Chorus. For that great exposition is a magnificent Rhapsody. It is called the Halleluiah Chorus, for it is in Praise of the LORD of Being. You may now understand how the motion of the Seven Thunders affected his planes. He had to sing Seraphicly.

Halleluiah! Halleluiah! Halleluiah!

For the LORD GOD Omnipotent reigneth.

And HE shall reign for ever and ever.

Halleluiah! Halleluiah! Halleluiah!

It is a proclamation. It is not made to the Divine; it is from the Divine to listeners. It is a song of the Universal Heavens. It is a

*The Lord
God
Omnipotent
Reigneth*

combination of the glorious intonations of the Heavens, proclaiming
the glory and regnancy of HIM Who is the LORD of Being. It is a
Divine Rhapsody or enrapturement, prophesying of the day when all
shall adore HIM Who is the LORD, and when HE shall reign forever
and ever! And what Handel heard had even more exalted meaning
than can be intonated. The Rhapsody as we have it, is but a partial
transcription of what he heard; and it is given in order to reveal
something of the glory of Angelic and Archangelic motion.

Beloved ones, I asked if I might take you with me into the
Heavenly places. Our own Sanctuary has been and still is full of the
Presences, and encompassed from the Divine World. It ceased
to be, in its compass, a merely earthly Sanctuary. It partook of the
glory of the inner vision. Thence we proceeded into the Angelic
World to behold Worship there. Divine Rhapsodies of Angelic Love
and Wisdom we have heard. We have witnessed the Glory of Worlds
such as Solar embodiments. We have been upborne even into the
Innermost Realms whither our vision was carried in the flight of
the Spirit. I asked you to accompany me that what might be permitted
to be given in the unveiling, might so enrapture you as to fill you
with the music of the Spheres, and enable you to make of your life
a glad Divine Symphony interpretive of the motion of the Spirit;
or a sublime Sonata interpreting the Divine Wisdom as expressed
in creation; and that in the hours of your spiritual upliftment you
might even be filled with the motion of the Angelic World to express
a Divine Rhapsody of Praise and Worship, that others might behold
something of the Divine Joy in you, the Radiance of that Joy, and
the power of its outflowing streams; that with head and eyes, lips and
hands and feet, your whole Being should be in motion as the result
of the Overshadowing of HIS Presence and the influx of HIS Streams,
and that their flow through you would be unto the making of your life
a blessed Symphony; a beautiful Song; a motion which is all praise;
a service which is all worship; and a Life that is, from the morning
hour to the evening hour, and from the evening hour to the morning
hour, an Adoration of HIM.

216

O Transcendent Lord! O Wondrous One! O Presence with glory ineffable! O Loveliest Fashion! O most Sacred Mystery! We adore Thee.

More fully would we adore Thee, even unto the estate wherein we might be the perfect revelations of Thy Love and Wisdom.

Ever would we bless Thee. We would be enraptured of Thee. Our whole Being would be in motion from Thee, unto Thee, and from Thee in blessing unto all whom Thou dost send unto us to bless!

May the fruitage of this hour be that all Thy children shall have received of Thy Glory, with a fuller vision of Thee, and greater empowerment for ministry for Thee.

Alleluiah! Alleluiah! Alleluiah!
Hallelujah! Hallelujah! Hallelujah!
For the LORD GOD Omnipotent Reigneth!

INDEX

TO

THE MYSTERY OF THE LIGHT WITHIN US

TITLES OF MAIN ARTICLES ARE INDICATED BY CAPITALS

ASTERISKS DENOTE PRINCIPAL REFERENCES

PITY   COMPASSION   LOVE

SELF-ABANDONMENT   SELF-SACRIFICE   SELF-DENIAL

REDEMPTION   REGENERATION   ILLUMINATION

The Order of the Cross

SPIRITUAL AIMS AND IDEALS

THE Order is an informal Brotherhood and Fellowship, having for its service in life the cultivation of the Spirit of Love towards all Souls: Helping the weak and defending the defenceless and oppressed; Abstaining from hurting the creatures, eschewing bloodshed and flesh eating, and living upon the pure foods so abundantly provided by nature; Walking in the Mystic Way of Life, whose Path leads to the realization of the Christhood; And sending forth the Mystic Teachings unto all who may be able to receive them — those sacred interpretations of the Soul, the Christhood, and the Divine Love' and Wisdom, for which the Order of the Cross stands.

SERVICE   DEVOTION   PURITY

SYNOPSIS OF MAIN PUBLICATIONS

THE MASTER sets forth the Inner Meanings of the Master's Teachings and gives a true picture of Him as He was in His Life, public and private. The Birth Stories and the Allegories of the Soul are revealed in their true setting; with the Teachings on the profound Mystery of the Sin-offering, and the Allegories of the Soul's Awakening.

THE LOGIA contains the chief utterances of the Master, in the form in which they were spoken by Him. Here they are restored, including the real Mystic Sayings, found in the Synoptic Records, the Gnostic Record, the Pauline Letters, and the Apocalypse, containing remarkable histories of the Soul, the Planet, the Ancient Christhood Order, and the Oblation or Sin-offering.

LIFE'S MYSTERIES UNVEILED gives the Path of Discipleship and Aids to the Path of the Realization. It includes definitions of terms in their relation to these Teachings and many answers to questions asked at Healing and other Meetings. The principal theme of the volume is Initiations of the Soul.

THE DIVINE RENAISSANCE, Vol. I. i. The Message. The Divine Adept. The Superstructure of Man. ii. The Eternal Mystery. A Divine Apologia. The Seat of Authority. iii. The Path of the Recovery. The Redemption. The Divine Purpose of the Oblation. The Mass and the Oblation. Altars and Sacrifices. The Flame before the Altar.

THE DIVINE RENAISSANCE, Vol. II. i. Unto the Great Silence. Science and Religion. The Angelic Realms. Corpus Christi. The Sabbath of the Lord. ii. Beginnings of Historical Christianity. Pentecost. The Advent of Paul. The Stone the Builders Rejected. The Church of the Living Christ. The Seven Sacraments. iii. A Renascent Redemption. The Seven Thunders. The Healer, Manifestor, Redeemer. The Obedience of Christ. Our Lord and Our Lady. The Three Altars. iv. A Divine Oratorio. The Ministry of the Gods. The Divine Government. The Cosmic Consciousness. The Regnancy of Christ.

THE MESSAGE OF EZEKIEL. *A COSMIC DRAMA.* The Office of a Prophet. The Purport of the Book. The Divine World Unveiled. The Distinction given to Israel. The Mystery of Tyre and Zidon. The Pharaoh of Egypt. The Arising of Israel. The *Logia* of the Prophet Ezekiel: with extensive Notes to the *Logia*. *The Logia of Israel*. Vol. I.

THE MYSTERY OF THE LIGHT WITHIN US. *With 17 coloured plates by Amy Wright Todd Ferrier.* i. The Luminous Cross and the Cross of the Elohim. ii. The Spectra of Souls and Stars. The Solar Fashion. iii. Auric Glimpses of the Master. iv. Celestial and Divine Estates. v. A Holy Convocation. Jacob's Ladder. The Adamic Race. The Secrets of God. The Girdle. The Blessing of Israel. A Divine Rhapsody.

ISAIAH. *A COSMIC AND MESSIANIC DRAMA.* i. The Unity of Divine Revelation. ii. The Prophecy. iii. The Word of the Lord. iv. A Divine Drama. v. The Mystery of the Sin-offering. vi. A Momentous Promise. vii. The Triumph of Adonai. viii. The Drama of Israel. ix. The Sign of the Cross. x. The Daysman of Israel. xi. The Appointed Redeemer. xii. The Five Cities of Egypt. xiii. The City of the Sun. xiv. The *Logia* of the Prophet Isaiah: with extensive Notes. *The Logia of Israel*. Vol. II.

PUBLICATIONS

By the REV. J. TODD FERRIER:

THE MASTER: *His Life and Teachings*	Large Crown 8vo			624 pp.
THE LOGIA: *or Sayings of The Master*	,,	,,	,,	436 pp.
LIFE'S MYSTERIES UNVEILED	,,	,,	,,	480 pp.
THE DIVINE RENAISSANCE, Vol. I	,,	,,	,,	402 pp.
THE DIVINE RENAISSANCE, Vol. II	,,	,,	,,	560 pp.
THE MESSAGE OF EZEKIEL: *A Cosmic Drama*	,,	,,	,,	280 pp.
THE MESSAGE OF ISAIAH: *A Cosmic and Messianic Drama*	,,	,,	,,	436 pp.
THE MYSTERY OF THE LIGHT WITHIN US With 17 plates.	Large Crown 4to			240 pp.

THE HERALD OF THE CROSS (Bound volumes)
Vols. VIII upwards   Large Crown 8vo

HANDBOOK OF EXTRACTS of the Teachings of The Order of the Cross, from the Writings of the Rev. J. Todd Ferrier.
Vol. I: Extracts A to D; Vol. II: Extracts E to J.   Demy 8vo
Further volumes in preparation.

LETTERS TO THE CHILDREN	,,	,,	238 pp.

SMALLER BOOKS (Paper Bound)

THE MYSTERY OF THE CITY UPON SEVEN HILLS	Demy 8vo		80 pp.
GREAT RECOVERIES	,,	,,	80 pp.
THE FESTIVAL OF THE MASS OF ISRAEL	,,	,,	72 pp.
THE STORY OF THE SHEPHERDS OF BETHLEHEM	,,	,,	72 pp.
SUBLIME AFFIRMATIONS	,,	,,	64 pp.
WHAT IS A CHRISTIAN?	,,	,,	64 pp.
THE EVANGEL OF ST. JOHN	,,	,,	40 pp.
THE GREAT TRIBULATION . THE WORK	,,	,,	40 pp.
THE CHRIST FESTIVAL . THE WAYS OF GOD AND THE WAYS OF MEN	,,	,,	36 pp.
THE CROSS OF A CHRIST . THE RESURRECTION LIFE	,,	,,	36 pp.
THE CONTINUITY OF CONSCIOUSNESS	,,	,,	28 pp.
IF CHRIST CAME BACK?	,,	,,	24 pp.
THE LIFE IMMORTAL	,,	,,	20 pp.
THE ORDER OF THE CROSS	,,	,,	16 pp.
THE MESSAGE AND THE WORK	,,	,,	12 pp.
THE INNER MEANING OF THE FOOD REFORM MOVEMENT	,,	,,	8 pp.
ON BEHALF OF THE CREATURES	Crown 8vo		128 pp.
THOUGHTS FOR THE DAY	,,	,,	52 pp.
THE SECOND COMING OF CHRIST	,,	,,	48 pp.
THE ABRAHAMIC STORY	,,	,,	20 pp.

By E. MARY GORDON KEMMIS:

THE "GREATER WORKS" (Cloth bound)	Crown 8vo	64 pp.

FOR USE IN WORSHIP

PSALMS AND CANTICLES FOR WORSHIP (Paper or Cloth bound)	Demy 8vo		96 pp.
HYMNS FOR WORSHIP WITH TUNES	,,	,,	256 pp.

THE HERALD OF THE CROSS

Vols. I to VII (published 1905-11) are now out of print. Vols. VIII (1934) to XXI (six issues a year) and Vols. XXII upwards (four issues a year) are available separately, paper bound, in limited quantities. (Vols. VIII to XVII, No. 4, edited by the Rev. J. Todd Ferrier: subsequent issues edited according to his instructions.)

All prices on Application

Please address all communications regarding Literature, and make remittances payable, to THE LITERATURE SECRETARY, THE ORDER OF THE CROSS, 10 DE VERE GARDENS, LONDON, W.8.

Loan copies of any of the publications may be applied for to THE LIBRARIAN.

MEETINGS

Regular meetings are held, at which all seekers after the Divine way of life are welcome, in the Sanctuary at the Headquarters of the Order of the Cross, as below, every Sunday at 11 a.m. and Wednesday at 7 p.m. throughout the year (except during the Summer Vacation); and there are Groups or Reading Circles for the study of the Teachings at:—

Aberdeen; Belfast; Birmingham; Bournemouth and Christchurch; Bradford; Brighton; Bristol; Cardiff; Colchester; Dundee; Edinburgh; Glasgow; Gloucester; Guildford; Inverness; Leicester; Leigh-on-Sea; Letchworth; Liverpool; Manchester; Newport, Mon; Nottingham; Reading; Sheffield; Stockton-on-Tees; Stratford-on-Avon; Sunderland; Tyneside; and also in the London area, at Croydon; Epping Forest; Hampstead; Kensington Gardens; Kew Gardens; Pinner, Middlescx; Westbourne; Woodford, Essex. Also at Melbourne, Australia; Auckland, Christchurch, New Zealand; Los Angeles, Salt Lake City, San Francisco, U.S.A.; Paris, France.

COMMUNICATIONS

Communications regarding the Literature of the Order should be addressed, and remittances made payable to, "The Literature Secretary," at the Headquarters.

Further information concerning the Order of the Cross and its activities will be given gladly to any inquirer, on application to:

THE SECRETARY

THE ORDER OF THE CROSS
10 DE VERE GARDENS, KENSINGTON,
LONDON, W.8

The Order of the Cross

FOUNDED OCTOBER 1904

AIMS AND IDEALS
(FOUNDATION STATEMENT)

TO ATTAIN, by mutual helpfulness, the realization of the Christ-life, by the path of self-denial, self-sacrifice, and absolute self-abandonment to the Divine will and service:

It is of these things that the Cross as a symbol speaks. It stands for the Sign of the Order of the Cross, because its three steps are those which have to be taken in order to arrive at that Estate which it symbolizes. It speaks of the quest after the humble spirit and the pure heart. It speaks also of that further state of realization when the Soul gives itself in absolute abandonment for the Divine Service. The Three Steps are:—

PURITY OF LIVING
PURITY OF THE MIND
PURITY OF THE SOUL

Thus to endeavour by example and teaching to win all men to the love of Truth, Purity and Right-doing.

To proclaim the Brotherhood of Man, the essential one-ness of all religious aspirations, and the unity of all living creatures in the Divine.

To teach the moral necessity for humaneness towards all men and all creatures.

To protest against, and to work for the abolition of, all national and social customs which violate the teachings of the Christ, especially such as involve bloodshed, the oppression of the weak and defence-less, the perpetuation of the brutal mind, and the infliction of cruelty upon animals, *viz.:* war, vivisection, the slaughter of animals for food, fashion and sport, and kindred evils.

To advocate the universal adoption of a bloodless diet, and the return to simple and natural foods.

To proclaim a message of peace and happiness, health and purity, spirituality and Divine Love.

EXECUTIVE COUNCIL (1904)

J. TODD FERRIER, *Founder, Editor,* "The Herald of the Cross."
ROBERT H. PERKS, M.D., F.R.C.S. (Eng.), *Secretary.*